PRAISE FOR *How to Get a Job You'll Love*

'In a difficult job market, this updated edition of *How to Get a Job You'll Love* is like a map and compass for anyone seeking a change of career direction. It's packed with wisdom, insight and practical advice.'

Graham Snowdon, Editor, *Guardian Work*

'John Lees' excellent book provides all you need to not only find a job you love, but to discover what kind of work you really want to do. Whether you're searching for your first job, the next step up or a whole new direction, this book provides practical, effective strategies for success.'

Maureen Rice, Launch editor, *PSYCHOLOGIES*

'John Lees approaches career transition in a completely novel and inspirational way. This landmark book is an indispensable guide to career transition and it really does what it says. Anyone following the guidance will get the best job for them. Highly recommended.'

Clare Withycombe, Senior Consultant, Talent, Performance and Development, British Council

'John Lees is consistently at the forefront of the latest research and thinking about career coaching. He provides high quality, focused, pragmatic advice that is highly relevant to today's world of work.'

Jo Bond, independent coach and former MD Right Management UK and Head of Coaching Cedar Talent Management

'John Lees has produced a superb guide to getting in the driving seat of your career. With a powerful and unusual combination of straightforward, practical tips and insightful and empathic understanding, this is a career guide that provokes and prepares you to go out and get a job that you'll love.'

Stuart Lindenfield, Head of Transitions Practice, Reed Consulting, and co-author of *Confident Networking for Career Success*

'John Lees book can play a vital part in helping you turn job loss into an opportunity. We spend so much of our lives working that the next role shouldn't just be another job, but a job you will enjoy – because if you enjoy your work you'll be more successful and you improve your work life balance. At CMC we are totally behind the challenge of "How to get a job you love" – we regularly give copies to our clients.'

Robin Wood, Director and Senior Consultant, Career Management Consultants Ltd

'With this new edition John Lees demonstrates that he is still the pre-eminent careers author. His books are based on common sense, are easy to read and full of valuable tips and advice. We recommend him to all our clients.'

Dr Harry Freedman, Director, Career Energy

'I regularly recommend *How to Get a Job You'll Love* to candidates I meet who are going through career transition. It is a practical workbook to help you through that important and sometimes bewildering time.'

Joëlle Warren, Managing Director, Warren Partners Ltd

'John Lees has long been one of the UK's leading authorities on the field of career change. John *really* knows this field and his book is packed with easy to understand information for anyone looking for a job or planning a career change. I am delighted to see that the new version has sections covering a range of topics including the growing use of social media. This book is the ideal gift for anyone you know who has career issues – which is likely to be more than half the population!'

Bill Pitcher, Director, Pitcher Solutions Ltd, and former President, ACPi

'My long experience in the recruitment sector convinces me that this book unlocks secrets that most career changers never discover – in terms of how the market operates and the new mindset you need to make changes happen.'

Jeff Grout, Business consultant & speaker and former UK MD of Robert Half International

PRAISE FOR EARLIER EDITIONS OF *HOW TO GET A JOB YOU'LL LOVE*

'No matter how many barriers – real or imagined – are currently preventing you making the career change you know you need, this book will help you demolish them more effectively than a wrecking ball. John's books are thought-provoking, stimulating, challenging and a pleasure to read – and this is no exception. It could well change your life.'

Steve Crabb, Editor, *People Management*

'A jewel of a book … through practical exercises and bags of encouragement Lees will put you on the primrose path. A must-read for everyone who wants work to be more than 9-to-5 drudgery.'

Management Today

'This book will certainly get you thinking. Being self-aware is a skill that all great leaders possess. John Lees teaches you how to develop your own self-awareness and how to use that awareness effectively to achieve career success.'

Carol Lewis, Editor, Career, *The Times*

'John Lees provides sound, knowledgeable advice, and coaching, especially in terms of the emotional and practical impact of career and, therefore life change events. Although I had activated my personal network to good effect, and felt I was in control of my own "destiny", I found John's counsel extremely helpful in "de-stressing" the situation. Having someone of John's calibre confirm and expand on the activities I was undertaking in the pursuit of a new career opportunity, and the explanation of the usual time-scales involved, provided a positive influence to my confidence about the short- and long-term future options.'

Kath Lowey, Head of Customer Service, Xchanging HR Services

'The popularity of John Lees' writing lies in his ability to connect with the sense many people have that they can be more than they currently are, and deserve greater job satisfaction than they currently have. What makes his work distinctive is his use of his wide experience in careers coaching to provide tools and ways of thinking that any motivated individual can easily use to take control of their working life.'

**Carole Pemberton, Career and Executive Coach
and author of *Coaching to Solutions***

'I am delighted with the revised edition. It is only if we enjoy and believe in our work that we have any chance, both of doing a good job and having a happy and satisfying life.'

Sir John Harvey-Jones MBE

'A rare combination of accessibility and thoughtfulness ... I wholeheartedly recommend it to those seeking insight into career management or embarking on a job search.'

Stephen Bampfylde, Chairman, Saxton Bampfylde Hever Plc

'An excellent book, challenging, thought provoking, enthusiastic. It is like having a good friend who has been equipped with the skills of empowerment and the wide ranging knowledge of a careers consultant.'

Career Guidance Today

FURTHER PRAISE FOR JOHN LEES' WORK

'I know first hand the joy that being in the right career can bring and I commend John Lees for his books and seminars which help other people do just that.

Rosemary Conley CBE

'John Lees inspires people to rethink the way they work: to work with greater purpose, meaning and life/work balance.'
Ben West, Editor *Daily Express* Careers

'Highly recommended – always practical, but never patronising.'
Ian Wylie, *Guardian Rise*

'John Lees writes in a clear thinking style about practical ways to manage a career journey in competitive times.'
Mark Venning, President, Association of Career Professionals International

'Career advice with a difference, John Lees delivers a clear and comprehensive step-by-step guide to making your dream job a reality.'
Sam Dukes, former Editor, *EDGE* (Institute of Leadership & Management)

'I love John's straight-up approach. There's nothing airy-fairy about the career advice in his books and yet the tone holds your interest, not the usual dry-as-a-bone business book banter. What I love most is that it's real-life, real-world stuff: first he guides you to making your own career decisions with passion and instinct but then he gives professional, realistic – and very grown up – advice about making those decisions happen. I can still remember reading *How to Get a Job You'll Love* as a young journalist fresh off the boat from Oz with zilch industry contacts. Now I am in my dream job – John's advice works, pure and simple.'
Anna Magee, former Health Editor, *RED*

How to Get a Job You'll Love

2011–12 Edition

John Lees

The **McGraw·Hill** Companies

London • Burr Ridge IL • New York • St Louis • San Francisco • Auckland
Bogotá • Caracas • Lisbon • Madrid • Mexico • Milan
Montreal • New Delhi • Panama • Paris • San Juan • São Paulo
Singapore • Sydney • Tokyo • Toronto

How to Get a Job You'll Love
2011–12 Edition
John Lees

ISBN: 9780077129934

 **Professional**

Published by McGraw-Hill Professional
Shoppenhangers Road
Maidenhead
Berkshire
SL6 2QL
Telephone: 44 (0) 1628 502 500
Fax: 44 (0) 1628 770 224
Website: www.mcgraw-hill.co.uk

British Library Cataloguing in Publication Data
A catalogue record for this book is available from the British Library

Library of Congress Cataloguing in Publication Data
The Library of Congress data for this book
is available from the Library of Congress

Typeset by Gray Publishing, Tunbridge Wells, Kent
Cover design by Two Associates
Printed and bound in the UK by Bell & Bain Ltd, Glasgow

McGraw-Hill books are available at special quantity discounts.
Please contact the Corporate Sales Executive

Mixed Sources
Product group from well-managed
forests and other controlled sources
www.fsc.org Cert no. TT-COC-002769
© 1996 Forest Stewardship Council
FSC

About the Author

John Lees is one of the UK's best-known career strategists. *How To Get A Job You'll Love* regularly tops the list as the best-selling careers book by a British author, and along with *Job Interviews: Top Answers To Tough Questions* has been selected as WH Smith's 'Business Book of the Month'.

As a career and outplacement coach, John specializes in helping people make difficult career decisions – difficult either because they don't know what to do next or because there are barriers in the way of success. John Lees Associates helps career changers across the UK, and John is a regular keynote speaker at UK events (including *One Life Live* and *Forum 3*), has presented at the world's largest international career conferences and at events in the USA, Switzerland, South Africa, Australia and New Zealand.

John is the author of a wide range of career titles, all published by McGraw-Hill Professional. He has a regular careers column in *People Management* and writes for *The Times* and *The Guardian*. His work appears regularly in the national press and also in *Management Today, Real World, Company, Cosmopolitan, Prospects, Psychologies, Eve, Red, Marie Claire* and *She*. His work and case studies have been profiled in *Coaching at Work* and *The Sunday Times*. He featured in the Cavendish Films DVD 'The CV Experts', broadcasts widely on radio, and his work has been featured on TV (he has featured on the BBC interactive 'Back to Work' programme and on BBC 2's 'Working Lunch').

John is a graduate of the universities of Cambridge, London and Liverpool, and has spent most of his career focusing on the world of work. He has trained recruitment specialists since the mid-1980s, and is the former Chief Executive of the Institute of Employment Consultants (now the IRP). He has worked with a large range of organizations including British Telecom, the British Council, CAFOD, Cahoot, Career Management Consultants Ltd, CIPD, HBOS, the House of Commons, HSBC, Orange, the Recruitment & Employment Confederation, the Association of MBAs, Marks & Spencer, NAPP Pharmaceutical, NIACE, Reuters, SCA, Tribal, as well as Business Schools across the UK. He has been elected a Career Management Fellow (CMF) by the Institute of Career Certification International and serves on its international board.

Alongside his careers work John serves as an ordained Anglican priest in the Diocese of Chester, working with candidates who feel they have a calling to ministry. He lives and works in Cheshire, with his wife, the children's writer, Jan Dean, with occasional visits from their two adult sons.

John Lees Associates provides one-to-one career coaching in most parts of the UK. For details plus information about talks and workshops given by John Lees visit **www.johnleescareers.com** or telephone 01565 631625.

ACKNOWLEDGEMENTS

This book is written standing on the shoulders of many career coaching giants, most notably Dick Bolles in California and Daniel Porot in Geneva.

As ever, my thanks to all those who have provided ideas, material or encouragement: Judith Armatage, Liz Baldwin, Gill Best, Jim Bright, Julian Childs, Stephanie Clarke, Claire Coldwell, John Courtis, Liz Cross, Liz Hall, Peter Hawkins, Barrie Hopson, Deirdre Hughes, Stuart Lindenfield, Stuart McIntosh, Brian McIvor, Andrew O'Hanlon, Bernard Pearce, Carole Pemberton, Stuart Robertson, Sital Ruparelia, Lorraine Silverman, Peter Sinclair, Philip Spencer, Ian Webb and Janie Wilson, as well as fellow members of the *LinkedIn* Career Coach Forum. Thanks to my brother Andrew Lees for insights into the way scientists think, and to Robin Wood of Career

Management Consultants Ltd, for giving me the opportunity to road-test many of these concepts.

I would like to extend my thanks for the creativity and energy of the McGraw-Hill team for coaxing this sixth edition into daylight: Emma Gibson, Katherine Wood, Sally Ashworth, James Heath, Bev Shields, and my editor Catriona Hoyle. Special mention is due after six editions to the two original technical reviewers Jane Bartlett and Stuart Mitchell and to earlier editors Elizabeth Choules and Julia Scott. Finally, thanks to my agent James Wills at Watson, Little for his unstinting support and to Sue Blake, still a very serious contender for the best publicist on the planet.

This book, like all five previous editions, is dedicated to my wife, Jan, for giving me space to find out.

Other careers books by John Lees published by McGraw-Hill Professional

Job Interviews: Top Answers To Tough Questions **(2008), £9.99, ISBN 9780077119096**
Lists over 200 interview questions typically asked by employers and recruiters including the kind that will throw you completely unless you have prepared carefully. Also a range of tips about multi-strategy job search and using your CV in the interview process.

Take Control of Your Career **(2006), £12.99, ISBN 9780077109677**
How to manage your career once you've got a job, learning how to read your organization, avoid career traps, re-negotiate your job role and enhance your future without losing control of your life balance.

Why You? – CV Messages To Win Jobs **(2007), £9.99, ISBN 9780077115104**
Building on an extensive review of what employers love and hate about CVs, helps you decide which CV format will work best for you and reveals the secrets of a strong, effective document that gets you short listed.

Career Reboot – 24 Tips for Tough Times **(2009), £9.99, ISBN 9780077127589**
Packed with quick-read, practical tips for rejuvenating your job search, this book is a must for anyone striking out into a difficult job market after redundancy or simply looking for new opportunities in a difficult market.

Contents

Preface: How to Use This Book

WHO IS THIS BOOK FOR?

This book is written for anyone who is trying to make conscious, informed decisions about career choice. All kinds of people have difficult career decisions to make.

This book can help you if you are:

- feeling 'stuck' and looking for new challenges, and wondering 'what on earth can I do?'
- ready to plan the next stage of your career
- facing redundancy and asking 'what do I do next?'
- leaving full time education or seeking work after bringing up a family
- unemployed and looking for better ways of identifying opportunities
- seeking work and short of ideas about job possibilities
- discouraged because you believe you have little to offer the labour market
- toying with the idea of making a complete career change

HOW THIS BOOK MIGHT HELP YOU

There are many 'how to' books about career change and job search. If you're looking for boxes to tick, 'to do' checklists, model CVs or letters, look at one of the hundreds of books available that will give you an organized, left-brain solution to career management. We all need good advice when it comes to managing our job search. These books work well if you have a clear sense of direction, and all you need is a more effective job search technique. However, they don't appear to help answer the most common career statement: 'I know I want to do something different, but I don't know what it is.' And just as important, the question: 'How do I take the first step towards making a change?'

The chapters ahead do something different. In these pages you will look at the way businesses and individuals generate ideas about products, services and organizations, and apply that creative energy to career planning. It will challenge your perceived limitations and help you to discover your strengths.

This book aims to unlock your hidden potential and apply it to your career and life planning, to make the way you spend your waking hours more creative, more meaningful, more enjoyable. Its focus is not on job change for its own sake. Quite simply, the aim is to help you to make connections between your natural creativity and the way you plan your life's work. As a result of reading it, you may discover tools to improve your present job and create career opportunities where you are now. Finally, the chapters ahead provide practical advice about making your chosen future happen.

Does the approach work? Appendix 2 looks at people who have used the book to help them make significant career changes.

You may find that a single exercise unlocks your potential, or you may gain multiple insights from using several ideas or exercises. One word of advice: if the exercise doesn't work for you, don't feel you have 'failed'. All it means is this: *the exercise doesn't work for you*. Put it aside and move on.

MAPS FOR THE JOURNEY AHEAD

Begin by asking the simple question **What Happened to My Career?** in Chapter 1 – take a sideways look at what has happened to the way we think about work in post-recessionary times. Then take a fresh look in Chapter 2 at your **career problems** – what's preventing you from getting a job you'll love?

Chapter 3 is written specially for those who will shortly be graduating or leaving full-time education: **Where Next After Finishing Your Studies?**

Before we move into the central section on working out your ideal career, Chapter 4 invites you to begin using creative strategies to revive your career by **Thinking Around Corners**. Then Chapters 5–8 offer you a step-by-step guide towards a deeper understanding of your career drivers, your chosen areas of **knowledge**, your preferred and hidden **skills**, and the key aspects of **personality** that will shape your career.

Next, some highly practical aids to achieving your goals – Chapter 11 offers a comprehensive range of **Creative Job Search Strategies**, and Chapter 12 is a brand new chapter which asks the question **Can I Find a Job Using Social Media?** Chapter 13, **Interviews and How to Survive Them**, does exactly what it says on the tin.

You'll find some unique tools to help you along your way, including the pivotal Chapter 10, **What About a Complete Change of Career?**, the **House of Knowledge** (Chapter 6) – an innovative exercise to capture the things you have chosen to know about, the **Field Generator** – a ground-breaking tool to generate potential fields of work (in Chapter 10), plus a range of supporting exercises including **skill clips** (Chapter 7) and a revised version of the popular **time balance** exercise (Chapter 14).

Career development is about much more than job search, so in Chapter 14 you will find help to **love the job you've got** – tips for renegotiating your present or future job from within, and making the best of your future career. If you are thinking about doing something unconventional, Chapter 15 on **Portfolio Careers and Beyond** might help.

Chapter 16, **Beginning it Here**, is a five-point plan to begin to transform your career, and also offers advice on using recruitment consultants and how to **find a career coach**.

The book closes with a series of highly **practical checklists** covering everything from CV design to online job applications, example CV material and recommended websites.

NEW IN THIS EDITION

As well as features which have appeared in previous editions, this edition contains revisions throughout, updating material in the light of the rapidly changing market. New material includes the following:

Chapter 1, **What Happened to My Career?**, reviews how we make career decisions in a market dominated by redundancies and downsizing, and also looks at the way we continue to get in the way of success. This chapter contains a brand new exercise – *The Path Not Taken*.

If you are leaving full-time education and looking for a job, look at the discussion on finding evidence of your employability in Chapter 3, **Where Next After Finishing Your Studies?** – which also contains new ideas about managing internships.

Chapter 9 (**What Kind of Work Would Suit You Best?**) and Chapter 10 (**What About a Complete Change of Career?**) both contain new material. You will find expanded discussion about the influences that push us towards certain career paths, and clear directions on the first steps you should take if you want to do something very different, plus a range of new exercises to draw out your personal values.

Chapter 11, **Creative Job Search Strategies**, contains a range of updated material on why people keep on making the same mistakes when they throw themselves at the job market, while Chapter 14, **How to Love the Job You've Got**, discusses new career thinking and trends including 'giga-nomics'.

Chapter 12, **Can I Find a Job Using Social Media?**, is a brand new chapter on making the best use of web-based networking tools – and why the Internet, alone, won't save your career.

Chapter 16, **Beginning it Here**, shows you how to make changes for yourself using the ADEPT model, how to avoid the traps of retraining, and how to find appropriate help, and much of Chapter 15, **Portfolio Careers and Beyond** is updated advice. The list of **checklists** at the end of this book now includes new material on **self-employment**.

Appendix 3 is an entirely revised and updated list of **Useful Websites** to help kick-start your investigation.

What Happened to My Career?

CHAPTER

1

This chapter helps you to:

■ Look at what has happened to career thinking in a downturn

■ Understand how self-managed careers are becoming increasingly necessary

■ Explore the way you have made career decisions in the past

■ Manage 'career blocks'

■ Invent strategies for coping with personal change

■ Handle the dark side: deal with the negatives

STARTING FROM HERE – CAREER MANAGEMENT IN AND AFTER A RECESSION

Before we move forward, we have to make sense of our starting position – coming out of one of the most difficult recessions in recent experience. Everyone appears to know someone who has experienced redundancy, or has coped with cutbacks in the workforce. Some have been forced to move into new jobs, often with difficulty. Redundancies have hit organizations in all sectors and regions. Youth unemployment has hit the headlines once again, and among all the effects of recession has the most worrying impact. Major sectors, including steel and motor manufacturing, have continued in a decline that goes back decades.

That's one perspective. It's important to distinguish between what has actually happened and the way we feel about it. For one thing, although unemployment has certainly increased, in general the UK has experienced levels of employment during recession that many of our European neighbours would have envied during the boom years. More than 9 out of 10 people who consider themselves to be in the workforce have been in a job, despite predictions of huge layoffs. In fact the downturn has had a positive effect on many. There are a lot of people out there saying 'if I'm going to lose my job I might as well find something interesting'. Naturally there have also been a good number of people saying 'I just need any kind of job', but often that simply reflects a low point in their job search cycle – they quickly discover that this undifferentiated message puts them at the bottom of shortlists. Employers are interested in your ability to match their needs, not the fact that you are looking for a job.

What else has happened? Our confidence about long-term job security has certainly weakened. This, too, will have positive and negative consequences. Repeated surveys have shown that more workers expect their job to change or possibly disappear, and as a result many believe they will not be in the same job in 5 years' time. A background trend is of course that fewer staff believe that their employers will manage their careers for them. The post-2007 recession, interestingly, enlarged our interest in 'alternative' careers. In every recession it seems that self-employment increases, but this time there has also been an increased interest in portfolio careers, discussed in depth in Chapter 15.

I was asked to write a New Year essay for *The Guardian* at the height of the recession, trying to make sense of where work was going. In it I looked not just at the state of the market, but also at the strategies we adopt as individuals. These matter more than ever in difficult times, because when the stock market is buoyed up by mergers and acquisitions and many employers are expanding, there are usually enough jobs around to fall over. Even the relatively passive job seeker will usually find something – jobs can be relied upon to come along at their own speed. When the market is difficult and organizations move from growth to retraction, in a short space of time jobs seem suddenly unavailable. This impression is deepened by another trend – fewer jobs are advertised in the press, and more jobs are being filled by word of mouth. Combine these various factors and you come to an immediate conclusion: not only do we have to make difficult career decisions, but we also have to work harder to make things happen using our own resources.

For some the recession has been a great excuse to put career questions on hold – being unhappy in work when times are hard may feel like the norm. If there are fewer jobs available, maybe staying put is a good strategy. Like all career strategies, there's at least a half-truth in the idea – the timing of your job move is always important. However, something else happens as the market tightens: once jobs are harder to find a new cynicism sets in – what's the point of managing your career? Even if you dislike your job intensely, it's easy to be convinced that nothing will change the situation. Set that against an equally powerful reality – we are good at avoiding taking career responsibility, and we love nothing better than a chance to put the blame somewhere. The recession has become the nation's favourite excuse for trashing our career goals. Watch this space: when employers are desperate for staff again and there are skill shortages, we will find other excuses for living an indifferent career. Any rationalisation will do if it means avoiding the bigger questions about where life is going.

SO WHAT HAPPENED TO CAREER PLANNING?

The idea that we have any choice at all in our careers is a fairly new one. It's only since the 1950s that the Western world has adopted the idea that we make career choices relating to our interests, personality types and backgrounds.

What is a career? To have a 'career' is largely an idea of the twentieth century. Before that, a 'job' was what we would now call an 'assignment' or 'project'; a short-term engagement. People had trades, and were 'jobbing' carpenters, masons, journalists or sailors. A permanent job was one that was attached to an income source arising from an endowment, e.g. a 'living' in a parish church or a royal appointment.

So what about career planning? The idea seems, for many, close to myth and legend. Other people seem to have highly developed career plans, but putting your own together either seems like very hard work or something that is going to be frustrated by the changing marketplace. How can you plan 20 years ahead when the market changes beyond recognition in a matter of weeks?

First, let's agree that career planning is an area we avoid. Most people spend more time planning a car purchase, one annual holiday or their new kitchen than they do thinking about their career. Generally speaking, we're not good at career planning at all. It's staggering how many people drift from one job to another with no clear idea of the way their career is heading.

It's easy to think of career management as a crisis activity. *I must get out of here. I've got to get a better job. I must find work. I have to get into a new career.* What this demonstrates is passive behaviour – waiting until external forces push you on to the next square of the game board. Clearly there are times when we have to make some kind of career decisions: when you leave full-time education, when you are out of work or when your job disappears. To manage a career on the basis of whether the economy is in boom or bust means accepting whatever comes along, rather than doing something to shape your own future.

Perhaps the decision is more pressing. You may have a strong impulse to move on, find a change of scenery or work with different people. You may want to keep learning, achieve success or make some other kind of progress so that each year recorded on your CV represents a fresh experience. Sometimes a sense of career crisis is expressed as an overwhelming need to do something more meaningful or relevant.

The Big Decisions

My colleagues and I specialize in helping people to make difficult career change decisions – difficult for a variety of reasons: people don't know what they want to do next, they can't see a way out of where they are now, or they know where they want to be but don't know how to get there.

If you manage your career, actively and consciously, you will make it work better for you. We've already discussed the limitations and false security of a long-term career plan. We need to think smarter about careers: planning ahead is far less important than being *awake* now – awake to the possibilities of change and the urgency of doing work which is more fulfilling and interesting. Those who make conscious decisions about their working lives are more successful and more satisfied. They have thought about the work they want to do and are actively pursuing it. Some have sought out the right job. Others have learned the skill of redesigning the jobs that they do, so that they play to their strengths. Sometimes it's about recognizing that some of the things you do outside work are important enough to play a bigger role in your life. Career development doesn't always mean changing jobs.

Career management has many dimensions, including:

▌ discovering the kind of work you find most stimulating and enjoyable

▌ discovering fields of work (including jobs you didn't know existed) where you can make a difference

▌ striking a balance between what you are looking for and what the world has to offer – setting out the steps on your journey

▌ setting goals – these may be financial, learning or personal goals

▌ achieving the right life/work balance – making room for learning, family, relationships and the things that matter most

▌ making sure that work provides the things that motivate you most – status, recognition, independence, learning, etc.

▌ renegotiating your job so that you can do more of the things that energize you

▌ planning for retirement or changes of lifestyle.

IS WORK THAT IMPORTANT?

Judging by the amount of time spent complaining about it, it must be. If it wasn't for work, we would have far less to moan about. We put a huge amount of energy into work, and rely on it for a large chunk of self-esteem. Far too many adults of working age in Europe are either unemployed or underemployed, even in boom times. Being underemployed is as worrying as unemployment: people who are underemployed or in the wrong kind of work become demotivated, depressed or even ill. Work matters. Finding the right kind of work matters even more.

If we begin with life and work, we should ask ourselves one question: do you **work to live** or **live to work**? If you believe that you **work to live** you may be more motivated by the things you do outside work than the things which earn you a living. You are living out your dream in a different reality, and your salary is there simply to fund your dream. A lot of people live that way, and can be happy.

The problem is that this ignores the huge amount of time that work consumes. If you work full-time hours you spend more of your life in work than in any other waking activity (if you live for 70 years, you'll spend about 23 of those years asleep, and 16 years working). Accounted for in another way, you will spend about 100,000 hours in work (that's just what Americans call 'face time', the time when your jacket is over your chair. Just think about all the other hours that go into preparing for work, worrying about work, complaining about work …).

If you feel that you **live to work**, it may be that you've found the best job in the world, or perhaps you haven't explored enough to find out what life has to offer. Perhaps work plays too important a part in your life? Those who suffer the greatest impact of redundancy are those who have made their work their only focus, perhaps at the expense of family or personal development.

One definition of the word 'career' is *movement in an uncontrolled direction*, as in 'the steering failed and my car careered across the motorway'. Rapid movement in an uncontrolled direction. Does that sound familiar?

The days of your life

In the past decade or so we have got used to the idea that we can make life choices – about how we live, the things around us, the activities that fill our days. Here's another perspective. In an average lifetime (according to www.statistics.gov.uk), a woman will live for about 29,800 days. Men get rather less, about 28,200 days. That's around 29,000 days to learn, work, play, raise a family, leave your mark on life and acquire wisdom. It doesn't sound a lot of days, does it? Certainly not a lot of time to be saying 'This isn't what I wanted to do when I grew up …'. How you spend those days matters – no matter what your spiritual perspective.

WHAT IS CREATIVE CAREER MANAGEMENT?

Valuing creativity

The first thing to recognize is that we are all capable of inventing extraordinary solutions to cope with life's problems. For most of us these problems are everyday: taking children in opposite directions in one car, paying this week's bills with next week's money, or mending using old bits and pieces rather than buying an expensive component. Sometimes it's the kind of thinking we take for granted, such as taking an engine apart and putting it back together, perfectly, without a diagram, or caring for three or four difficult children at their most unpleasant, or making dinner out of six things in the cupboard. We are all creative. We have to be: that's how humans have survived.

You will probably have come across many different ways of describing the way people think. However, for many of us lists, plans, diagrams and flowcharts don't work. We don't read life that way. We're inspired by conversations, by people, by movies; our natural creativity needs a different kind of kick-start.

The important thing to remember at this stage is this: we are all given a particular kind of creativity. Career choice is about unlocking what makes *you* a creative, energized person.

There is no point in work unless it absorbs you like an absorbing game.

D.H. Lawrence

What has creativity got to do with career exploration?

We normally use our creative brain to solve problems where ordinary solutions don't work. Isn't your career this kind of problem? You've tried to deal with it logically, by progressing in a sequence from A to Z. You've done the right courses, taken the right initial steps, gained the experience …. Does work provide the right answers? You've tried to look at career change as a business discipline, because you've been told that getting a job *is* a job. Did this approach get you the right results?

We need another method. Every day, business executives wake up and have to think of new ideas: new names for brands, new ways of selling old products, new ways of communicating with people. Where do ideas come from? The age-old question of the tired mind. Writers, designers, inventors and advertising executives all have the same dread: the blank piece of paper. Yet there are ways of learning how to generate ideas. We normally look for the 'right' solution, but creativity works better where we seek multiple solutions: first one idea, then another, then another. Creativity thrives on abundance.

The vital thing is not to confuse idea generating with decision making. How many meetings have you been to where the first good idea is shot down in flames? Ideas are tentative, fragile things that in their early stages can't stand up to the strong light of decision making. It's no use thinking 'I wonder about medicine …' if you immediately say 'Do I want to be a doctor, or don't I?'. Forcing a decision too early simply crushes creative thinking. Maybe not a doctor – maybe a medical journalist, or a pharmacist, or a physiotherapist … .

When a business enterprise is in decline and heading towards oblivion because it has nothing interesting to offer the marketplace, it needs to find a new way of thinking. Right now this business needs some smart thinking: how can it reinvent itself and turn things around? At times like this businesses throw out the rule book and become hungry for ideas that will generate new products and services. If your career is in the doldrums you may benefit from the same kind of thinking: you need to reinvent yourself, rediscover what you are capable of doing and being. As the saying goes, 'if you only live half your life, the other half will haunt you forever'.

Why do people avoid having great jobs?

There are more varieties of jobs out there than ever before, yet we still generally let our careers be shaped by accident, or accept second or third best because it's easier to stand still than to move forward. Most importantly of all, we insist on using the most limited kind of straight-line thinking in career planning and job search. Why? Essentially, we like to do what feels safe, even if that means being unhappy. There's a powerful part of the brain that says *stop here. It's dull, but it's comfortable. Out there looks difficult and strange.*

And then you find evidence to support your position. You focus on stories of people of your age and background who tried to make a change and failed. I have a theory. At times when change threatens we develop a personal radar that scans the horizon for information. Radar, as you know, is hungry for enemy objects. And we find them. You suddenly discover people who were made redundant and never found a job again. People beat a path to your door to tell you *don't do it … it will all come to tears.*

As you'll discover from reading this book, we come up with all kinds of negative messages to act as blocks to growth and change. If you believe 'I'm not an ideas person' or 'I'm not a leader', your brain is capable of making sure this is a self-fulfilling prophecy. If a golfer says, 'I bet I slice this ball', he probably will.

Adaptability

One of the odd reasons that we avoid doing the kind of job we'd love to do is that we are adaptable. Human beings have evolved to become highly adaptable creatures. We can live in temperatures from –30 to +50°C, we can survive in the most demanding, unhealthy and difficult conditions, and families can work, raise children and live good lives even under the most brutal political regimes. Perhaps because of this built-in survival instinct, some of us have the capacity to do something which modern society finds odd and most of history saw as the norm. We can hold down an uninspiring job for decades. Given a world of choice, the fact that we can, doesn't mean that we should.

I don't want to make the wrong decision

Planning a career that has no risk is a comforting 1950s fantasy of a workplace where you could find a safe job with a good pension. The idea 'I don't want to make the wrong decision' sometimes reflects what we have seen happen to others, but far more often speaks of our individual fear of doing something which is going to make us look foolish. Being motivated by safety is not being attracted towards something, but is about being motivated *away* from danger. Sadly that means that all your energy goes into avoiding the first steps which will lead to exploration, and trying to conform to some internal picture of a life that is sensible, low risk and conventional.

How many successful brands or products started life by being *conventional*? It is true that people have constraints: bills to pay, mouths to feed. It's important not to underemphasize that fact. However, what matters is that these basic requirements are seen for what they are – problems to be solved, not reasons for living. See also Chapter 8 on the word 'realistic'.

Put another way, incremental thinking only gets you incremental results. But if you don't take even the small steps, you can pretty much guarantee that nothing will change at all.

'I just need a job'

By now you may have come to the conclusion that creative career management might be a good thing for somebody else. Why not you? Because you feel that reality is harder and tougher than that. You need something real, right now, that pays the bills. You just need a job. This might be because you're unemployed, or because you're just not paid enough to make ends meet. This places you in a vulnerable position in the labour market. It forces you to become a job beggar, going round with your hat in your hand saying just one thing: I need a job. Desperately.

I spent some time in early 2000 working with a group of job seekers from one of the townships in Johannesburg. One of them, Gugu, was aged 17 and had given up looking for work. Why? 'There are no jobs in South Africa', she said. But new jobs are being created in that country every day ... 'Yes, but so many people are chasing them', she said sadly. Talking to her I realized that all over the world too many people fall into job beggar mode. Fortunately, Gugu and her fellow job seekers all found jobs as a result of a programme which encouraged her to focus on her strengths and actively talk about them to employers.

No, it's true: I just need a job

Do you really? How long will it be before you're back asking the same questions: What am I doing this for? Where's my life going? Soon you end up saying that there's no point thinking about your career, your skills, your future, *because there are no choices*. There are very few occasions when that's true. Just get some perspective on that statement. Compared with most of the world's population, past and present, people in today's developed world have a huge range of life choices, and more protection against failure. If you need money, just earn it. Don't pretend that's all there is. We all have choices.

Perhaps an inner voice is saying '*get real* – choosing a job because you enjoy it is self-indulgence, a daydream'.

Listen to successful people talking about the work they do. They don't often say 'Well, the money's good'. They talk about work being like a 'game', being 'fun' or 'the best job in the world'; they talk about the privilege of doing for a living what they would gladly do for nothing. Another interesting fact: during the decade up to 2007 the UK enjoyed low unemployment, and more people were employed than at any time in its history, yet people still said 'this is a really bad time to be unemployed'. Equally, people get brilliant jobs even in the depths of recession.

How many excuses do you need to have to ensure you stay miserable at work?

Effective career planning is about finding a job that works for you, matching who you are to the life you are going to lead. That's not a luxury: that's the clearest reality there is. Doing that provides you with a great career, and gives you a greater chance of contributing to life.

Working smarter rather than harder at career building

Some say that the right job is out there somewhere looking for you. Beware, this sounds like a strategy of 'I'm not getting excited until the perfect job comes along', but even if there's a job out there which is great for you, you can't sit at home and wait for it to knock on the door. The majority of us have to rely on a mix of good judgement, inspired guesswork and a pinch of luck. Luck has been described as two mathematical laws working together: chance and averaging. We can't control chance, but we can increase the odds in our favour. Invest in your future. Use your precious thinking time carefully, and learn to think openly, because a moment's inspiration can sometimes take you far, far further than a year's dull planning.

Setting objectives is a vital part of the process. Ideas without activity are daydreams. The danger is that we move too quickly to activity without really taking the opportunity to reinvent our careers. Equally likely, we may continue to have career daydreams without making the first step to find out anything at all about the possibility of change. You don't need a master-plan, an original idea, a lucky breakthrough or great contacts (although any of the last three will shorten the process). What you do need is to plan what you are going to do very soon, and then take the first step, and the step after that. That's what makes change happen.

Be experimental

Setting out means being prepared to make mistakes, and – ultimately – being prepared to make a change. However, the first step is simply finding out, and trying on new ideas to see if they fit.

Adopt the habit of being experimental. To think 'it's all experimental' is a great approach to life. It's an approach which values finding out and avoids blame when experiments go wrong. Experiment and failure, 'making mistakes', is a necessary part of creative thinking. It's a well-known fact that behind every new business idea there's a long list of things that didn't quite come off. Before every new invention comes a history of failed attempts. You can't make progress without getting things wrong some of the time. If you are going to focus on failure, then 'fail forwards' rather than 'fail backwards'; in other words, make your mistakes positive steps forward in your learning. Every successful product brought to market required a thousand near-misses. Experiment away.

No-one can persuade another to change. Each of us guards a gate of change that can only be opened from the inside. We cannot open the gate of another, either by argument or by emotional appeal.

Marilyn Ferguson

Exploring is an opening-out process. We tend to think along tramlines, moving logically from one stage to the next. Divergent thinking works rather differently. Let your imagination fan out: rather than making decisions too soon, look at possibilities. Try on ideas. Figure 1.1 shows how once you have really worked through the process of idea building, you will reach a point where you have enough information to start setting concrete objectives. At this point the funnel reverses,

Setting career objectives, making decisions

Exploring, opening out options, exploring fields, discovering what you have to offer

Figure 1.1   Career transition funnels

and you consciously close down options and aim for specific outcomes. This book takes you from the point of exploring to the point of setting real goals.

EXERCISE 1.1 – THE PATH NOT TAKEN

Two roads diverged in a wood, and I—
I took the one less traveled by,
And that has made all the difference.

Robert Frost, *Mountain Interval*

Draw a flow chart of your life so far, indicating all the most important steps and decisions. It might look a little like this:

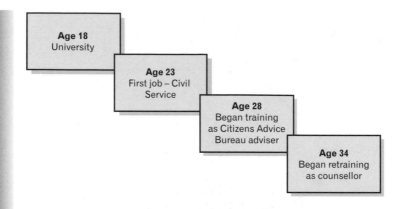

Figure 1.2   Life flow

Now think about the **paths not taken**. Look at each stage above and draw in as many alternative choices as you can ('the things I nearly did/ could have done') as below:

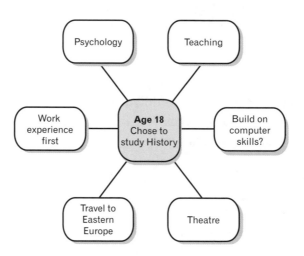

Figure 1.3   Possible choices at each turning point

EXERCISE 1.2 – MINDMAPPING YOUR FUTURE

You might find it helpful to use a **mindmap**. This is a technique pioneered by Tony Buzan which provides a tool for individual brainstorming. Place a topic at the centre of a large, blank piece of paper, and draw a line out of it to record a new idea. Start a new line, like the branch of a tree, to represent each new idea or connection as it comes up. Figure 1.4 shows a completed example.

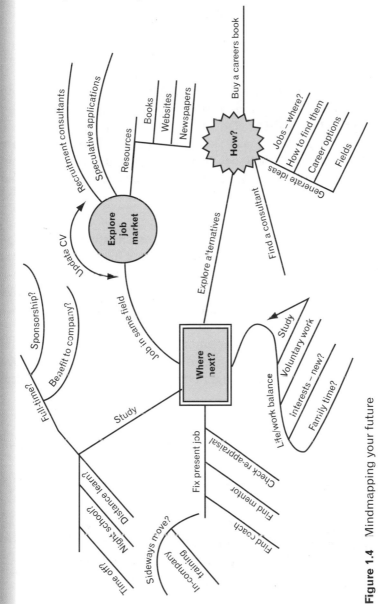

Figure 1.4 Mindmapping your future

EXERCISE 1.3 – FORCE FIELD ANALYSIS

This technique, devised by Kurt Lewin, presents a variation on traditional problem-solving techniques.

Draw up two columns. In column one list all the benefits that would be obtained if you manage to change your career, either by changing your job or renegotiating it. In column two list the negative forces, i.e. the forces against change. Figure 1.5 shows some typical examples.

Lewin argues that change is brought about when the driving force for change exerts greater pressure than the restraining forces that resist it. Driving forces are generally positive, reasonable and logical. In contrast, restraining forces are often negative, emotional, illogical or even unconscious. Both sets of forces are very real and must be taken seriously when dealing with any change.

Increasing the driving forces may bring results in the short term. As long as the restraining forces are still there, change becomes increasingly difficult. Think of it like pushing against a spring: at first it's easy, but the harder you push, the greater the resistance. Negative elements have a strong conservative factor. For example, it is often easier to stay where you are rather than face a set of difficult decisions. The fact that people dislike change is demonstrated by the fact that in the UK people change spouses more willingly than they move bank accounts, despite the huge growth in competition in the banking sector.

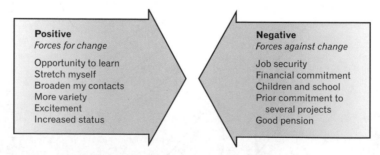

Positive
Forces for change

Opportunity to learn
Stretch myself
Broaden my contacts
More variety
Excitement
Increased status

Negative
Forces against change

Job security
Financial commitment
Children and school
Prior commitment to
    several projects
Good pension

Figure 1.5   Force Field Analysis and career change

Using Force Field Analysis to manage personal change

▪ Draw up your own list of positive and negative factors.

▪ Add as many new positive factors as you can.

▪ Next look in detail at your negative forces. How real are they?

▪ Give each factor a score from 1 (weak) to 5 (strong).

▪ Add up the total score on each side: which side is stronger at the moment?

▪ Now we are going to make the Force Field Analysis really work. See if you can strengthen any of your positive forces. If 'opportunity to learn' is a positive factor encouraging change, then ask yourself what your job will be like if this is taken away from you. This might mean that you increase the score for factors which you discover are really important.

▪ Can you add any new positive factors? They will only make a difference if they are both real and important.

▪ Can you reduce the negative forces in any way? This means really looking at them and seeing whether you can weaken their impact or turn them into positives. How transferable is your pension? Is your present job really as secure as it seems? If you are worried about the effect of change on your family, what would be the effect if you do nothing and remain unfulfilled? If you are worried about the risk of making mistakes in a new job, then look back at your work history and think of a time when you were worried about exactly the same thing: maybe as a result you achieved something which is now a central plank of your CV?

'MUST DO' LIST

☑ Reflect: have your career decisions been made consciously, or have you largely responded to opportunity and chance?

☑ Look at the Paths Not Taken – how much of your career is about regret or missed opportunity?

☑ Think about how you can use this book to help. Begin a hard-back notebook to jot down your discoveries and the results of the exercises in this book. Write down the steps you need to take in the next 2 months. Then take step one.

☑ Plan ahead. Look at the chapter headings and decide how and when you are going to set aside time to go through this process.

☑ Use the Force Field Analysis technique to help someone else with personal change, and then come back to try it again for yourself.

☑ Identify someone you know who is a champion of change. Find out how and why they do it, what motivates them and how they generate the energy to convince others.

What's the Problem?

This chapter looks at the following:

▌ The reason careers go off-line

▌ Why people follow careers they hate, and fail to get careers they would love

▌ The blocks between you and a great career

▌ Overcoming personal barriers

I DON'T HAVE TIME FOR A CAREER CRISIS ...

How many times have you heard someone talking about where they have 'ended up'? The truth is that most people are very passive about their career choices and leave job satisfaction very much to chance. It's easy to shrug off responsibility with a phrase like 'A job's a job. It pays the bills'. We are getting used to the idea of job mobility, and some people are changing jobs ever more frequently. New occupations are opening up all the time, and some people are sampling a whole range of them during the course of a single 'career'. Does this mean that people are happier in work or better at choosing career paths? It seems not. According to the American writer Studs Terkel, work is, for some, 'a Monday to Friday sort of dying'.

Where do the days go?

We haven't always done so, but since the 1990s British workers put in some pretty long working hours. In 2000 a British government report found that 80% of workplaces have employees who work more than their standard hours, and 39% without extra pay. It's a culture that can be damaging. According to Chartered Institute of Personnel and Development (CIPD) research published in 2009, just over a fifth of people in employment work more than 45 hours a week. One in three partners of people who typically work more than 48 hours a week feel that this has had a negative effect on personal relationships.

Studies on work satisfaction show that over the last 20 years or so we have become increasingly unhappy at work, and one of the most common reasons quoted is long working hours. Nevertheless, for a range of reasons we're increasingly dissatisfied with our jobs. This may be because we expect more from our careers, or a natural reaction to two decades of downsizing and job uncertainty. We are more prone to 'burn out', more in need of stress counselling as a result of work. It matters more than ever that we have a toolkit to help us to find a job we enjoy.

Why should people be happy at work?

It's easy to believe that work is not somewhere you are supposed to enjoy yourself. What happens if you believe this is that you create a world of compartments. *This is the compartment where I work. This is my family compartment. This small compartment in the corner is where I really enjoy myself.* It's all part of that either/or thinking we're so good at. I *either* have a job that pays the bills, *or* a job that's fun. I can't have both.

Career and coaching specialist Carole Pemberton talks about the Faustian pact we make in our careers – a deal you make that allows you to think in these either/or terms, like Faust's pact with the devil. A pact typically says 'I can only be successful if …'. Here are some examples: 'I can only be a top salesperson if I work long hours and eat badly.' 'I can only be a great manager if I don't empathize with my staff.'

Why should people be happy at work? Work isn't fun, your friends will tell you. Work is real. If this all sounds reasonable, look at the people who seem to have most fun in their jobs. They're often running their own businesses, making new things, meeting new people, sharing what they know and inspiring people. Sometimes they are in jobs which directly improve the lives of others. For some, it's about producing brilliant ideas, products, or great experiences for customers. Are these workers poor as a result? Sometimes. However, some of them are richer and more successful than most. Happiness and success don't always come hand in hand, but on the other hand being unhappy is no automatic route to success either. Unfortunately it's often the unhappy, unenthusiastic, low-energy people that companies get rid of first.

Why should people be happy at work? Take a deep breath. Read that question again. Work is where you spend most of your waking life. It's where you put about 80% of your personal energy. So that question really means why should people be happy? What do you think? Do happy people live longer, have great children and make a difference? You know they do. So let's stop that all-time Faustian deal: 'I can only get a great job if I forget about being happy at work.' That's a self-fulfilling deal. Be careful what you ask for in life, you might just get it … .

One of the symptoms of an approaching nervous breakdown is the belief that one's work is terribly important.

Bertrand Russell

Are some occupations more satisfying than others? We seem to have a constant fascination with the worst jobs in society, but research published in 2007 by the Economic and Social Research Council (ESRC) Future of Work Programme (see www.esrc.ac.uk) identified that some jobs are more likely to lead to job satisfaction. It seems that medical secretaries, childcare workers, cleaners, clergy, various managers and those offering personal services such as healthcare, travel and catering get top place. Low job satisfaction levels are recorded among journalists, mining surveyors, postal workers and Civil

Service executive officers. (For what it's worth, telephone fitters declared themselves Britain's unhappiest employees.)

Happiness – goal or accident?

It's worth saying a little more about happiness. Many of us think that happiness is a vague, subjective and entirely individual state of mind. Others believe that we can do very little to influence or adjust happiness.

Richard Layard's book *Happiness: Lessons from a New Science* is one of several that reflect on the research undertaken into what makes some communities and some nations happier than others. This research begins with the principle that when people say they are generally happy or very happy in life, this is something that can be measured. Layard looks at the major factors in life which contribute to happiness, and the results are fascinating. First, being happy seems to contribute directly to good health. Second, being rich doesn't make anyone happy. Many countries in the developing world with low income levels per capita are just as content as developed nations, and in some cases happier. Internationally, once people achieve an average income of about $15,000 per year (that's dollars, not pounds) anything they earn above that level doesn't make them any happier.

Layard defines his 'Big 7' factors that affect happiness. The first five are in order of importance:

1. **Family relationships** – countries with the highest rates of divorce and family break-up have relatively unhappy populations.

2. **Financial situation** – not earning enough for your needs, or feeling pressurized to earn competitively for reasons of status tends to lead to less happiness.

3. **Work** – being underemployed or economically inactive makes us unhappy; doing relatively fulfilling work acts as a positive. Layard writes: 'When people become unemployed, their happi-

ness falls much less because of the loss of income than because of the loss of work itself.'

4. **Community and friends** – having active friendship groups and being involved in community activity and associations increases happiness.

5. **Health** – ill-health, particularly where it involves pain and distress, naturally leads to unhappiness.

6. **Personal freedom** – having some independence in our life decisions helps us to be happy.

7. **Personal values** – being of service to others, contributing to society and having a personal faith are all factors which increase happiness.

It's worth revisiting what Layard has to say about work:

'Work is vital, if that is what you want. But it is also important that the work is fulfilling. Perhaps the most important issue is the extent to which you have control over what you do. There is a creative spark in each of us, and if it finds no outlet, we feel half-dead. This can be literally true: among British civil servants of any given grade, those who do the most routine work experience the most rapid clogging of the arteries.'

Richard Layard, *Happiness – Lessons from a New Science*
(Allen Lane 2005)

The good, the bad and the just plain awful

In 2009, Gallup reported that 'more than 80% of British workers lack any real commitment to their jobs, and a quarter of those are "actively disengaged" or truly disaffected with their workplaces'. This research recorded that as many as 61% of workers were 'not engaged' – i.e. not psychologically committed to their roles and likely to leave if an opportunity presents itself.

What are the things at work that give you the greatest buzz? The sort of things you go home and talk about? Write them down. It's worth recording the good things. Take a blank piece of paper and divide it into three. Write down everything that you would include under each heading:

1. THE REALLY GOOD STUFF   Things you find stimulating
                                    and enjoyable

2. THINGS I COULD LIVE   When do you find work boring
    WITHOUT   or dull?

3. THINGS I PUT UP WITH AT   What aspects of work fill you
    WORK THAT I NEED   with dread or loathing?
    LIKE A HOLE IN THE HEAD

Table 2.1 shows another way of measuring work happiness. Not all of the statements will match your personal situation, and you may have your own that you would like to add. Which category in Table 2.1 describes you best?

Table 2.1   How happy are you in your work?

A	**Dream job**
	I can't wait to get into work. Work is the place where I grow and learn most, where I am set healthy challenges, where I am valued and appreciated. A great deal of fun and self-esteem are centred in my work, which fits my values, talents and personality. I *know* that I make a difference. I express who I am in my job. The rewards are right, and I would be happy to be paid less if necessary. I love the part work plays in my life.
B	**Thumbs up**
	I enjoy work most of the time, but sometimes there are headaches and problems. My work feels useful and contributes to my self-esteem. My contribution is clear, acknowledged and significant. My career is a good match to my talents, personality and values. I am appreciated by others. I feel that I make a difference, and that I add something positive to the organization. I find supervision helpful, but my boss is more a mentor than a supervisor. I lead a satisfying career which contributes to all parts of my life.

C **Mustn't grumble**

I accept the work I do. Sometimes I feel valued, other times exploited or ignored. Work is stable, largely unexciting, doesn't interfere with my inner life too much. New ways of doing things are sometimes discouraged. I may be in the right line of work, but in the wrong organization. I am valued for some of what I do, but not always the most important things.

D **Someone's got to do it**

I work because I need to. Otherwise I don't feel I owe a great deal to my employer. Several parts of the job are unpleasant/boring/demeaning/pointless. Real life begins at 5 o'clock. I'm not learning anything. I try to make a contribution but sometimes hit a brick wall. Some of my best skills are getting rusty. Sometimes I feel I would just like a quiet life.

E **Wage slave**

There are days I almost have to drag myself to work; every day and every moment is miserable. I feel a huge mismatch between the person I am and the person this job requires me to be. I feel trapped. Each day makes things seem worse. I dread the prospect of Monday morning. I take all my sick leave because the job makes me ill.

If you're in box A, congratulations. Recognize what's good about your work and ensure that it remains that way. Generally only 30% of people place themselves in group A or B. Indeed, surveys repeatedly show that as many as 70% of people are unhappy with the work they do. If you're in box E, make a review of how you can change things. Soon. You may not be in box A for a while, but moving up the scale is possible for most people in work.

Nothing has a stronger influence psychologically on children than the unlived lives of their parents.

Carl Jung

YOUR WORLD VIEW

Careers specialists have long talked about *motivated skills*; in other words, the skills you relish using, the skills you would exercise for next to nothing, even for free. There's a huge difference between doing something because you know how and doing something because you actively choose to do so. That difference is the power of motivation. Motivation turns a task into a joy, an errand into a quest, a job into a vocation.

The key ingredient in your career exploration is the degree of motivation you apply to the process. *You get out what you put in*. Read that last sentence again. Your success in gaining a stunning career depends as much on your own personal motivation as it does on any other combination of factors, internal or external.

Where does that motivation come from? Think about your **world view**. Think about what makes up that picture. It contains your memories, your history, elements of the world views held by your parents, friends and loved ones. In it you'll find your preconceptions, your fears, your values. A world view is made up of sentences as well as pictures. We have an all-too familiar script running most of the time: 'charity begins at home', 'if you want a job doing properly, do it yourself', 'keep your cards close to your chest'. Look closely at the picture you hold of yourself, the script you run in your own personal soap opera. Do you see the glass as half full or half empty?

Ah, that depends …. And it does. It depends on the way *you* look. Look at the signals you receive during the course of a day. How many times do you receive praise and ignore it? How many times do you hear neutral or objective data and take it the wrong way? How often do you hear criticism and clutch it to yourself as the last, final and totally accurate picture of *you*? The reality is that most of us have an impressive talent: to ignore positive information, distort neutral information and attach ourselves to negative information.

Where you put the energy matters. If you put your energy into believing the glass is half empty, what you see is emptiness, absence, insufficiency. If you choose to put your energy into seeing the glass as half full, you will see fullness and abundance everywhere.

Information is neutral. But where do you put your energy and attention? You fill your personal bubble with evidence of what you lack: 'I can't do that ...', 'I've never been good at ...', 'Nobody's interested in me when I ...'. You have a natural, inexhaustible ability to hang on to these favourite ideas. Those who understand the secrets of motivation are generally masters of two areas of personal growth:

1. They know who they are, and what they are good at.

2. They know when to ignore negative data, when to accept a neutral picture as simply neutral, and when to remember and act upon all the good things they ever learned about themselves.

At this point you may be hearing two words in your head:

YES, BUT ...

About now the **YES, BUT** area of the brain is kicking in. We all do it. It's a part of the human psyche that psychologist Ned Herrmann called the *safekeeping self*. The safekeeping self is the senior committee member who faithfully attends every meeting in your brain and says: 'We've heard all this stuff before', 'It'll never fly', 'I'd be taking a risk', 'It might work for somebody else', 'Show me the statistics', 'It might work in London, but ...'.

'Yes, but' thinking is the biggest block to career transition. Saying 'Yes, but' is a good way of avoiding an issue and avoiding change: 'Yes, but I have to earn a living', 'Yes, but in the real world ...'. It's often a sign that the speaker is not listening positively – it's a classic defence mechanism, a way of avoiding having to face issues.

Normal is getting dressed in clothes that you buy for work, driving through traffic in a car that you are still paying for, in order to get to the job that you need so you can pay for the clothes, car and the house that you leave empty all day in order to afford to live in it.

Ellen Goodman

PROBLEMS FOR THE CAREER DOCTOR

Time to discuss your various 'Yes, but' symptoms. The Career Doctor will see you now.

Too long in the same job

The 'same job' could have been a 20-year history of change, variety and development. We're not demotivated by being in one job or one organization. We're turned off when things start repeating themselves and we're not learning or changing.

Even if you're in a great job that you love doing, you may not want to do it forever. Most careers need a reboot from time to time.

The side benefits are good

In one firm an employee stayed on for several years because somebody in the office brought in an excellent cake every day. We all have our reasons for staying and our reasons for leaving. The million-dollar question is: are these the *real* reasons? People are very good at finding excuses for avoiding the real issues, or justifying decisions. If you find yourself saying 'the pension scheme/the medical insurance/the gym is so good ...', then the question should be: *but is this why I'm here*? Side benefits go quickly in times of trouble.

Talk to people after they have retired. Do they talk about the salary and benefits, or do they talk about the good relationships, the fun, the excitement, the feeling of doing meaningful work? When you're on your deathbed, are you going to say 'I wish my pension had been just a bit bigger' or 'Why did I waste 20 years in that office watching the clock?'

I'll stick it out

'The job's okay, and a lot of things are good about it, but …'. This general sense of dissatisfaction needs focus. Is it really the whole job that doesn't suit, or part of it? Is it just some of the people you work with? Are there problems elsewhere in your life (partner, health, family) and work provides a convenient dumping ground for your troubles?

The answer to these questions takes a little time to work out, but you can begin by asking:

▌ What parts of the job do I enjoy?

▌ What parts do I *really* enjoy? When does the time pass quickly?

▌ If I could change something using a magic wand, would it be the people, the place, the rewards, the tasks I do? Make a list, then look at what you can actually change, and be aware of the difference between what can be changed, and what can't.

A word of warning: it's all too easy to believe that the only solution to dissatisfaction at work is job change. Often all that work dissatisfaction shows you is that there's a mismatch between who you are and what you are doing. That mismatch shows, if not to ourselves, to others. But the real answer is **career growth**: moving towards a closer match between yourself and the work you do. Career growth may be something you can achieve exactly where you are already.

I'm too old

Yes, employers are wrong-headed about age. But time and time again they buy experience, know-how, reliability. Look at the information the employer is sending in the job description: do you hear steadiness, reliability or short-term energy? Try to match who you are and what you have to offer against the job. Look at Table 2.2 for a range of strategies for those who feel that age is a barrier.

Remember this: employers who discriminate on the grounds of age are either too young to appreciate that anyone can have an original idea over the age of 30 (so show them ...) or old and tired and assume that everyone over 40 is equally old and tired. If the employer wants a 21-year-old he can burn out in 2 years, do you want to be there anyway?

Table 2.2   Age and work: how big is the problem?

The negative side *The key facts on age and employment*	**The (more) positive side** *Ways of compensating by changing your approach or thinking*
Workers over 50 are now less likely to be working than they were 20 years ago. Few people now assume that they will stay in their present job until the age of 65. About one-third of people between the ages of 50 and 60 are unemployed or inactive, despite being in relatively good health.	The working population is ageing. There are fewer young people around. Four out of 10 workers nationally are over the age of 45. There are just not enough bright young things around. New legislation on age discrimination makes it harder for employers to screen out older workers.
Men are more likely than women to become economically inactive over the age of 55.	And how many of those men relied simply on physical fitness to achieve a living, and allowed themselves to be passive flotsam in the job market, employed one day, unemployed the next? Even in times of recession you can find stories of older workers who got back into doing worthwhile work. Seek

	out those people. Find out how they did it. You'll discover that it was a mix of determination and positive thinking.
Approximately 50% of men aged between 60 and 65 are not working.	Percentages? A proportion of people are always doing something or not doing something. Don't be a statistic.
A high proportion of workers are retiring before their company's normal retirement age.	… often because they have become tired and unhappy, and because they have stopped learning.
Employers think that younger people are more adaptable, learn more quickly and have more energy to dedicate to work.	OK, and statistically they will be more likely to drink to excess, have hangovers and decide to go off backpacking round Australia. Older workers are more reliable, steadier and, if they package themselves right, better able to offer a blend of learning and common sense. Adaptability is something you claim and show evidence to support. Learning can be demonstrated by your current interests. All too many older workers are happy to say 'All this computer stuff is beyond me …' and don't hear the door slamming shut.
There seems some evidence to suggest that older people are likely to be out of work if (a) they are in the bottom 25% of earners or (b) they are in the top 50% of earners and also in an occupational pension scheme.	… which shows that some age problems are simply economic, and some caused by employer pension policies, which sometimes make it more convenient to encourage early retirement as a comfortable way of 'downsizing'.

Many areas of work are perceived as 'young' jobs.	Age discrimination is unlawful in the UK, and a great many employers conform to equal opportunities policies. It's worth asking, explicitly, 'what is the likely age range for this post?'
Other research reflects a widespread belief that those close to retirement have less to lose through redundancy. and job loss, and that the risk of displacement from work is higher among people who are older. In other words, workers over 45 are more vulnerable to job loss, and find it harder to get back into work.	Employers gain all kinds of irrational, negative pictures about all kinds of people: students, single mothers, vegetarians. The key thing is not to feed the flames of prejudice, but to concentrate on what you have to offer. Sometimes it's helpful specifically to address the age issue: 'What kind of experience are you looking for?', 'How long is this project?', or even to ask specifically 'What's the *minimum* age/experience requirement for this job?'

Key advice for older workers

First of all, acknowledge that age discrimination is real. The reason for beginning there is that if you know something is real, you can begin to compensate. If you're not a natural with numbers, compensate by finding tools to help. Concentrate on who you are, and what makes you special.

Employers value a number of things that older workers have in abundance: experience, reliability (a 'safe pair of hands'), credibility, maturity, financial stability (you won't be asking for a pay rise every 6 months).

Here's some of the best advice around, from John Courtis, head of executive search and selection firm John Courtis & Partners, to whom I am grateful for permission to print the following from his Candidate Newsletter:

Too young? Too old? Does your age matter?

- Only if you keep on about it
- Only if you look it
- Only if you bring it up and apologize for it in your covering letter
- Only if the photo you've attached to your CV makes you look significantly older/younger than the chronological date would suggest
- And last – only if you don't distract the reader from it with all the *good* things you have to offer – recent relevant achievements, unique selling points, etc.

I don't have the qualifications

Formal qualifications are often far less relevant than people think, particularly in flexible environments like Britain and the USA. Two considerations here: there are now so many young people obtaining degrees, diplomas and certificates that employers can't tell one from another, and they have no idea whether the qualification equates to workplace performance.

In the (rarer than you might think) event that a particular qualification is a non-negotiable requirement, then get it, or a recognized equivalent. With most roles you can explore the alternatives – other ways to prove your acceptability. Can you train on the job? Can you buy the training somewhere? What kind of parallel experience might be accepted?

Where an employer mentions a specific qualification you don't have, don't despair, and don't send in your application anyway, saying nothing, hoping that your lack of a Certificate in Astrological Science won't be noticed. Ask yourself, 'why do they need this? – what problem will it solve?' – and then address the issue directly by communicating what you know and what you can do: your answer to the problem posed by this job.

I'm not IT literate

If you are even tempted to use this statement, do something about it. At one time using a PC, the Internet and email was a specialized skill. Now it's common currency. It's not rocket science. As a minimum target, get yourself connected and acquire an email address you check at least once a day.

There are a million things the Web makes easier: research, finding people to speak to, discovering new ideas, tracking down former colleagues, seeking recommendations and endorsements. To do all this and to keep people updated about what you are doing without using the Internet is like trying to cook a three course meal over a candle flame, avoiding those dangerously modern tools electricity and gas. An interesting challenge which leads to indifferent results very, very slowly.

I'd need to retrain/go back to university/college

Almost every time a journalist rings me for a quote about career change, they usually say 'what about the cost of retraining?'. It seems they think that someone can only have a bright future if they stop working to study or retrain full-time. This is another example of old world thinking struggling to cope with twenty-first century reality. In the past almost every career path required an apprenticeship or qualification, now the majority don't. Even those occupations which require entry qualifications often allow alternative ways in. Ask, and keep asking, and don't let 'I'd need to retrain' become a job myth that stops you finding out.

Your second line of defence might be *I don't have the time or energy to study*. Is that true? If the job you do takes so much out of you and leaves nothing left for learning, maybe it's the wrong job, or maybe you're doing the right job the wrong way?

If retraining is required, look at the range of options available from home study through to full-time education. Information on courses and qualifications is widely available. Bookshops have miles of texts telling you how to do things. There are thousands of choices in education today: part-time study, open and distance learning. Try to talk to both those who teach the course and those who have taken it in the past to find out whether it's as good a passport as the college brochure says. Take soundings from recruiters about whether the qualification is going to improve your employability or simply put a hole in your bank balance.

Chapter 3 – Where Next After Finishing Your Studies? – has more discussion on this topic.

I'll never earn what I earn here

The trouble with the rat race is that even if you win, you're still a rat.

Lily Tomlin

This one's the kiss of death, because it's really saying 'I'm over-paid here and nobody else will let me get away with it'. This is usually wrong-headed. Very few people are overpaid for more than a short period. Whatever you're earning (or have earned) is a reflection of what someone, somewhere, feels is the justi-fied cost of your presence and activity.

Being found out

It's surprising how many people in senior jobs share a common fear: that they are only pretending to be good enough to do the job, and one day they'll be found out. It's known as the **Impostor Syndrome**. This was first recognized in the 1970s, and it's widely experienced. A significant number of senior staff believe they have got a job largely through luck, they are 'faking it' daily, and one day their boss will say: 'OK, we know it's been a big pretence. Just leave now and we'll say nothing more about it.' A worrying number of people would leave the building without protest.

Insecurity is everywhere. The strange thing is that everyone seems to assume that people who are more senior in the organ-ization are immune to it. In fact, many senior staff feel so isolated that they spend more energy than anyone else coping with their impostor syndrome.

I can't get motivated to make the change I need

You don't have to make a big change on day one, but you *do* need to do something. It's true that sometimes we can't get round to doing the very thing that we know will make life better. Why do we fail to take the first step? If it's a direction you know you want to take, then the usual answer is fear of failure, which can include fear of rejection. There's a simple trick I use with many clients: imagine you are making enquiries for someone else. A colleague has offered you several thousand pounds to find *her* ideal career path. If you accepted that brief you wouldn't be going back every five minutes saying 'this won't work for you', 'this isn't as exciting as I thought' or 'this is a difficult sector to get into'. You'd keep exploring, keep looking for variations and angles, press on by asking questions like 'what else is there?', 'who else could I talk to?', and 'what are the unconventional ways into this field?'.

I don't interview well

What does *interviewing well* really mean? If it means that you're negative, that you talk yourself out of every job you apply for, then this isn't a matter of technique, but just a trick you play. The trick is this: you think you'll fail, so you set the game out to ensure that you do. That way you won't be disappointed. Employers in general buy experience, but they also love enthusiasm. That's not the same as false confidence, but conveying a simple statement: *I like what I do. I do it well. I can do it here, for you.* Chapter 13 has a wide range of tips.

EXERCISE 2.1 – UNDERSTAND YOUR CONSTRAINTS

We all have constraints, but each of us thinks that our constraints are uniquely limiting. Tick the constraints that you feel apply to you.

☐ I am too old

☐ I am underqualified

☐ My experience is all in one industry

☐ Travel to work distance

☐ Travel as part of the job

☐ Nights away from home

☐ Lack of information about the job market

☐ The stigma of unemployment

☐ No clear career goals

☐ Financial commitments

☐ Family/personal problems

☐ Fear of approaching people

☐ Few measurable achievements

☐ Attitudes/needs of family members

☐ Lack of confidence selling myself in person

☐ I worry about taking risks

☐ Worry that I will repeat old problems

☐ Worry that I will be out of work for a long time

☐ Fear of employer's attitude to redundancy or unemployment

☐ I have health problems

☐ Lack of up-to-date skills

☐ I am out of touch with the market

☐ Fear of rejection

☐ Lack of relevant qualifications

☐ Worry about having to retrain/go back to full-time study

☐ My job search to date hasn't worked

☐ Don't want to make the wrong decision at my time of life

☐ Want to get a job that looks good on my CV

☐ I want a safe job

☐ I have never had to apply for a job before

☐ I don't interview well

Look at the constraints you have ticked. Take a highlighter pen and mark the ones which you think are most critical or most limiting. Record against each one a time when you overcame this constraint in the past, and the steps you can see to help you to overcome this barrier in the future. If you feel you have constraints that you can't overcome, that's a good reason to find help.

'MUST DO' LIST

☑ Career problems are sometimes concrete, but usually strategies for avoiding the issue of change. What are your favourite 'Yes, but' defences?

☑ You can be happy at work. What would be the first step you could take to achieve that? How would your friends and colleagues notice the difference?

☑ Look at your CV, your interview style, your attitude to work. You complain that employers see negative things about you. How many of these messages are actually composed and delivered by you?

Where Next After Finishing Your Studies?

This chapter looks at ways of:

▊ Using this book if you are leaving school, college or university soon

▊ Building on your academic achievement

▊ Composing a CV when you have little or no work experience

▊ Translating what you know and can do into employer language

Of course, it is very important to be sober when you take an exam. Many worthwhile careers in the street-cleansing, fruit-picking and subway-guitar-playing industries have been founded on a lack of understanding of this simple fact.

Terry Pratchett

A 10-STEP CHECKLIST FOR SCHOOL LEAVERS LOOKING FOR THEIR FIRST JOB

1. Choose your subjects for further study carefully. Avoid being press-ganged into a subject because someone else thinks it's a good idea.

2. Areas of further study should meet two benchmarks: (a) the qualification will be a reasonable stepping stone, and (b) you will be motivated to study the topic (this works best if you really enjoy what you are studying).

3. Accept all ideas for career pathways gratefully, but make up your own mind based on evidence. Talk to real people in real jobs. Ask around: family, parents of friends, anyone you know in the world of work.

4. Where your studies are related to work, use them as a platform for your investigation. Most organizations will let you speak to someone if you are carrying out some research.

5. Take work experience and short-term work assignments seriously – write down the skills you use and what you have learned.

6. Be very clear about your qualifications – why did you study them, what are they, what did they cover and what are your grades? BUT when you apply for a job list them *after* your skills and work experience, however limited that is.

7. Stuck for a career idea? Use this book to help, but begin by looking at two big areas of life for clues:

   ▌ what you enjoy doing (how do you spend your free time? what activities motivate you?)

   ▌ what do you enjoy thinking/talking/learning about?

8. If you are totally stuck about career choice, look at what you love doing and try to find the opportunity to try it out on a work experience basis.

9. Use temporary work as a way of gaining skills and relevant experience.

10. Don't accept secondhand information – from websites, teachers, family, careers advisers – find out for yourself.

'I DON'T KNOW WHAT KIND OF WORK I WANT TO DO'

If you have recently qualified, or you are thinking about your future while still in full-time education, you may feel you are facing a bewildering range of choices regarding possible jobs and careers. Your problem may in fact be that you don't know enough about work to know which parts you are going to dislike. You may have little experience of work, or you may feel that your experience is not appropriate or useful to the new career you are hoping to begin.

On the other hand, many people in their 40s and 50s say 'I wish I'd thought more carefully about career choice when I was young'. It's up to you. If you add up the number of hours, days and weeks you put into achieving qualifications, it's rather surprising how little attention people give to the question 'what kind of work would really suit me?'.

Begin with some background thinking:

▋ Look at all the subjects that have interested you, and translate them into potential fields of work using Chapters 9 and 10.

▋ Look at all your experience of work to date. What has motivated you or excited you? Where is your sense of *flow*? (See Chapter 4.)

▋ Look at the subjects you have just studied. What would you like to know more about? What skills have you developed while studying?

▋ Conduct an audit: what do you actually know about work? How can you find out more? Who can you talk to? Appendix 1 shows you how you can use REVEAL interviews to help.

Next, *think research rather than job search*. Don't miss out on the obvious sources of information:

▋ Your university careers service or any of the organizations offering specialist careers guidance to young people and adults.

▋ Lecturers and subject specialists.

▋ Text resources, including the hundreds of career books and guides to specific occupations which are available.

▋ Reference libraries (the staff can be enormously helpful).

▋ Websites relating to employers, industry sectors and career entry.

■ Professional and trade associations (see the website listings in Appendix 3 for ways in).

Next, undertake the kind of investigation that most people leaving full-time education don't do:

■ Talk to students a year ahead of you who have found work.

■ Ask around – friends, parents of your friends, former teachers and lecturers.

■ Talk to people who have employed you in the past.

The first item on this list may sound painfully obvious, but very few *current* students make use of alumni associations. Talking to someone who has qualified in your subject and is now in work can help you enormously in your thinking, especially if you are trying hard to work out (a) if you will enjoy the work they do and (b) how you can persuade an employer that you have transferable skills.

WHAT CHOICES DO I HAVE APART FROM FINDING A JOB?

Undertaking 2 or 3 years' **further study** may seem like the most comfortable option. Indeed, many students choose this as the 'default' mode, but is this the right step? Taking a higher qualification can give you a late start on the salary ladder, but is it an essential requirement for the career you have in mind? Are you continuing simply because you have been offered a grant or a place, or because you don't know what else to do? Ask yourself the real motives for continuing your studies.

Taking time out may also appeal. Again, the question is whether you want to delay your career start merely to indulge yourself, to put off a decision, or whether there are things you really want to do. There is probably no other time in your life when you will be able to travel with so few restrictions, but think hard about what you will learn from the experience. Employers need to see the relevance of your time out, and what you learned from the experience. Sometimes you can successfully combine travel with work.

Thinking rather than drifting

Whatever your career stage, it's vitally important to be active rather than passive in your job search. If you are entirely passive, taking what the labour market offers, it is rather like planning a long journey by turning up at a bus station and jumping on the first bus to arrive. If you start that way then job change often becomes a question of jumping on whatever vehicle happens to come along at a time when you feel dissatisfied.

Your first full-time job makes a big impact on your career. Many people take 'fill-in' jobs after qualifying. The danger is that this kind of work can quickly lead to the idea that 'this is all there is' or 'this is what work is like'. You may develop the idea that the work you do will never be linked in any way to your studies. 'Fill-in' jobs can quickly become permanent posts unless you keep your goals in mind.

Ideas are powerful. Career counsellors will tell you that one of the difficulties they have in dealing with young people or those with little work experience is that, essentially, all work looks the same. Very often it's only after some work experience that you get a 'feel' for the kind of work you would really like to do.

The advantage of traditional graduate trainee programmes was that they allowed entrants to gain experience of many different parts of a business before choosing to specialize. The number of schemes has decreased significantly in the past 20 years, and it may be no coincidence that research from organizations such as The Work Foundation shows that workers have become less satisfied. Do you want to be one of those casualties of work? Assuming that you don't, how can you replicate for yourself the opportunities and experiences provided by a good graduate entry programme? Starting to negotiate your options at an early stage in your career makes a big difference.

YOUR SKILLS KITBAG

Table 3.1 lists a range of competences seen by employers as vital for workers competing in the twenty-first century labour market. The information comes from the Association of Graduate Recruiters, but this list of skills and qualities is useful to anyone beginning a career.

Table 3.1   Career management and effective learning skills

Self-awareness	Being able to identify your own skills, values, interests and strengths, seek feedback from others, and seek opportunities for personal growth.
Self-promotion	Being able to define and promote your own agenda, i.e. actively communicating your 'message' (see Chapter 7 on presentation statements).
Exploring and creating opportunities	Being able to identify, create, investigate and seize opportunities.
Action planning	Goal-setting, organizing your time effectively, and preparing contingency plans along the way to achieving goals and targets.
Networking	Being able to define, develop and maintain the support network for advice and information (see Chapter 11).
Matching and decision making	Finding a match between opportunities you meet and your own core skills and knowledge; making informed decisions based on constraints and opportunities.

Negotiation	Negotiating the psychological contract to achieve win/win.
Political awareness	Being aware of hidden tensions and power struggles within organizations (sometimes defined as spotting the most likely person to stab you in the back).
Coping with uncertainty	Adapting goals and your mindset in the light of changing circumstances.
Development focus	Being committed to lifelong learning and your own personal development.
Transfer skills	Applying your skills, and communicating them, to new contexts. See 'Translation', below.
Self-confidence	Having an underlying confidence in your abilities, in terms of both past success and your innate qualities.

Adapted from *Skills for Graduates in the 21st Century*, reprinted with permission from the Association of Graduate Recruiters (AGR).

AGR Chief Executive Carl Gilleard says: 'We ask our members what skills they are looking for in graduates when they're recruiting. And not surprisingly, top of the list, come interpersonal skills and the ability to communicate effectively, the ability to work in teams, and customer awareness. We also find that employers very much look for candidates who have had work experience; that carries a high premium these days. And let's not forget the old-fashioned attributes of enthusiasm, motivation and commitment – all of these things still carry a lot of weight with employers.'

WHAT TO SAY IF YOU HAVE LITTLE OR NO WORK EXPERIENCE

When you are leaving full-time education, finding good-quality evidence for your CV can feel like a tough job. You may feel you don't have many skills, or you are not sure what an employer finds valuable. You may have a fairly good idea of your personal strengths and feel that these are the only things you can write about. You probably haven't yet really understood how to communicate your skills to an employer, and although you know that employers are interested in evidence of achievements, you don't feel you have many worth mentioning.

For all the reasons mentioned above, most school, college and university leavers write an upside down CV – all the important message is at the wrong end. You can read more information on what goes wrong in such CVs in *Why You? CV Messages To Win Jobs*, but in summary too many documents major on recent academic success and don't say anything about skills, know-how and achievements until page 2 when a rather thin-looking work history is presented. The problem with such a CV is that it essentially says 'I am a student who has had the occasional job' rather than 'I am ready to hold down a job'.

Identifying achievements

Your achievements can range from building a tree house to backpacking in the Himalayas – not just working activities. Now look for the *skills* and *personality traits* that you demonstrate. Remember that employers are looking for flexibility, resilience and imagination, as well as traditional skills and know-how. Try to say something user friendly and interesting about your main qualification. A subject title is rarely helpful to an employer. A recruiter makes assumptions about the usefulness of your qualification unless you specifically state what you most enjoyed about it, what special projects you undertook and what you got out of it. The **skill clips** exercise in Chapter 7 can help.

Look at your activities outside study. Perhaps you organized complicated or exciting social events, competitions or sporting activities, or you may have been a member of a society or club.

Think about the transferable skills that you acquired from these experiences, and make sure that they are mentioned in your CV.

Some academic subjects are, sadly, off-putting to potential employers. Think about ways of selling the subject, for example explaining why the topics you have studied are relevant to a modern workplace. Even if you have done something fairly obscure and academic, you will have gained considerable experience of researching, organizing and analysing data, consulting experts and presenting information concisely and coherently in speech and in writing. Table 3.2 offers some advice on ways of composing a winning message.

Table 3.2 Ten steps to a winning message when seeking work on leaving full-time education

1 Experience	An employer is trying to measure potential, but provide what information you can about relevant experience (e.g. work, travel, time out). Indicate what kind of challenges you faced, what you learned and what you achieved.
2 Skills	Be honest, which means neither bragging nor hiding your light under a bushel. Identify your skills and state your level of competence. Give examples of what you have done with these skills (e.g. leading an expedition of 10 people for a 20-mile trek).
3 Key achievements	Make sure that you include achievements. Think about your accomplishments in different contexts: study, work, leisure time, voluntary activities. Try to present your achievements in interesting terms, explaining them as mini-narratives if necessary (see Chapter 7 for further details).
4 Qualifications	Explain, translate, communicate. Don't assume that an employer is automatically interested in your academic achievements. Don't overemphasize poor results.

5 Education and continuing professional development	Don't forget to include details about non-academic courses and training, even if they are uncertificated. If you have the skills but not the qualifications, give an indication of what you have achieved with them (e.g. producing a complex spreadsheet).
6 Work history	What did you actually do? What problems did you solve? Look at any work you have ever done and find a way to communicate the skills you used and the contribution you made.
7 Support skills	Think about the support skills you can offer, and an employer's expectations (e.g. IT, word processing, customer service or sales skills). Don't miss out anything, particularly IT skills. Indicate your standard of competence.
8 Fields of work	Work out what kind of work interests you. Communicate enthusiasm to employers: show them that you really want to work in their field, not that they happen to be the first to have a vacancy.
9 Interests	Include a good range. An employer won't expect you to have a long work history, but will expect you to be a rounded person with an interesting life outside work. Focus on interests and activities that include other people or develop skills that may be relevant to work.
10 Profile	This is a short paragraph of no more than four sentences saying what sort of role you have in mind, your current role or position, your key experience to date and what you can offer an employer in broad terms. This will form the first part of your CV. Avoid flowery adjectives or claims you can't support. See Chapter 17 for outline CV advice, and look at the range of CV models presented in *Why You? – CV Messages To Win Jobs*.

TRANSLATION

The single biggest problem with CVs of university or college leavers is a failure to translate qualities, know-how and experience into terms that are meaningful to an employer. This isn't just a problem for people leaving full-time education; it's very difficult for people to leave teaching, the health service or the armed forces for exactly the same reason. You find yourself immersed in a particular language, and then fail to perceive the need to help others to understand what these terms mean.

I sometimes use the term 'bridge thinking'. What you essentially want a recruiter to do is to form a bridge between your experience and the world of the hiring company. You want an employer to see not just skills, but transferable skills. You have to do the bridge thinking for the other person. For example, if you simply write that you produced a 6000-word dissertation on fish farming, you may get a fairly blank response. If, however, you talk about the problems of gathering data, interviewing people, keeping up with the latest developments in your subject area, and working under pressure to achieve the project by a fixed deadline, then your interviewer starts to get interested. You have started to talk the same language.

INTERNSHIPS

If you find it difficult to gain paid work experience in your chosen field of work, consider working as a volunteer. An internship offers you the chance to gain work experience by working for a short period for nothing. There are a growing number of internships, and even if they are not formally offered you might want to suggest one. However, make sure that an internship doesn't become a career habit – ask around for what seems like a long or a short time as an intern, and be careful about not doing too many. If there really are no paid jobs in your sector, you might be better off gaining experience in another, related, sector for a couple of years. If you work for nothing, always ask for something in exchange, even if it is only learning opportunities, a reference, names of contacts, and always ask for feedback about how you have done and where else you could go.

KEEP A RECORD

Work experience isn't just for your bank balance. Build up your own personal portfolio of what you have done, including details of your role, the company, the contribution you made and where you made a difference.

Look in detail at all the times you have had exposure to work:

▮ placements during a sandwich course

▮ overseas work or study placement

▮ work during term-time

▮ work experience elements in a course of study

▮ vacation work

▮ workplace visits or tours.

BECOME HUNGRY FOR EVIDENCE OF YOUR EMPLOYABILITY

You will find that your job search will be easier if you are able to offer concrete evidence of skills and achievements. Increasing numbers of students are working while studying. Sometimes this is just during vacations, sometimes students work up to 20 hours a week or more during term-time. Again, make sure that you talk about more than your job title – while you are doing the work seek opportunities to enlarge your skill set, and learn to communicate these skills to employers.

RETURNING TO WORK AFTER TAKING TIME OUT TO STUDY

Those who have taken a career break to take a full-time course usually need to think carefully when trying to return to the workplace. Taking time out to study places a gap in your CV, and doesn't always communicate employability; for a start, you have to convince an employer that you really are motivated to return to paid employment.

The key thing to remember is that you need short, focused answers to three questions:

1. Why did you decide to give up work to take this qualification?

2. What did you get out of it?

3. What do you hope to do next as a direct result of your studies?

If you fail to give an adequate answer to Question 1, a recruiter starts to worry that you make random decisions in your career, or that you might be in danger of becoming a life-long student. Question 2 requires you to think about *translation* (see above), but also requires you to talk with enthusiasm about what you enjoyed while studying (after all, if you didn't enjoy it, why did you do it?). The third question requires you to communicate a clear, straightforward data-burst about the way this recent experience adds to your CV and has helped to reshape your career path.

Special advice to holders of postgraduate business qualifications

Those who have taken time out to study for postgraduate degrees or diplomas in business-related areas, including MBAs, often need particular help. This is ironic, because people often take such qualifications to improve their employability.

Business Schools, in order to persuade you to part with substantial fees, will make claims about their alumni and the kinds of jobs they have acquired. It's easy to feel persuaded that having the right business qualification is an instant passport to success.

When students come to the end of a very intensive course they know that they have to hit the deck running and find a job. One problem they face is that the work they do next may not be as challenging and demanding as the course they have just completed. I have met MBAs who, as part of their course, have worked alongside main board directors of blue chip European companies. Their course of study has given them this unique access, but one of the things the new MBAs have to get used to is the fact that they are unlikely to work at this level immediately upon qualifying.

The next problem (based on feedback from a number of recruiters) is that holders of postgraduate business qualifications assume that the qualification speaks for itself. We're back to the basic questions above, but this time the questions (whether spoken or implied) are slightly different:

1. Why did you decide to suspend your career and your money to study for this qualification?

2. What did you learn on this course that has added to your skill set?

3. How do you hope to use your qualification in the next stage of your career?

4. *Why you*, in a market flooded with qualified people?

Question 1 naturally has more impact if you have spent a large amount of money gaining a qualification, putting your career on hold for a while in the hope of greater success in the future.

Question 2 again requires *translation*, but this time you should have pre-rehearsed, impressive answers about particular projects and achievements, particularly where they relate to work you have done with real organizations.

Question 3 needs you to be highly focused indeed: where did you want your new qualification to take you? Unclear answers around this topic sound very weak indeed – why have you spent so much time and money doing something with an unclear outcome in mind? Recruiters often have a prejudice that fresh MBAs don't stay in organizations for long. This isn't just based on a hunch: Business Schools regularly reveal that a high proportion of MBAs change career shortly after graduating.

Finally, to Question 4. Why you? You'll have a hard job selling your qualification just on the reputation of your Business School. Although this sometimes works, you have to be able to communicate what you learned, and how your experience allows you to offer something different from all the other candidates out there with exactly the same qualification from Business Schools all over the world.

Recruiters will tell you that too many qualified candidates just don't have well-constructed answers to these interview questions. You have to remember that the person interviewing you might love to have your opportunity to study full-time, or might have bad experience of people holding particular qualifications (as employees or as management consultants).

'MUST DO' LIST: HOW TO USE THIS BOOK IF YOU HAVE JUST QUALIFIED

Think about how you are going to choose your career. If you have no idea about what kind of work you would like to do, use the various exercises in this book, particularly in Chapter 10. Draw up a shortlist of ideas, and then talk to as many people as you can. This is more important now than at any stage of your working life. Find out what careers other people like you have gone into, and ask them how they got there, what they enjoy, and what kind of applicants do well in the selection process.

To work smarter at your career, start with the principle of *leverage*. A small amount of time now spent seriously thinking about career possibilities will have an enormous impact on your future life. What negative messages are holding you back at the moment? How many of them come from other people? How many of those thoughts are accurately informed by objective information about the real marketplace? How are you going to create real ideas about your career future?

Examine your **Career Hot Buttons** (Chapter 5) and draw up your personal wish list. You may find it important to think about the likely values of organizations you will be talking to.

What do you have to offer? Look seriously at your skills. Build carefully – based on what you have done and the work that becomes available to you in the short term. Catalogue the skills and achievements you have acquired from *all* parts of your life. Almost any kind of work experience is valuable at this stage for you to experiment and work out your preferences and potential.

Use the **field choice** exercises in this book to help generate possible pathways. Don't give up too early on career choice, and don't shelve ideas until you have taken the opportunity to talk to real people about real jobs. Research what's out there, otherwise you're planning a journey with blank maps.

Prepare now for **interviews**. Don't believe that interviews are a matter of luck. Prepare. Work out what the employer is really looking for, and work hard to communicate your strengths and your enthusiasm.

Thinking Around Corners

This chapter looks at the following areas:

▌ How you normally solve problems

▌ Breaking out of A–Z thinking

▌ Aiming for career breakthrough

▌ Moving towards positive solutions

The most successful people are those who do all year long what they would otherwise do in their summer vacation.

Mark Twain

PROBLEM SOLVING, AND WHAT GOES WRONG

How can you solve the problem of your career? Well, if you use the strategies you have learned so far in your life, you'll probably try a structured approach such as undertaking research and working out possibilities logically and systematically. Such *structured* approaches usually rely on what you have learned about organizing information and ideas. We categorize problems. We write out lists. We prioritize. We time plan. We write out pros and cons. That's a sound, business-like way of working things out, isn't it?

A–Z thinking

In school and in work we learn *straight-line thinking*, a logical progression from one step to the next. This is the mindset that says every book must be read from front to back, from A to Z. From problem to solution: this was the language of a great deal of post-1945 management training: analyse the problem and work out a logical sequence of actions to form a solution.

Businesses all over the world are discovering that this kind of thinking doesn't help in every situation. Sometimes, survival depends on thinking very differently. Many businesses have taken non-linear thinking to new heights: they turn problems on their heads. They seek innovative solutions. They invent new concepts, not just new products. In the twenty-first century, this is the kind of thinking to apply to our working lives.

This might be about being just a little less subject to tunnel vision. Accept that you can come up with new ideas for your future, and just try things out. For some it's about being open to *inspiration*. When you are inspired something larger than you moves within, whether that's the spirit of God, the spirit of life or something untapped in the human mind. How are you going to plan to be inspired? This sounds absurd, like planning to be spontaneous. You *can* plan inspiration, in the sense that you can open yourself up to possibilities, and you *can* learn to use both conscious and unconscious techniques to teach you how to break down barriers and begin to grow.

VARIETIES OF CREATIVE THINKING

Chapter 1 introduced you to the fact that everyone has their own form of creativity. It's important to remember that there are several kinds of creative thinking. Some of them come naturally to some people, but most can be nurtured or actively learned, as Figure 4.1 shows.

Straight-line creativity
This is step-by-step, detailed, methodical. It's fairly close to A–Z thinking, but ensures that you don't jump to one immediate conclusion. It's about defining a problem and looking for a variety of effective outcomes. This kind of creativity is great for questions such as 'who can I talk to about physiotherapy?' or 'what should I remember to take to the interview?' It can be done alone or in groups.

Used in career decisions it ensures that you use research, investigation and the full range of tools and techniques available to you.

Provoked creativity
This derives largely from the work of Edward de Bono, who even invented a new word for the purpose: *po* (read 'Serious Creativity'). The idea is that you can use an unexpected and unrelated prompt or *provocation* to make the mind switch gear: this may be an analogy, a metaphor, a word chosen at random or a picture. For example, think of your favourite pop song. What do the lyrics of that song make you think about? How can that help to solve your problem or create a new approach? Provoked creativity can be learned, and can be used by individuals or groups.

Used in career decisions it helps you to make unexpected connections. It's great for exploring fields, and for overcoming the 'Yes, but' barriers described in Chapter 2.

Freestyle creativity
This is free-flowing, fast, exciting. It relies on open-ended, **discontinuous thinking**: What else? What other ways are there of looking at this? What happens if I turn the problem on its head? Examples include brainstorming and idea creation. This kind of thinking tends to work best with other people to bounce your ideas off. This is the kind of thinking found in organizations who claim to be 'creative'.

Used in career decisions it generates positive possibilities and connections, and great ideas for researching jobs, fields, possible employers, etc.

Flash creativity
Sometimes known as 'Aha!' or 'Eureka!' moments, these are times when you get a sudden insight or moment of illumination. These often happen at a time when we are doing or thinking something entirely unrelated to the problem at hand, possibly having a bath or digging the garden. Flash creativity results in totally new ideas, approaches, products and ideas that did not exist before. There are no steps, no rules, no predictable outcomes. One way of aiding the process, however, is to feed your favoured natural intelligences (see Chapter 8 – Who Are You?)

Used in career decisions this kind of thinking occurs rarely, but the vital thing is to recognize the possibilities in the daydream, and test them out using one of the other forms of creative thinking.

Combine and conquer
It's important to realize that these kinds of creative thinking are not exclusive; they work best in combination with each other. Brainstorm possibilities using freestyle creativity. Use provoked thinking if you get stuck. Explore the range of positive practical outcomes using straight-line creativity. Reflect on a problem unconsciously by doing something that engages other parts of your brain: jogging, listening to a piece of music, stripping down an engine … (see Exercise 10.2 on discontinuous thinking).

Figure 4.1   Different styles of creative thinking

Go with the flow

Psychologist Mihaly Csikszentmihalyi coined the term **'flow'** to describe a state of existence you reach at times when you are totally absorbed in an enjoyable and fulfilling activity. Csikszentmihalyi describes several characteristics of enjoyment, including those outlined in Figure 4.2.

FLOW

The following lists examples of times when you might experience 'flow' in your work.

Where did you experience it? What were you doing?

1. There were clear goals every step of the way

2. There was immediate feedback (you knew how well you were doing)

3. There was a balance between the challenges you faced and the skills you possess

4. Your concentration was entirely focused on what you were doing

5. Time appeared to pass quickly

6. The activity was an end in itself. You did it because you enjoyed doing it.

Figure 4.2   Flow

Getting unstuck

First, review where you feel a sense of dissatisfaction at work. Perhaps it's about knowing you could do more, or you would like to be valued more. A feeling that you don't quite match the life you're leading. A vague sense that there is more to life than this, that your work should have some meaning ....

Having got to this point, it's quite common for people to feel stuck in a rut. The worst kind of rut is the **velvet rut**: you hate its confines, but it's just too comfortable to move. You may get channelled or stuck in your ways, not just in work, but stuck in your thought processes, your career planning. You know that something needs to change, but what? What's needed is breakthrough thinking, something to take you from where you are to the next stage. You need to think up ideas.

The best way to get a good idea is to get lots of ideas.
                    Linus Pauling, Nobel prize winning scientist

There are a few ground rules for idea building:

▌ Believe that the solution to your career block exists, either within you or somewhere out there.

▌ Allow yourself to generate a range of ideas, without self-criticism.

▌ Learn how to focus on both questions and solutions.

▌ Don't restrict yourself to tools that you find easiest or the most comfortable. Stretch yourself.

▌ Believe in your ability to succeed. Self-belief is vital.

Rule 1: **Behaviour follows belief**. The greatest barriers between you and an inspired career are not in the marketplace or on your CV, but in your mind. And if getting your ideal career requires positive thinking, then getting the ideas to put your career plan together takes even more; it's vital that you learn to accept your brain's own ability to create ideas, possibilities, connections. Accept that this is not only a natural gift for the chosen few, but (as thousands of businesses have discovered over the past 30 years) something you can practise and train your mind to do.

It's often said that the creative mind can hold contradictory ideas at the same time. So to Rule 2: **Belief follows behaviour**. This is certainly true in the very first stages of working on your self-belief. Dick Bolles, author of *What Color is Your Parachute?*, has said: 'It is easier to act your way into a new way of thinking than to think your way into a new way of acting.' This has all kinds of implications. For example, if you have to make a public presentation, then decide to act, walk and talk as if you already have the full attention of your audience. Sometimes the thing that works is to act and behave as if you are already successful. Walk the walk, talk the talk, and something happens – you physically act your way into a new way of looking at yourself. That's why it's easier to have authority if you are dressed professionally, and why people are more assertive on the telephone when they stand up. If you act confident or proficient, eventually you become it.

Finding new life in the old clichés

Too many businesses misuse the idea of creativity, and pay lip service to the idea of genuinely open thinking. Even the word 'creative' can become a cliché.

Clichés have their usefulness. 'Thinking outside the box' was a term used in the advertising industry to think outside the rectangular frame of an advertising billboard. 'Pushing the envelope' comes from the field of aviation. The 'envelope' is the box-like shape on a graph representing an aeroplane's maximum speed and range. Behind the tired language lie some very real business concepts.

What happens when there is a mismatch between your talents and your work? For creatures other than us humans, the answer to this question is extinction. Because we are so adaptable, we survive, but at a terrible cost. What gets extinguished is the pure joy of doing something that comes perfectly naturally. The further you get from fully expressing your talents and abilities, the less likely it is that you will enjoy your day on the job.

Nicholas Lore

CAREER BREAKTHROUGH TOOLS

Here's a range of tools from different sources that work well to help you to achieve career breakthrough.

Focus on what's working, not what isn't

Trainee airline pilots are taught, in an emergency, not to focus on what has failed, but to make a quick assessment: 'What do I have left working which will get me safely on the ground?' In the same way we need to learn to put our attention on the things we are doing which are working and the things we have in our toolkit which can help. Otherwise it's easy to spend all your time and energy focusing on conversations that haven't worked, applications that fell at the first hurdle, or people who won't return your call. Everyone gets knock-backs. If you are the kind of person who takes rejection personally, don't beat yourself up about it, but recruit some support.

Set real goals

Stephen Covey's book *The Seven Habits of Highly Effective People* advises us to 'begin with the end in mind'. Many people believe that all you need to make the future happen is to set long-term objectives and stick to them with fanatical commitment. In his inspirational book: *59 Seconds, Think A Little, Change A Lot*, Richard Wiseman debunks ideas around goal setting. Wiseman demonstrates that it's a myth that writing down life-changing goals has a recordable effect. However, there is evidence to suggest that another kind of goal setting is very effective indeed.

Real goals are ideas that require a first, second and third step. Active commitment to short-term goals that have long-term ends in mind is the most effective strategy. Those people who break a task down into short-term goals and reward themselves for achieving them are more likely to achieve their goals. Your goal might be to be self-employed within 3 years. It can remain a goal until you retire, or you can take the first step – an informational interview, perhaps (see Appendix 1). Better still, set out an action plan of research and face-to-face meetings over the next 3–4 months – the more detailed, the better.

Ask others to support you (and call you to account if you don't do what you promise).

Whether you think you can or you can't, you're right.

Henry Ford

Distinguish between goals and dreams

We're all great at having 'safe' dreams – ideas we like to play with, assured that we will never have to do anything about them. They are daydreams that keep us warm on cold winter evenings. Goals are things we can do something about. For some people dreams become goals when logical/planning thinking is applied to them: 'What do I do next?'. However, it's important to remember the dream as well, or the original impulse is lost.

Take happiness seriously

If you have reached career crisis, you'll already be in tune with this point. It's fairly central. If you don't believe in being happy, you probably don't believe in enjoyable work. If you're unsure, look at it this way. As the work of Richard Layard and others has demonstrated, happiness isn't a passing fancy but is measurable, and there are things you can do to improve it. Being in work which feels worth doing *and* you have some control over is one of the key factors. Secondly, be pragmatic – if you are in work that makes you happier, you will probably be more motivated, more productive and potentially better paid. There really isn't much of an argument in favour of prolonging misery.

Theologian Sarah Maitland says that the word 'joy' comes from the same source as 'jewel'. We all seek some kind of hidden treasure in life – that missing 'something'. Often all we need is a better search method.

DIY

A huge jump in understanding demonstrated in career clients is that they, and only they, are responsible for their happiness.

Try a change of vocabulary. Describe the glass as half full, not half empty. Practise a register shift, from No to **Yes**.

The language of NO	The language of YES
It'll never work	Let's look at our alternatives
It's how I am: I was born that way	I can try a different approach
She makes me behave like that	I control my own feelings
It's against the rules	I'll invent a new rulebook
I'm forced to	I will choose
It's just not me	What shall I try next?
In the real world …	I make my world real by …
Another mistake	How interesting …
If only …	Let's try …
Never	It's all experimental

Stick to your guns

The key word here is 'integrity', which isn't just about doing the right thing, but *wholeness*. Once you know who you are and what you have to offer, try to resist offers that really don't match that discovery. I work with clients on the 70% principle. This is measured by drawing up your wish list in terms of work values, career hot buttons and the skills you would like to exercise, and then comparing it with the employer's stated wish list in the job description or advertisement. If there is a 70% overlap between their list of needs and wishes and a job opportunity, there's enough for it to be a healthy stepping stone. If not, watch out.

Follow real leaders

Interview successful people and one factor frequently emerges – at some stage they worked around a great leader. A real leader – not someone interested in status but someone capable of inspiring people. If you're not sure what that means, look at research from the UK's Work Foundation published in January 2010 which showed that many of the best leaders listen to others and are acutely aware of the impact they have on people around them, consciously modelling positive behaviours in the workplace. Sometimes it's good when old-fashioned ideas come around again.

Following great leaders is often the foundation for a great career – firstly these people are great benchmarks, secondly they attract attention, and thirdly if you are lucky enough to gain advice from such a leader it will often influence the way you conduct yourself in the rest of your career.

Look for synergy

It's a habit of life: look for connections. Carl Jung talked of *synchronicity*, a sense of things coming together in a pattern of significant coincidences. Those of faith may call them *Godincidences*, but you don't need to have strongly defined beliefs to become aware of synchronicity. Once you start to make connections, patterns in life start to emerge, and you become more aware of synergy. At a most basic level, the more you discover about yourself, the more you discover that many others around you are on a similar journey, with anxieties very similar to your own. Such people make good support partners.

EXERCISE 4.1 – SETTING GOALS USING THE IDEAS GRID

Once you have generated a number of tentative goals or career ideas, you'll need to find some way of focusing on those that will really work for you.

This idea originates with the 7×7 technique, developed by Carl Gregory. It helps if you can use blank postcards or small index cards. What works even better is to put a strip of Velcro on the back of each card and stick them up on a piece of material pinned to a wall or notice board.

1. Begin by writing out all the goals that seem important or attractive. Don't exclude anything because it seems unrealistic. Write them all on separate cards.

2. Combine ideas that are virtually the same. You might have both 'serving the community' and 'putting something back into society'.

3. Sort your draft goal cards into columns. Give each column a heading (e.g. financial, learning, personal).

4. Place the most important column on the left, the least important on the right.

5. You might want to apply a timescale, e.g. discard anything that you can't achieve within 2 years. So 'Find time to write my novel' might have to go on the back burner for a year or two. It's up to you.

6. Put the ideas in rank order within each column, with the most important at the top.

Now stand back and look at your results. Better still, go away and do something else for an hour, then come back and look. What you have is a draft *prioritized* grid, with the most important, critical or immediately relevant ideas in the top left-hand corner.

You can use the same technique to come up with ideas to solve a problem. For instance, if your problem is 'How can I change my career without going back to full-time study?' you can come up with a range of potential ideas and solutions, without self-criticism or feeling forced into a decision too soon. Reward yourself for off-the-wall ideas. Sort, re-sort, reflect.

'MUST DO' LIST

☑ Review Figure 4.2 and write down details of the times when you found 'flow'. What were you doing? What skills were you using?

☑ Learn how to think in different ways. Try a range of techniques for idea generation and problem solving (start by using them on everyday problems and then adapt them to career planning).

☑ Take dreams seriously, and see which ones will translate into goals. Write them down, somewhere, and tell someone you've done it.

☑ Write a Plan A for the next 12 months. Things to include: first steps on the journey, measurable goals, the critical steps you need to follow to make things happen (writing articles, going to conferences, talking to people, getting your CV rewritten, finishing that book ...).

Your Career Hot Buttons

This chapter looks at ways of:

▌ Identifying workplace turn-offs

▌ Measuring your career satisfaction

▌ Looking at money and motivation

▌ Piecing together your jigsaw job

▌ Discovering your career drivers

TURN-OFFS IN THE WORKPLACE

Go back to 'The good, the bad and the just plain awful' in Chapter 2. Think about your hate list: the 10 things you would like to change most (about the work you do, or the way you are at work). Write them down.

You might find it helpful to categorize some of your dissatisfactions: physical work environment, location, people you work with, management style, status, recognition, people, tasks, variety, values of the organization, and so on. Make sure you have recorded all the things that demotivate or irritate you.

'I NEED THE MONEY'

Psychologists will tell you that money is rarely the primary motivator in changing jobs. People are often persuaded to take only a minor increase in salary, or even a pay cut, in order to get the 'right' job. Money only motivates in the short term: once you've got your fast car and the key to the executive washroom, the buzz fades pretty quickly. However, poor rewards can quickly demotivate, particularly where there is a sense of injustice. The thought 'I'm worth more than this' may begin from an awareness that you are underpaid.

How do you have any sense of what you are worth? I have known individuals being interviewed for £40,000 and £80,000 jobs in the same week, with little real difference in responsibility or complexity. Markets often do very odd things with salaries. Have you ever calculated what you really cost your employer, including overheads, and then calculated what value you add to the bottom line, whether actual in terms of profits or metaphorically in terms of your invisible contribution?

You ask what is the proper limit to a person's wealth?
First, having what is essential, and second, having what is enough.

Seneca

When asked 'How much money do you need to feel that you have enough?', I'm told that most people name a figure which is double their present income, whether they earn £15,000 or £150,000 a year. However, most careers books ask you to work out the minimum you need to pay all your bills and to eat. Unfortunately far too many people confuse this figure with what they are worth.

Write down a figure in answer to each question below.

WHAT DO YOU NEED TO EARN?

When you have added up all your monthly bills, travel, insurance, health and food costs:
What do you need to live on?

£

What would you need to earn to be relaxed about what you spend each month?'
What would be ENOUGH?

£

How do you value your skills, knowledge and commitment? What do other people like you earn in your chosen field? If you know the earnings range, what do you have to do to be in the top 25%?
What are you worth?

£

On the basis that you have a greater chance of achieving something if you write it down:
What do you really want to be earning in 5 years' time?

£

WHAT *REALLY* MOTIVATES YOU?

In order that people may be happy in their work, these three things are needed: They must be fit for it. They must not do too much of it. And they must have a sense of success in it.

John Ruskin

Recruiters will tell you that the first answer to that question is usually 'money'. The reason is that it's easy, convenient shorthand. In my interview training programmes I always try to get interviewers to probe to the next level. You may not be motivated by money at all, in fact. Throwing money at a problem does not make satisfied workers. Once money issues are resolved, deeper motivators kick in, such as being respected for what you know, seeing the job through to the finish, variety, making a difference, learning and work/life balance. If you want to check this out in more detail, try the Motivations Checklist in *Take Control of Your Career* or at www.johnleescareers.com.

What recruiters know is that everyone has Career Hot Buttons, but most of us are not good at identifying them (Exercise 5.2 will help). If you're asked why you want to leave a job, it's convenient to use shorthand: 'the job stinks', 'the money's rotten', 'it's the way they treat you'. We all have our convenient shorthand for the things that go wrong in life: work, car, house, marriage. To build on that experience it helps to ask 'What went wrong? What parts did I find uncomfortable or unhelpful?' and then actively seek the positive.

Knowing what you don't want is helpful, but only as a first step. This book is here to help you discover what you do want in your career, and to help you get it.

EXERCISE 5.1 – YOUR JIGSAW JOB

Here's a way of discovering what your ideal job looks like.

People find it difficult to describe their ideal job because it requires too big a commitment: a job title, a field of work, a potential decision. An easier way in is to use the jigsaw job technique.

You buy a jigsaw from a charity shop, but this is a jigsaw puzzle that comes in a plastic bag. You have no box, no picture, no title. You have no idea whether you have a picture of a cottage, a seascape or a kitten. So, in order to make the jigsaw you have to use other rules. You'll probably begin with the edges and the corners, but in the early stages of assembly you have to let go of the question 'what is this a picture of?'

Defining your 'jigsaw' job is like making a jigsaw without a box or the picture. You begin by making edges, corners and recognizable shapes. The analogy in career terms is that you forget about job titles and fields, and build the job up from the inside. Imagine you are in a really fulfilling job, but forget about what it says on your business card or on your door. Build the picture up from the edges, just thinking about each element in turn. Look at the example jigsaw job in Figure 5.1, and then fill in your picture using the same or similar headings.

My jigsaw job will contain the following ingredients:	
Location, setting	Urban. Aesthetically pleasing. Flexible. Involves travel and meeting people
Hours	Generally Monday to Friday, but hours flexible
General details	A firm that's large enough to help me grow, small enough to support people
People	A role where I am mentored. Trusting, co-operative environment. Team working environment. Sharing ideas, thinking collectively
The way I manage	More a mentor than a supervisor
The way I am managed	I am given opportunities. My boss is direct, honest, sees my potential. Keeps me on the straight and narrow
Skills I use	Being the face of the organization. Liaising, explaining; translating complex ideas into straightforward terms. Communicating/influencing. Using creative and analytical thinking
Problems	Trying to help people with their problems. Completing work on time
Challenges	Competition: something to drive me. The job is testing/stretching. Learning about managing/leadership
Values expressed	Strong ethos. Clear sense of purpose/meaning
Likely/attractive outcomes include	Getting a team result. Bringing the best out of people. Delighting the client
The job will be rewarding because	I will be achieving something. It will be fun
How work contributes to life outside work	Comfortable lifestyle. Health. Well-being
Work will allow time and energy for me to do these things outside work	Spending time with family and friends. Enjoying the theatre and cultural events again

Figure 5.1   An example of a jigsaw job

EXERCISE 5.2 – DISCOVER YOUR CAREER HOT BUTTONS

Table 5.1 provides a profile to check what motivates you in your career choices. First read the category title and questions. Against each category, circle a score on the scale of 1 to 10. Try to use the full scale rather than bunch all of your scores in the middle.

Table 5.1 Career Hot Buttons

1. Financial rewards

How important is the money, really? How much would you be re-energized if your salary increased by 10%? 20%? How long would that feeling last?

How motivated are you by financial rewards such as bonus payments?

If you could do more of the great things about your job and fewer of the dull things, would you be just as happy with less money?

When you're at a party and listening to people talk about their jobs, do you always want to know how much they earn? How much does it matter to you?

Financial rewards are:

1	2	3	4	5	6	7	8	9	10
Unimportant			Moderately important				Very important		

2. Influence

How much do you enjoy exercising the skills of leadership, persuasion or motivation (high influence)?

How much control do you like to have over people, situations, problems?

You know how you like things done. Do you prefer to be in charge (high influence) or are you happy to follow a good leader (low influence)?

How much do you like to have a say in change?

A high degree of influence is:

1	2	3	4	5	6	7	8	9	10
Unimportant			Moderately important				Very important		

3. Expert

How much do you like that feeling of being knowledgeable, skilled, an expert?

Are you happy knowing a lot about a focused area of knowledge?

Do you enjoy a reputation as a specialist (high expert) or a jack of all trades (low expert)?

Being an expert is:

1	2	3	4	5	6	7	8	9	10
Unimportant			Moderately important				Very important		

4. Independence

How far do you prefer a mentor to a supervisor?

Are you a self-starter? Do you like to set your own deadlines?

How much control do you like over how you spend your time?

Do you like to have control over what you do (high independence) or are you happy to accept intelligent supervision (mid to low independence)?

Independence in my work is:

1	2	3	4	5	6	7	8	9	10
Unimportant			Moderately important				Very important		

5. Relationships

How important are close relationships at work to you?

Do you tend to make friends through and at work?

Are you more productive working in a team (high relationships) or quietly on your own (low relationships)?

How important is it to you to trust and be trusted?

Relationships at work are:

1	2	3	4	5	6	7	8	9	10
Unimportant			Moderately important				Very important		

6. Security

How far do you need to feel you are financially secure?

That you have a nest egg, a safely barrier – a cushion against ill fortune (high security)?

How happy are you to take on risks of varying kinds (low security)?

How important is it to you that you know what you will be doing next week/next year?

Security in work is:

1	2	3	4	5	6	7	8	9	10
Unimportant			Moderately important				Very important		

7. Status

How much of you is contained in your reputation?

How far do you seek recognition from your colleagues, your profession, your community (high status)?

How far are you happy to work in the background, getting the job done, not minding who gets the credit? (low status)?

How important is it to you to have a job title that reflects the level and impact of your job?

Status is:

1	2	3	4	5	6	7	8	9	10
Unimportant			Moderately important				Very important		

8. Meaning and purpose

How strongly do you feel about the value your work adds to your community, the world?

How aware are you of the damage your work might be doing to others, or to the environment?

Do you hear yourself saying that your work should be meaningful (high meaning)?

Are you happy to seek meaning outside your working life (low meaning, as far as work is concerned)?

My search for meaning through work is:

1	2	3	4	5	6	7	8	9	10
Unimportant			Moderately important				Very important		

9. Imagination

How good are you at discovering new ideas, new ways of doing things?

Do you prefer to let others come up with the good ideas while you do the detailed planning?

Do you prefer to follow a system or set of rules (low imagination)?

Or do you like to invent new solutions to problems (high imagination)?

Using imagination at work is:

1	2	3	4	5	6	7	8	9	10
Unimportant			Moderately important				Very important		

Your Total Scores

Career Hot Buttons	Total	Rank Order
1 Financial rewards		
2 Influence		
3 Expert		
4 Independence		
5 Relationships		
6 Security		
7 Status		
8 Meaning and purpose		
9 Imagination		

Write down your total scores, and then work out a rank order. If you have given equal scores to more than one button, balance one against the other. For example, if your scores for 2 (Influence) and 7 (Status) are the same, ask yourself 'Would

I prefer a job where my ability to influence or control others was *marginally* more important than my status?' If you have 3 or 4 equal, play 1 off against 2, then 3, then 4. It works, but if you have equal scores for some headings, no matter.

What are the implications? Match your top three career drivers against your present or most recent role. What is the degree of overlap? What is missing that you would like to add into your present job, or you will be actively seeking in your next post?

Occupational psychologist Stuart Robertson has been kind enough to build on my Career Hot Buttons when designing his very interesting **Career Motivation Indicator**. See www.sr-associates.com.

'MUST DO' LIST

Now you have identified your Career Hot Buttons, look back at what you discovered so far in this book:

☑ What really motivates you?

☑ What do you find unstimulating, unacceptable and demotivating?

☑ What might move you up the career satisfaction grid?

☑ How will you deal with 'Yes, but' and the limits it puts on your life?

☑ How far does your present job match your top three Career Hot Buttons?

Your House of Knowledge

This chapter helps you to:

▌ Tap your hidden knowledge

▌ Understand how your preferred interests provide huge clues about career satisfaction

▌ Make new connections between what you know, and what you can do

WHAT DO YOU KNOW?

Just as we all have hidden skills, we have concealed but vital areas of knowledge. What's powerful about your hidden knowledge is not just what you know, but why you know it. A certain amount of knowledge is inflicted upon us in school, but from the age of 14 or so we begin to make choices about our academic subjects. All the subjects we read, learn and think about in our own time tell us a huge amount about our personality, aspirations and interests.

However, one point to beware: don't ignore the possibilities of new areas of knowledge you have yet to discover. One of the benefits of a demanding and eclectic education system is that it forces students to be exposed to subjects, materials and ideas that, at first sight, don't seem to be interesting at all. It's one of the reasons why exercises focusing on skills and knowledge don't tend to work with young people – they just haven't explored enough yet.

EXERCISE 6.1 – YOUR HOUSE OF KNOWLEDGE

This exercise helps you to identify, record, value and communicate the things you know about. It is also a vital step to help you to identify your areas of interest that may provide strong links into fields of work. What we choose to learn about is a vital part of who we are.

What do you know about? Ask that question of someone you meet on a train or in a pub, and most people talk first of all about the areas of knowledge most frequently used by their current job. They will often talk about their educational specialization. Therefore, 'My degree was in Spanish, but I'm an accountant now.' This is merely scratching the surface.

Look at the three-storey house in Table 6.1. It has a ground floor, first floor and second floor. It has an attic and a basement, and a garage at the side. Each level of that house represents something of what you know.

The exercise runs as follows. Like most exercises in this book, it works better if you have one or two people to ask you questions as you go along.

1. Begin with the **basement** of your house, the firm foundations provided by your home and school. The following questions will help:

   ▮ What did you learn from your parents? What was your favourite subject at school?

   ▮ What projects or activities engaged you outside the classroom?

   ▮ What was the first thing you wanted to read when you put aside your textbooks? What was that about?

Table 6.1 House of Knowledge

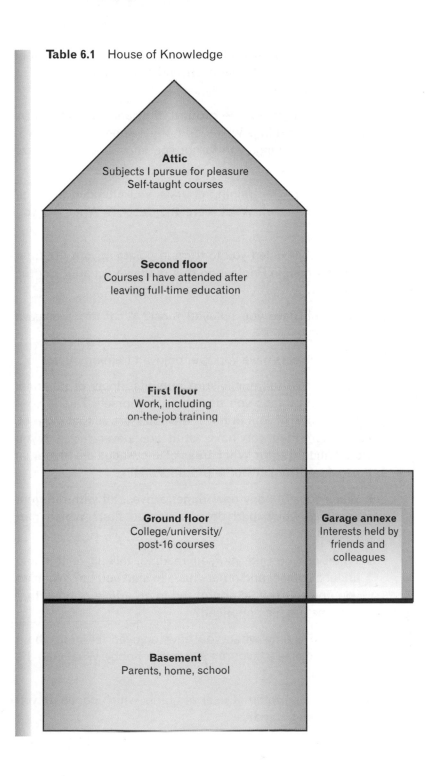

■ When were you so enthusiastic about a subject at school or college that you went off and found more to read in your own time?

2. Complete the list for the **ground, first** and **second floors**. Try to think of things which do not yet appear in your CV – including the things you forgot you know about. Here are some prompts:

   ■ Think about the training courses you attended that you got most out of. What were they about? What did you learn?

   ■ What subjects led you to turning points in your life (that night school in Photoshop that made you change degree course …)?

   ■ What job have you enjoyed most? What did you learn from it?

   ■ What subjects have you ever enjoyed training others in?

3. Move on now to your leisure pursuits, areas of personal interest and things you have taught yourself. This is your **attic**, the part of your brain where you store all that old junk you've forgotten you have, stuff you never thought you would find a use for. What areas of knowledge are hidden in those dusty trunks? Some prompts again:

   ■ When your Sunday newspaper arrives, fat with different sections, which part do you turn to first? Which part second?

   ■ When do you find yourself reading, talking or thinking about a subject and others have to shut you up? When do you find yourself so engrossed in an article or book that the time passes unnoticed?

   ■ Think of a time when you have enjoyed learning about someone else's favourite subject or hobby. What was the subject?

   ■ If you are an Internet user at home, which pages do you have bookmarked?

■ If you were accidentally locked into a large bookshop for the weekend, in which section would you camp out? Once you got bored, where would you go next? And next? Write down the headings that would appear on the book-shelves.

■ Given a free choice, what would you choose to talk about over a relaxed meal?

■ If you could teach a workshop on any subject in the world, to any audience, and given unlimited preparation time, what would that subject be?

■ If you received a bequest from an aged relative that would fund a return to full-time education, what would you study?

■ If you could learn about any subject in the world, from any teacher, what would that subject be?

■ If you won the lottery and didn't have to work, you'd spend a few months indulging yourself, but eventually you would get bored. What would you actually do to fill the time?

4. Last but not least, the **garage**. It's on an annexe at the side because it's about vicarious interests, living life through the eyes and minds of other people. Think about close friends whose interests you share. My friend Peter Maybank has a long-held interest in the First World War. I've joined him on battlefield trips to both Verdun and the Somme, and I realized through this experience how important the knowledge of others can be in shaping my own.

5. Look at your complete house. What have you missed out? It'll probably be things you consider 'trivial', such as cooking, homemaking or family history. If you enjoy it, include it.

It's important to remember what you are *really* interested in, and to remember all the things that you have chosen to know about. This tells you a great deal in terms of motivation and subject interests, and can lead you on to potential areas of work (moving from personal subjects in which you are interested into fields of work). This step is important because it's about recovering parts of your past which you undervalue, and interests that will give you energy and enthusiasm in the future.'

'KNOWING ABOUT' AND 'PASSIONATE ABOUT' – THE THINGS THAT WON'T LEAVE US ALONE

The attic of the House of Knowledge potentially reveals more about us than any other part of the building. This is where we store away the special projects, the things that call to us from time to time and just won't go away. When work feels like this we have our strongest sense of 'flow'. I had the chance to work with the Liverpool-based photographer Colin McPherson some time back and asked him in passing 'do you still enjoy taking photographs when you're not taking them for a living?'. 'Oh yes', he said, and showed me a card with one photograph on it, part of his long-term project photographing the last working salmon net fishermen on the east coast of Scotland (see www.colinmcpherson.co.uk).

'MUST DO' LIST

☑ Look at your completed house of knowledge. What activities in your past filled you with energy? Where is that energy today?

☑ Sit with someone else while they explore their own house of knowledge, and your partner's ideas will probably jog your memory.

☑ If you've caught yourself saying 'Ah, I *really* used to enjoy …', then look at why you dropped the activity or interest. Is there a 'Yes, but' in there somewhere?

What do You Have to Offer?

CHAPTER 7

This chapter helps you to:

I Map your hidden skills – the parts of your experience you took for granted

I Discover your potential, undiscovered, uncharted and motivated skills

I Communicate your skill set to your colleagues, managers or potential employers

I Identify your achievements and express them as mini-narratives

I Compose brilliant presentation statements

My work is a game – a very serious game.

M.C. Escher

WHY IS LOOKING AT SKILLS SO IMPORTANT?

You use and observe skills every day, and you may think you're expert at cataloguing your own skills. Ask most people and they'll tell you 'it's obvious … it's just a matter of knowing what you are good at'. One of the greatest reasons people fail to achieve motivated careers is that they only ever see half the skills they actually possess. They only really know and develop 25% of those skills, and they only communicate a fraction.

If you want to make sure you never get a great career, one of the best strategies is never to reveal your full set of gifts. If you're determined to continue doing work that fails to stretch you or match your aspirations, that will do the trick.

Also, we are not simply what others see in us. It's too easy simply to accept the skill set that others describe – your friends see and affirm the skills they value; they don't always see the skills that motivate you.

Example: Bill uses his computer every day, but his real interest is natural history. He gives time freely to his local school, which asks him to come in to fix computer problems or advise on software. If he is invited to do anything with the children, it usually involves explaining something about computers. He's great at it: probably the best person the school can find. But what he really wants to do is to talk to the kids about pond life.

First impression list

Divide a piece of paper into four boxes as in Table 7.1: Things, People, Information and Ideas.

Table 7.1 Skill categories

THINGS	PEOPLE
INFORMATION	IDEAS

Now write, in any of the four boxes, the skills you think you use most frequently. The following descriptions may help you to make sense of your results of performing an initial skills sort:

■ People who work mainly with **things** (and animals) – this includes engineers, machine operators, nature reserve wardens, vets, carpenters, car designers and gardeners.

- People who work mainly with **people** – this includes teachers, social workers, counsellors, trainers, salespeople and personnel officers.

- People who work mainly with **information** – this includes scientific researchers, librarians, auditors, archivists, editors, researchers and systems analysts.

- People who work mainly with **concepts and ideas** – this includes e-business pioneers, marketing professionals, artists, writers, campaigners and systems designers.

UNWRAP YOUR GIFTS

One of the ways we know that we live in an abundant universe is that we have a rich set of skills. We all have. If you're spiritually minded, you may have discovered that God or the universe has sent you a particular set of *gifts*. It's useful to think of our skills as gifts, because it reminds us that what we do with those skills really matters – we have a responsibility to use them well. Many cultures believe that every person is born with a gift, and the purpose of our lives is to realize that gift in some tangible way. Unwrapping your gifts, exploring and celebrating the talents you have been given, is not just about work, or fun or duty. It's about discovering why you are here.

Few of us see what a well-equipped skills toolbox we've been given. We use skills without recognizing or crediting them, and we fail to bring out our latent talents, blinking, into the light. You have been given a unique set of talents. Unique not because of one, primary, virtuoso skill that commends you to the world, but because of the way all your skills are uniquely combined in you. Unique because you are the only person with your skills, exercised through your personality, your history, your viewpoint. No-one else can be you, in your particular situation in life. You can always find somebody who can employ a particular skill better than you, but they can't be *you*.

STEPS TO SKILL AWARENESS

The experience of helping career changers suggests to me that most of us have skills that we know well and are comfortable with, but there are huge areas of unmapped territory. You may find your own personal categories, but try these:

How many of your skills are:

Unconscious	Undiscovered
Undeveloped	Undervalued
Unsung	Unfulfilled
Unpolished?	

Unconscious skills

Unconscious skills are unseen skills, used so often that we hardly ever see them. Another way of describing them is 'wallpaper skills'. When you put up new wallpaper you're very aware of it for a month or so, and then it gradually becomes invisible as you get used to it. It springs back into focus when someone else notices it.

Example: Amy's great skill is making people feel better about themselves by talking to them. Others see her do it: it's oiling the wheels, increasing a sense of community. She does it so often she's unaware of it. She had never thought of it as a skill until a friend said, 'Do you know what you do most of the time? You're the cement between the bricks of our community.'

Key: You are more likely to spot your 'wallpaper' skills when you ask others to remind you what you're good at and where you have made a difference.

Undiscovered skills

Undiscovered skills are skills you use only occasionally, perhaps under pressure or in special moments. You often don't notice exercising these skills in the heat of the moment, or you don't claim ownership: things just happened. In an emergency, for example, there is often someone present who has great clarity of mind, organizing people, calling an ambulance and preventing panic.

Example: Maureen's great skill is untangling messy personal situations. She works quietly in the background, helping people to see things clearly, encouraging the parties to put anger aside and seek common ground. She never gets the opportunity to use these skills at work, so the opportunity only comes along very occasionally.

Key: Remember that sense of surprise – something changed because of your involvement. Why? What did you do? Ask yourself (or someone who saw you operating), not 'what happened?' but 'what did I do?' and 'how could I use this skill more often?'.

Undeveloped skills

You possibly may see only the beginnings of undeveloped skills in yourself. Look for potential in clues, small seeds that may grow into something stunning.

Example: Norma has never been able to walk past a piece of fabric without touching it. She has a good eye for texture, colour and pattern, and for matching materials simply and cheaply to make a room look great. She has a knack of walking into a room and knowing how to make it look more welcoming, more 'together' by making a few simple changes. Last year her friend brought out these 'wallpaper' skills and found a set of undeveloped and marketable skills underneath – becoming a 'house doctor', helping other people to sell their homes quickly by reading the mind of the buyer and offering a series of low-cost, high-imagination solutions to make a home look great and sell quickly.

Key: Think about materials you love to work with, words you enjoy hearing. Stretch yourself. Read books and go on courses on new subjects.

Undervalued skills

Undervalued skills are skills you are aware of but you feel are of little value. You will hear yourself say 'I can do this, but who would be interested?' You enjoy using these skills, but you feel they have little currency, so you don't put any energy into cultivating or broadcasting them to the world. Sometimes these skills have become unappreciated by others. What if your skills are invisible to others, and that has changed the way you feel about them too? If you do something regularly, and do it well, ask yourself 'Do I need to do something else, something differently, or do these things somewhere where they will be appreciated?'

Example: You're great at making a calm, tidy space in your home. But does anyone appreciate what you do? So you tidy, clean and dust with heaviness. How would you feel if your work was appreciated? If your job was to make a reception area look comfortable and welcoming – if your efforts made a difference? Are these skills you would love if someone else loved them, too?

Key: Look for fulfilment levels in the skills you use. To find an inspired career there should be a metronome ticking inside you, repeating *These are the things I love to do and can do well. These are the things I'd love to do more often.*

If you are in demand for skills you don't enjoy using, either learn to love them or learn to say no. Tell people what you enjoy doing, and ask for opportunities so you can learn by doing. If you want a middle way, train someone else who will *really* love to do the things you can do well. Pass the skills on.

One of the things I have always said while training recruiters is that there are no unmotivated people out there. There are those who show their motivation at work, and those who are motivated by exercising skills which they feel are of no value to employers. Often they will think of these as 'hobby skills'.

Example: Sue's hidden passion is ballroom dancing. She has never put it on a CV because she feels it is entirely irrelevant. One day she heard of a college lecturer who taught business skills through ballroom dancing. Formal dancing teaches timing, responsiveness, leading and following, reading signals, anticipating change, paying attention to personal space. Sue realized that using these skills at work was what made her a brilliant PA.

Key: If the skill is valuable to you, make it valuable to others. Look again at your undervalued skills – they are probably there somewhere in your working life in an undeveloped state. Learn to make better connections between the skills you love using outside work and the roles you perform best in the workplace.

When love and skill work together, expect a masterpiece.

Charles Reade

Unsung skills

Unsung skills are skills you have identified and valued, maybe skills you feel do have some relevance to the world, but you don't broadcast them. You haven't yet discovered the right language to talk about them in a way that communicates them to someone who 'matters'. Job-changers often say 'I talk to my friends about this stuff all the time, but I don't know where to begin to tell an employer'.

These are often so-called 'soft' skills. This is a fine example of split thinking in the business world – hard skills are directly useful (selling, making, pushing, doing), soft skills are ten-a-

penny and there in the background (imagining, feeling, training, sharing). We are often frightened that our 'soft' skills
sound vague or prissy.

Example: Sally has held a number of voluntary positions,
connected with school, church or Girl Guides. In the last 10 years
she has acted as treasurer, leader, resource manager, transport
co-ordinator, catering manager and team leader. She condenses
this into a throwaway phrase on her CV: 'voluntary interests'.

It's true that employers often suspect that work done in a
voluntary environment is pressure-free, unconnected with the
real world. Show them it isn't: give examples of working to
deadlines, under pressure, to budget. Communicate how difficult it is to manage volunteers where you have to rely on
persuasion and example rather than work contracts. Voluntary
work often grows brilliant managers and self-starters.

Key: Look for those moments when you say 'things just
happened … it all came together at the last minute'. Who
made it come together? If it was you, how did you do it?
Finally, spend time discovering your skills; it's an inner journey
worth taking because:

*The minute you begin to do what you really want to do, it's really a
different kind of life.*

                                                    Buckminster Fuller

Unfulfilled skills

Your unfulfilled skills are the skills you dream about using,
things you instinctively feel you might be good at if you only
had the chance. Listen to those dreams calling you. I always
wanted to … paint watercolours, ride a horse, write my auto-
biography, run a soup kitchen, build my own house ….

Don't confuse longing with fancy. You might dream about
becoming a test pilot, but the test of longing is that the idea
won't leave you alone until you do something about it. The

crunch comes when you find an *activated desire* – in other words, a desire you can act upon. Want to be Prime Minister? Join a party, achieve some kind of elected office, take the first steps towards becoming an MP.

Watch particularly for tasks you dream about. I sailed as a boy and often dreamed about sailing again. At the age of 40, I did. It was everything I'd dreamed about, but better: because I had practised sailing so often in my head, I was actually better at it. I've heard this phenomenon called 'learning to ski in the summer, learning to swim in the winter'. All kinds of sports research has also confirmed that training by visualization is almost as good as the real thing. If that's true, then imagined skills are more powerful than you think.

Nothing is as damaging as a ruthless policy of ignoring your unfulfilled skills. Try things out. Try a job on a short-term basis. Work for nothing just to get the feel of it. Shadow someone doing the job to find out if it's what you'd really like to do. Take a short course rather than a 3-year degree.

Warning: These skills are most easily dampened by others. People will try to steal or suppress your dreams.

A new idea is delicate. It can be killed by a sneer or a yawn; it can be stabbed to death by a joke or worried to death by a frown on the right person's brow.

Charles Brower

Unpolished skills

Unpolished skills are rather like undeveloped skills, but with one important distinction: you are fully aware of these skills and value them, but you have settled for competence when you know you are capable of far more. The skill is stuck at a fixed level. It's not growing, and nor are you.

Example: Kate learned through her job in customer services to deal with complaints – and when to refer difficult calls to managers. She had learned the job inside out, but hated any change: new products, new support services. She had failed to stretch herself, to see what she was really capable of, because she had never looked at the underlying master skill: *keeping customers happy*. Once she learned to develop that skill, to invent new ways of helping people, she began to grow and was promoted to supervisor.

Example: When you learn to swim, you begin by thinking of it as organized movement. Somewhere, you think, there's a special combination of movements that will keep me above water and move me forward. The barely competent swimmer achieves that, and no more. *That'll do. I can swim.* Bill broke through that stage when he realized that swimming wasn't about movement or power, but a form of guided floating. With that idea in mind, he progressed to swimming several lengths. Then he discovered that it was also about timed breathing. Control the timing and breathing, and you can continue swimming just like you can continue walking. The first skill breakthrough will rarely be the last.

Key: Look for the underlying principle. Why are you doing this? What's the overall concept behind it? If your skill is selling, is the underlying principle profit, people, adding value, sharing a good idea … ?

SKILL CLIPS

Think of your life as a movie. Your personal movie contains everything you've ever done, every moment when you've exercised any kind of skill.

When you want to communicate who you are and what you can do, you will tend to edit. You will show only short, quick scenes to your viewers. You edit your life like a movie editor, disposing of whole scenes, cutting, abbreviating.

The **skill clips** exercise sends you back to the cutting room floor, and fine-tunes your skills as a movie editor. When a distributor wants to persuade you to watch a movie, you get to see a trailer – the whole plot condensed into 30 seconds. That's your CV, if you like: a condensed, all-action version of you.

When a film critic wants to convey the character of a film, he will show you a film clip: an extract that shows a key scene, a special moment. In the movie of your life, what are the key moments? They may be the kind of events that you recorded in your photograph album. Go back and look through them. Do any of those occasions tell you anything about skills you have exercised in the past? (Incidentally, use your family photo album to remind you of areas of knowledge and interests – if you enjoy doing something, there's probably a photo of you doing it, somewhere.)

Fix on one event. Start with an occasion when you felt a great sense of success or achievement (maybe a 'flow' moment: see Figure 4.2). Picture your 'clip', and give it a title. Then ask yourself the following skill discovery questions:

What obstacles did I have to overcome?	What did I have to do to achieve this?
What was the task or challenge?	How did I work with others?
What planning did I need to do?	What was my best moment?
What skills did I see myself use?	How did I surprise myself or others?
What skills did others see me use?	What did I do personally?

Figure 7.1 shows you a skill clip example. Your skill clip begins with a title, like any good movie, but it also has a concise storyline – rather like the 'pitch' a writer has to make to a Hollywood studio to get an idea accepted.

Title: 'Top of the World'			
PITCH			
I've always been frightened of heights. I was pretty unfit. My work team challenged me to climb Cwm Clogwyn in Snowdonia.			
[Scenes] **Opening shot: The problem**	**First step**	**Main action**	**Ending**
Panic! Fear of failing. Sponsorship for a good cause convinced me to go ahead.	Weighing up the problem. Deciding what I needed to learn and practise.	Setting off – the real thing. Putting theory and training into practice. Scary!	I made it! Photograph at the summit. Elation.
Skills I used Recognizing my limitations. Overcoming fear.	**Skills I used** Learning from friends, practising on a climbing wall. Learning to climb and belay, understanding equipment. Risk management? Anticipating and measuring problems	**Skills I used** Working as a team, learning to rely on others. Responding (fast!) to instructions. Helping others to cope with their fear. Keeping people's spirits up with humour!	**Skills I used** Celebrating – enjoying what we had achieved as a team, and my special role in our success. Reflecting on what I had managed by overcoming fear and relying on my colleagues. Insight: new ways of working together.

Figure 7.1   Example skill clip

Home movie rules for editing and composing your skill clips

1. **Zoom in as tight as possible** – avoid long sequences. One day is good. One hour is better. Keep it concise. Like a movie clip, it's got to convey a lot in a short space of time.

2. **Use slow motion** – reveal the action as it happens by thinking about what you did and how you did it.

3. **Use a good screenplay** – does this scene convey a message about skills, about overcoming obstacles?

4. **Keep the star in shot** – make sure this scene is about the hero: you.

5. **Make sure the clip has a happy ending** – an achievement or a skill revelation.

Some prompts for your skill clips:

▮ Think of times when you achieved something you are proud of. This doesn't need to be a work-related achievement. How did you do it? What difference did you make? Turn the event over in your mind until you see the skills, particularly those which are **unconscious** or **undeveloped**.

▮ Now look at your achievements from your non-working life. Times in the past when you overcame the odds, did something that surprised yourself. Look in particular for skills that are **undervalued**.

▮ Think about both **activities** and **accomplishments**.

▮ Think about work-related clips that demonstrate the full range of skills: things, people, information, concepts, etc.

▮ Finally, what's your favourite skill?

Keep drawing up these skill clips, either alone or, even better, with a friend or fellow career developer. If you show a series of movie clips from the work of Alfred Hitchcock, you see similarities of style and content. After five or six skill clips you'll start to notice a pattern of skills, or a set of *master skills*, and you'll get a strong sense of what you are really good at *and* enjoy doing.

Express your achievements as mini-narratives

You can build on the skill clips exercise by learning how to remember each achievement as a mini-narrative. A good story is short and memorable, and has a clear topic. A good statement of your achievement has the same structure, as outlined in Figure 7.2, with a short explanation of the problem, a brief overview of what you did, and an indication of the outcome.

Story: Beginning	Middle	End
The problem My company needed to simplify its accounting system and save money.	**What I did** Identified, researched and introduced an off-site central accounting function.	**The outcome** 25% savings, and the new accounts centre came on line to budget and on deadline.

Figure 7.2   Achievement as mini-narrative

Using mini-narratives has great advantages. First of all, it's easier for you to remember good material to use at interview. You're providing yourself with a mental portfolio of useful evidence. Secondly, a well-constructed mini-narrative is easier to listen to and remember than a long, rambling tale. Thirdly, you don't have to think this stuff up during the interview. Trying to remember good examples in the interview room is hard work, because you have to apply several filters at once ('Will this sound interesting/relevant/impressive … ?', 'Will it come out right?', 'Can I remember enough detail to answer supplementary questions?'). Having this information ready in the front of your head actually means that you can give more attention to using your interview radar, working out the *real* agenda (see Chapter 13 for more on interviewing).

Presentation statements

I am indebted to my colleague Bernard Pearce for the idea of presentation statements. At interview and when networking it's vital to give brief, upbeat responses to key questions. Being brief prevents you getting bogged down in possibly difficult details. Being upbeat focuses the listener on the positive, and interviewers in particular are far too good at remembering negatives. A presentation statement also allows you to communicate your skills and successes. This is something you work on a long time before you go anywhere near a decision maker.

Compose a brief statement, using your own words, to cover each of the difficult questions outlined below.

1. **Why do you want to change career?**
   Explain why you are looking for a new opportunity. Don't dwell on past problems or uncomfortable relationships, but discuss positive reasons for change.

2. **Where is your career going?**
   Describe the job you are looking for and why you find it exciting. Say why you believe you are suited to this kind of work, and stress how what you have to offer will help a prospective employer.

3. **'Tell us about yourself'**
   Compose a brief summary of who you are, what you do, and what skills and experience you have: encapsulate traits, skills and accomplishments to build a positive image in the mind of the listener.

4. **Summarize your career to date**
   Keep this to no more than 2–3 minutes, starting and ending with your present or last role and covering all the positive aspects of your experience that are particularly relevant for the position you are seeking.

5. **What are your strengths?**
   A concise overview of the skills and abilities that are likely to be of most interest to prospective employers. Remember that this is not a list of the job titles you have held or the companies you have worked for, but a shortlist of your main skills.

6. **What are your weaknesses?**
   This is always the toughest question. Avoid giving away any huge negatives. Usually it works if you admit to being something of a perfectionist or saying that you push yourself and others too hard. Be prepared to talk about times when things didn't go so well at work, and talk about what you learned and what you would do differently next time.

7. **What are your main achievements?**
   Prepare more examples than you will actually need. Learn how to communicate achievements as mini-narratives (see above). State the ultimate benefits to the organization, including measurable results.

8. **What motivates you?**
   Be prepared to talk about what you have to offer rather than what you want to gain – talk about valuing the chance to use particular skills, opportunities to learn and grow or try out ideas. Stress the benefits to the organization.

9. **Why should we hire** *you***?**
   How your skills, know-how and experience combine together in a unique way. This is your unique selling point (USP) – the reason(s) why you are the best person for the job.

10. **Why do you want to leave your present job?**
    Alternatively, this may be a question about why you left your last job. Whether you were pushed or decided to leave for your own reasons, keep your answer as short and upbeat as possible. If you were made redundant, a phrase such as 'the organization restructured and laid off a number of staff' usually works. Talk about what you want to do next as soon as possible. Avoid saying anything negative about a previous employer.

(Also see 'Your Two-Breath Message' in Chapter 13).

It usually takes more than three weeks to prepare a good impromptu speech.

                                                                    Mark Twain

How employers see skills

Employers see too many candidates who claim to be skilled but fail to provide back-up evidence. An employer is not interested in skills that are not grounded in real situations. For example: *I am a good communicator.* What kind of communication? What do you mean by good? Improve the way you describe your skills by providing evidence of what your skill achieved. Employers see skills in terms of a context: how, where, when, why? Don't just name your skills – say something about the level of skill you have achieved, and also something about the context – problems and outcomes: *I regularly communicated difficult messages to team members, keeping them informed and motivated – resulting in improved staff retention over a 3-year period of organizational change.*

EXERCISE 7.1 – MOTIVATED SKILLS

What skills do you really enjoy using? Think about a time you were so engrossed in a task that you lost all track of time – moments when you felt completely yourself.

Look at skills you have identified and record them in a grid laid out like Table 7.1.

Skills in the darkest grey box are those you should be using and developing. If not, watch out for the consequences.

Table 7.1 Your motivated skills

	Skills I love using	Skills I quite enjoy using	Skills I don't enjoy using
Skills I perform well			
Skills I perform reasonably well but need to develop			
Skills I do not perform well			

EXERCISE 7.2 – SKILL CIRCLE

Take your identified top 12 skills and write them in a circle, like the 12 points of a clock, as in Figure 7.3.

Try combining skills. Ask yourself, 'When have I ever used these two skills together in an exciting or impressive way? What sort of work would benefit from a combination of these two skills?' You might, for example, combine 2, Managing people, and 7, Inventing solutions. This might mean: inventing new management systems, devising new ways of looking at management issues, such as giving people the tools to solve their own problems.

Combining 12, Challenging assumptions, with 6, Fund raising, might make you think about turning the whole idea of fund raising on its head. You might look at the question, 'how can we persuade more people to give us money?' and turn it around: 'how can we get people to persuade us to take their money?' Your fund-raising campaign may find a way of empowering people to select charities that exactly match their values.

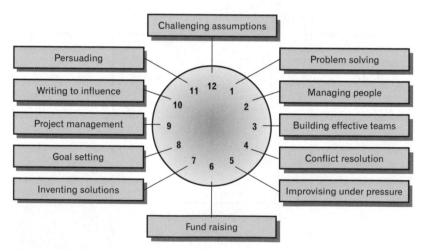

Figure 7.3 Skill circle

'MUST DO' LIST

☑ Find the best way for you of discovering your hidden skills. Enlist the help of a good listener, a patient friend or a professional career coach.

☑ Look at the connections between your dreams, your interests and the skills you love using. There's a magic combination somewhere ... .

☑ Try at least four skill clips. Write out the skills you discover. Look at the skills that keep coming up time and again – what are your **master skills** – in other words, the skills that are central to you as a person?

☑ Identify achievements for the different stages of your career.

☑ Plan, write down and rehearse your presentation statements.

FURTHER HELP TO IDENTIFY YOUR SKILLS AND ACHIEVEMENTS

It's virtually impossible to capture all your own skills. Most people need the help of a colleague or career coach. However, I have developed a set of skill cards that you can use on your own to give you a list of your **Top 10 Motivated Skills** and linked achievement stories. The cards come with a full set of instructions including several exercises you can use to help you understand and communicate your skills.

For full information about the **JLA Skill Cards** toolkit, designed to you identify your top skills and communicate them to employers, visit **www.johnleescareers.com**, and for further tips on communicating your skills at interview, see *Job Interviews: Top Answers to Tough Questions* by John Lees and Matthew DeLuca (McGraw-Hill, 2008).

Finally, please note that all of the examples given in this chapter come from actual career clients. For further, detailed case studies of people who have read this book and moved on to new and exciting careers, see **Appendix 2**.

Who Are You?

This chapter helps you to:

▌ Explore your work and life values

▌ Understand what motivates you

▌ Gain insights into your personality

▌ Discover your different intelligences

Happiness is not having what you want, but wanting what you have.

Rabbi H. Schachtel

We looked in Chapter 2 at your *world view* and the way it affects your career decisions. Now we're going to explore some of the ways to help you to become more self-aware. The people who are most successful in their careers are:

▌ aware of who they are, and happy in that knowledge

▌ conscious of their motivated skills

▌ clear about the way these skills will be helpful to the world

▌ filled with something more than a surface confidence, but a deep-down confidence about what they have to offer.

Table 8.1 looks at a typical menu of options that a career might bring you, and looks at possible points of comfort and discomfort. Table 8.2 lists a range of typical **personal barriers**, and creative strategies to overcome them or get round them.

Table 8.1   Your personality in the workplace

	Comfort	Discomfort
Work role	The majority of the tasks you undertake and your overall role match your skills, temperament and areas of enthusiasm.	You find yourself doing too many things that seem meaningless, trivial or boring.
Work values	Your work relates closely to your wider life ambitions, your beliefs and your sense of purpose. You receive more than a short-term buzz. There is a sense that you are doing something important or meaningful, and your small part of the world is improved by the fact that you're doing it.	You feel that there is something missing. Maybe you're almost there, and what you need to do is to add other voluntary activities to your work portfolio. Or maybe there is something hollow about you: efficient on the outside, but empty in the middle?
Skills	You do things well and enjoy what you do. You have a sense of **flow**: time passes quickly and you are absorbed in your activity and proud of the results.	There is a significant mismatch between what you know, can do well and enjoy doing, and what your work role actually demands of you. You are doing some things extremely well, but discover that you really don't enjoy doing them.
Work context	Where and how you exercise your skills	A good benchmark of your discomfort is the

	matters. Do you prefer to work with people, things, information or ideas?	question *do you actually enjoy talking about your job*? This is not the same as the question *do you enjoy complaining about your job*?
Organization	Do you respond best to a small organization which offers variety and challenge or where you need to be self-reliant, or are you happier in the more defined structure of a larger organization?	Do you feel constrained by too small a firm, or by being an anonymous cog in a large concern? Perhaps you have struck the wrong balance between growth and security, between variety and structure.
Career drivers	See Chapter 5 for your **Career Hot Buttons** and compare your primary career drivers to what your job has to offer. How far is your present role in tune with your primary drivers?	If there's a mismatch, what would happen if you addressed your strongest scoring driver first? How would your present job change? What would be your next move?
Working conditions	Think about how your working life is affected by the following: location, travel, the kind of building you work in, what you can see from your office window, where you spend your lunch hour.	Now look at the same list in terms of the things that irritate and rob you of energy.
Growth, variety learning	Does your job keep feeding you? How are you different now from 12 months ago?	How do you begin to manage your career if you are in a job which does not offer growth or learning opportunities?

Career potential	Is your present role a useful stepping stone to the future? Do you have a clear plan for the next 5 years? Do you need one?	How would a recruiter see your present role: as a dead end, a side alley or a building block in your career?
Pace	Every job has its own sense of pace and speed. Does your organization make things happen quickly enough for you?	Are you being pushed at a speed which is faster than your natural or comfortable rate? How do you feel about leaving things half completed?
Change	Change, development and new opportunities fill you with energy.	You find change frightening or threatening.

DISCOVERING THE BEST YOU THERE IS

In the spirit of lateral thinking, I want to look at personality using the kind of 'what if?' thinking businesses use to re-invent themselves. Here are a few ways of starting a small revolution in 'You Plc'.

A fresh look

Look at Table 8.2 and ask what your working life would be if you assumed a completely different mindset for each box. To take a fresh look is to see things as if you had just landed on the planet, or as if you were an inquisitive child: 'What does this do? Why do you do this?' It breaks you out of your habitual ways of thinking. Look at what normally energizes you in life. If you obtain your energy from contact with others, then look at ways of finding your own company more enjoyable and productive. Just as you should get out of your normal physical environment from time to time, it helps to step outside your own personality.

Table 8.2 Personal barriers, and creative ways to overcome them

Lack of confidence	The key to getting an ideal job lies as much in your confidence as your skills or the state of the labour market. Seek out positive feedback and record it somewhere so you can retrieve it when you feel low. Resist every temptation to put yourself down.
Being held back by your CV	You would be surprised to realize how many very senior people feel uncomfortable once they have prepared their CV. They feel that an employer will 'see through it'. They are worried about all those positive claims, and feel they are exaggerating. The reality is that employers, just like you, are good at latching on to negative pieces of information. So, don't give them the opportunity to do so. In your CV and at interview you should be the *best possible version of **you** that you can be*.
Fear of making mistakes	The world's greatest inventions are the result of mistakes. Mistakes are simply feedback on our performance. Winners make far more mistakes than losers – they get more feedback as they continue to try out more possibilities. The more timid mind stops after one mistake. Thomas Edison failed to invent the light bulb several thousand times before coming up with a version that worked. IBM chief Thomas Watson once said 'the way to succeed is to double your failure rate'.
Fear of rejection	Statistically you will be rejected more times than you are accepted. This is a fact of life, not a reflection of what you have to offer. The positive career changer looks at every interview, every discussion, as a learning opportunity. The most important question is 'what did I learn from this?' If you find

	yourself thinking 'all I learned was that people don't want me', then look again.
I don't know if I want the job	Research, and find out. Compare your 'I wish' list to the employer's 'We want' list. If it seems right, throw yourself at the opportunity with enthusiasm. If there are difficult decisions to make about moving house, or whatever, don't worry about them until the job offer is actually in your hand.
No achievements	Everybody has achievements. It's all relative. It is part of human nature to have goals and to overcome obstacles. The point is to recognize your achievements and to celebrate them, rather than assume they are of little worth and of no interest to others.
No clear direction	Not a problem, but a continuing opportunity. It simply means you have not yet finished exploring. Remember, though, that an employer is not interested in hearing about your areas of uncertainty. Do not use the job search process as a way of seeking answers to the questions you hold most deeply – all you will do is increase an employer's perceived risk.
Image	Find as many ways as you can to improve your own self-image (see the note on self-confidence above), but also learn to see how the world sees you. Ask your friends how they and others perceive you; most people find this feedback rather surprising.
Modesty	Many European cultures see the skills discovery process as boasting or self-aggrandizement. It's not. Boasting is when you come to the conclusion that you have something better than everyone else, and ram it down their throats. Discovering your true skills, talents and attributes is following

a road to contentment, i.e. wanting what you have got. Objective self-criticism can be helpful and is sometimes painful, but should be a short-term burst of activity not a way of life. The human brain is finely attuned to living out negative messages, and we all gravitate towards our dominant thoughts. If you keep telling yourself 'I'll never be a manager' you will subconsciously use every ounce of energy to make sure that it becomes a self-fulfilling truth.

The shock of the new	It takes courage to make dramatic career changes, and courage to throw yourself into an entirely new job. Try to remember times in your past when you made similar leaps. How long, in fact, was your adjustment period? We are actually quite good at adjusting to new conditions. Even the most demanding and strange environment can become familiar and routine within a matter of months.
The expectation of others	Don't let other people live your career for you. Everyone does it – parents, teachers, friends and colleagues. They paint a picture of the future and you feel obliged to live it out. They often do so on scant information. You need two kinds of people to make these decisions properly: (a) skilled professionals who can help you to identify where your career is going, and (b) a core team of supporters who can positively encourage you to make it happen.
Lack of information	I talk to a great many people who try to imagine what new fields of work will be like. Imagination can be a helpful step in reaching a goal, but in an age full of information we can take solid steps towards finding out a great deal more. Talk to people

	who are currently doing the job. Find out what a job feels like from the inside.
Everyone I know is in the same boat	This particular mental block is common among school leavers and graduates. They effectively take a small sample of the population, which is the group of friends they socialize with. Every step forward or backward is judged in relation to that small peer group. There is often an interesting dynamic which holds back everyone except for the very strongest individuals. An antidote is to broaden your perception, increase your network, and try to find people who are living successful and balanced lives. Role models can be informative and inspiring.
Be careful what you ask for	One peculiarity of the brain is that we attract what we fear. If you see a small child carrying a glass of water and then say 'be careful you don't spill that', what happens? The child's focus goes from carrying to spilling. The drink is spilled. If you concentrate on the things you fear, you unconsciously put energy into a negative outcome. It sounds corny, but there really is power in positive thinking.
No goals	Set goals. More important still, start with small goals, and stick to them. Plan your week ahead: apply for a course, read a book, get an appointment with someone who works in marketing, increase your typing speed.
It's a dog eat dog world	*Competition brings out the best in products and the worst in people.* David Sarnoff Don't make the mistake of thinking you're in competition with everyone else. You're not.

	You're up against the requirements of a particular job and the needs of a particular employer. Co-operation is far more productive than competition. Pass on the lessons you learn about your own career explorations, and help others on their way. Beginning a network based on co-operation is the secret to a successful career.
Commitment	You need to think about what you really want. You need to think about the dreams that are simply dreams, and the dreams you can act upon.

You will also find it helpful to review your personal constraints using Exercise 2.1 (Chapter 2).

Protecting your ideas about your future

New ideas need 'greenhousing'; when we have new ideas some-times the worst thing we can do is to share them with the wrong kind of people and have them dismissed or trashed. Cultivate ideas quietly.

We all need rather more 'what if' thinking. Suspend judgement for a while; just let the idea ferment undisturbed, and stir the pot occasionally. Keep thinking up alternatives, possibilities, extensions.

Drains and radiators

In life there are two types of people: *drains*, who absorb the energy around them, and *radiators*, who push energy out. It pays to spend time with radiators when you are looking for career development energy. Radiators will say 'go for it'. Drains say 'that will never work'. Drains tell you to be 'realistic', which usually means doing next to nothing in the hope that some-thing good will come along.

Being 'realistic'

Let's look again at 'realistic', the most dangerous word in the career changer's vocabulary.

Listen to everyday career conversations going on around you in coffee shops. Someone asks the question 'what are you looking for?' and the answer often begins, 'Well, in an ideal world....'. As the thought develops, watch the body language as the voice becomes more downbeat. Whether voiced or not, a presence stalks – that word 'realistic'. On the one hand, that interesting 'ideal' world where work would feel like fun. On the other a rather less exciting option – a compromise that looks and feels like trading down.

Applied too early in the process, so-called 'realistic' thinking can stop you at the first hurdle. Advice which says 'just dream the dream' or 'you can be anything you want to be' doesn't cut it, even in a buoyant market. The reason the word *realistic* is dangerous is because it is rarely about what is real. It's usually secondhand information – someone else's picture of the way the world works. This doesn't mean that your next move should be made without any reference to the real world of employers and hiring decisions. It's vital that you understand yourself, and how the world will react to you.

This advice is *not* encouraging people to try to shift into a fantasy world that doesn't exist. All work is a compromise between what you want out of life and what your employer wants out of you. Good career coaching finds the right balance between inspiration and what is actually out there. An inspired career coach (see Chapter 16) will be able to bring out the best in you *and* tell you how the market will react – to your CV, your interview performance, your 'pitch'.

Many great ideas for career change are trampled by other people's 'Yes, but's', or by the jaundiced, narrow perspective of people who really do see the glass as half empty every time. What's real is this. If you get half a dozen seasoned recruitment consultants telling you that even with the best CV rewrite in the world you will never break into sector X, that's data. Everything else is just experiment. In short, keep pushing, keep finding out, and keep looking.

From imagination to reality

Captain Jean Luc Picard, second generation Star Trek Captain, executed his commands with three simple words: *make it so*. There comes a point where we have to make our ideas work. From 'what if' move on to 'how could I make this work ... ?'. Try thinking in terms of pilot schemes and experiments. In businesses these provide effective safety valves for introducing new ideas. We can apply the same thinking to our own careers by finding opportunities to try things out. One way is to extend yourself by going on courses, studying in your own time. Another is to take up some form of voluntary activity outside work in order to experiment with your career longings. Short-term or temporary employment can sometimes help to provide a useful 'laboratory' for your career plans. There is one useful principle here for everyday experiment: 'don't think, just leap' – don't give up, just do it and see what happens.

Keeping the energy going

When a business hits a flat patch, often habit, inertia and passivity combine to make sure that new things do not happen. You can see the same forces operating in your own life. You need to recognize that your initial energy will start to fall away, and inertia, or sometimes apathy, will take hold. Try to harness momentum by setting short-term goals, and tell other people what commitments you have made so that they can help you to stick to them.

Include plans for ways of re-energizing yourself when you feel flat, because it's inevitable. The most confident-looking people hit low points when they are trying to make a difficult change. If you get a brilliant idea for career investigation, in some

3–4 weeks' time you will start to lose confidence. Plan *now* to talk to someone positive at that critical time.

Learn how to think

Expand your range of thinking styles. Edward De Bono offers us **six thinking hats** which work well in the context of career planning, as described in Table 8.3.

Table 8.3 De Bono's six thinking hats applied to career transition

White hat	The information collector. What more facts do I need? Who else could I talk to?
Red hat	Emotions, feelings, intuition. What do I really feel about this? How far do I let these feelings affect my behaviour and my decision making? What gets in the way of change?
Black hat	Judgement, caution, conformity, truth. Will it work? Is it safe? How big is the risk? (Warning: Black hat thinking can easily become 'Yes, but' thinking and suppress new ideas.)
Green hat	Seeking alternatives, exploring, extending the art of the possible. How can I look at this differently? How can I generate new ideas for my career?
Yellow hat	Advantages, positive benefits. What would be the advantages? Why would it be good for me? How could I make it work?
Blue hat	The hat you use for thinking about thinking. The blue hat controls all the other hats, i.e. tells me 'isn't it time I used some yellow hat thinking, agenda setting here?'

Adapted from: Edward De Bono, *Six Thinking Hats*, Penguin Books, 2000.

Inventing your future

It takes bravery to take time out to think laterally and flexibly about the way your life is going. It takes even greater courage to tell other people about your discovery. It takes maximum courage to begin to put your discoveries into action. Those with higher self-esteem find it easy to adopt and explore new ideas, because those new ideas are not threatening their core selves. But don't make the mistake of trying to do it alone. Ask yourself this question: *did you buy this book in order to avoid a conversation?* In order to avoid picking up the phone and finding out?

CELEBRATING OUR DIFFERENCES

He that is good with a hammer tends to think everything is a nail.
Abraham Maslow

Understanding your personality can be a self-centred and unproductive activity if it simply affirms an 'I am what I am' mentality. We're given clues about our personality types not in order to fence ourselves off from the world, but in order to build bridges.

Table 8.4 gives you a chance to record some broad indicators about your personality. Think about the way you see yourself, the way others see you, and the way you react under pressure.

After completing Table 8.4, ask someone who knows you well to judge how far you have produced an accurate self-portrait. Use this information to increase your level of awareness of the way your personality operates in work.

Personality tests

There are a number of standard tests available. Tests such as the Myers-Briggs Type Indicator (MBTI), the 16PF5 Questionnaire, or the Occupational Personality Questionnaire (OPQ) should be conducted by a qualified practitioner. You should be given a clear introduction to the nature of the test, how it is to be used and who sees the results. You should be given objective, independent feedback.

Table 8.4　Personality profile

Your understanding of yourself will help you to see where you will thrive in your next career. Where would you place yourself on each scale? (Avoid the mid-point, and please note that there are no 'right' answers – just prompts to give you an insight into the way your personality fits the world of work):

How would you describe yourself?

Confident — Cautious

Head in the clouds — Practical

Abstract — Concrete

Logical — Intuitive

Emotional — Analytical

Optimistic — Pessimistic

Open to change — Reluctant to change

Self-reliant — Need the approval of others

Emotionally vulnerable — Self-assured

Follower — Leader

Solo artist — Team player

Steady — Flexible

What energizes you?

People — Solitude

Activity — Calm

Thinking — Doing

Schedules — Improvisation

Groups or teams — One-to-one

There are also many other personality tests out there which are not delivered by qualified practitioners. Hundreds of them are online variants of dubious validity (how well results connect to reality) and reliability (consistently providing accurate information). Some recruiters use tests which do not require a trained user. Any of these tests may give you useful information, but the results should be treated with care. If you are unsure about feedback you have received, arrange to be tested by someone qualified to Level B by the British Psychological Society.

The second problem with personality tests is that they give you a fairly clear picture of *how* you are, but there is no straightforward connection between personality type and the fields of work you might enjoy. When you are given your test results pay attention to where each of your scores fits on the overall scale. For example, no-one is entirely an extravert or an introvert. Secondly, reflect on your test results in terms of the way that others see you – how are you different from others? Finally, you will learn to 'read' other types around you and begin to see their preferences and the way they respond to situations. This gives you better strategies for communication and bridge-building with people who see the world very differently to you.

It's vital that you should not feel pigeon-holed by your results. Career explorers are vulnerable people, and will attach a great deal of significance to any job titles that are generated by career-related personality tests – you should certainly not conclude 'because I am an ESFJ, I should become a …'. In any occupational group you will find many personality types.

EMOTIONAL INTELLIGENCE

If you are all wrapped up in yourself, you are overdressed.
Kate Halverson

The concept of emotional intelligence has provided an important contribution to the understanding of the human mind.

Where there was IQ, we now also have EQ. The ideas of EQ derive from the work of Yale psychologist Peter Salovey, who develops and expands on Gardner's ideas of interpersonal and intrapersonal intelligence (see Exercise 8.1 at the end of this chapter). One popularizer is Daniel Goleman, who suggests that people with well-developed emotional skills are 'more likely to be content and effective in their lives, mastering the habits of mind that foster their own productivity; people who cannot marshal some control over their emotional life fight inner battles that sabotage their ability for focused work and clear thought'.

There are five elements to an increased awareness of emotional intelligence:

1. **Knowing your emotions** – being able to monitor and describe a feeling as it happens.

2. **Managing emotions** – handling feelings as they arise, coping with our emotional reactions to setbacks and upsets.

3. **Motivating yourself** – marshalling emotions in the service of a personal goal.

4. **Recognizing emotions in others** – the fundamental people skill of empathy; being attuned to others' needs and the way they express them.

5. **Handling relationships** – managing and responding to emotions in others and displaying various forms of social competence, social skills, communication and leadership.

One of the most important features of any personality test is the way it measures your ability to cope with change, stress and working under pressure. Sometimes this is referred to as your emotional stability – an important factor when choosing your work culture.

Using your whole brain

You will often hear talk of 'left brain' and 'right brain' personality types. This is, of course, a metaphor; our brains are not ordered so simply. There are, however, some people who are more inclined to 'left' brain ways of thinking (organized, logical, systematic) and others who are more naturally 'right' brain thinkers (free-flowing, unstructured, abstract). In some personalities 'left' or 'right' may be dominant, but we are all a complex mix of both sides of our brain. The important thing is to discover your natural inclinations and build on them, and to learn how to communicate with those who see the world very differently.

EXERCISE 8.1 – DISCOVERING YOUR STRONGEST AREAS OF INTELLIGENCE

Professor Howard Gardner argues that intelligence is not a single faculty that can be accurately measured, for example by an IQ test. He believes we have several separate but related intellectual capacities, each of which deserves to be called an intelligence.

The following **inventory** helps you to discover your strongest intelligences, and matches them to your preferred style for developing ideas or managing problems.

Completing the Seven Intelligences Inventory

Please note carefully: the inventory which follows is not a psychometric test. The results are not intended to limit your occupational choices or give you a distinctive personality 'type'. Its aim is to add to your understanding of the way you see the world, and suggest further areas of exploration in terms of:

∎ the way you learn

∎ the way you interact with others

∎ the way you respond to different personality types, e.g. in a team

∎ the skills you enjoy using

- interests that might develop your 'weaker' intelligences

- fields of work where you might develop your primary intelligences.

Under each of the seven headings is a list of characteristics. Tick any sentence that describes what you are like most of the time. There are no right or wrong answers – if in doubt, put a tick. Then give yourself a score between 1 and 5 after reading the longer description of each intelligence.

Add up your total score out of 15 for each category, and transfer your scores to the final panel. At the end of the inventory write down your three strongest intelligences.

Linguistic intelligence		TICK
1	I enjoy language and word games	
2	I enjoy crosswords or other word games	
3	I like telling stories or jokes	
4	I enjoy reading for pleasure	
5	I enjoy choosing the right word	
6	I like listening to spoken word programmes	
7	I enjoy intelligent debates	
8	I hear words in my head before I speak or write	
9	I can often remember exactly what was said to me	
10	I rehearse things verbally in my head	
Total number of ticks/10	**Score** ⇨⇨⇨ ☐	

Linguistic people enjoy reading and writing, love word games, and are responsive to the spoken or written word, and the richness of language. They often have a good memory for names. They possess a wide vocabulary and speak and/or write fluently.

Give yourself a score between 1 and 5 in terms of how well this paragraph describes you

Not me at all   Spot on

1   2   3   4   5   **Score**   ⇨⇨⇨ ☐

Linguistic intelligence	**Total combined score/15** ⇨⇨⇨ ☐

Logical–mathematical intelligence

		TICK
1	I am good at mental arithmetic	
2	I enjoy games or puzzles which require logical thinking	
3	I enjoyed maths and/or science in school	
4	I enjoy practical experiments	
5	I enjoy strategy games like chess	
6	I like things to be clear and well organized	
7	I think things through logically	
8	I am interested in new developments in science	
9	I like to have prioritized lists	
10	I believe that most things have rational explanations	

Total number of ticks/10   **Score**   ⇨⇨⇨ ☐

Logical–mathematical people respond well to patterns and structures, and prefer to do things in a sequential order. They organize experiments to test theories, and enjoy opportunities to solve problems. They reason things out logically and clearly.

Give yourself a score between 1 and 5 in terms of how well this paragraph describes you

Not me at all   Spot on

   1   2   3   4   5   **Score**   ⇨⇨⇨ ☐

Logical–mathematical intelligence   **Total combined score/15**   ⇨⇨⇨ ☐

	Visual–spatial intelligence	
		TICK
1	I can interpret plans or diagrams easily	
2	I quickly understand symbols on signs, instrument panels and equipment	
3	I enjoy cartoons	
4	I like to draw, sketch or doodle	
5	I enjoy photography	
6	I have a good sense of direction	
7	I prefer books with illustrations and diagrams	
8	I am good at giving road directions	
9	I am good at reading maps	
10	I feel strongly about the layout and 'look' of a document	

Total number of ticks/10   **Score**   ⇨⇨⇨ ☐

Visual–spatial people tend to think in images and pictures. They enjoy visual puzzles and mazes, and tend to organize ideas visually in their heads, drawing maps or networks to connect ideas.

Give yourself a score between 1 and 5 in terms of how well this paragraph describes you

Not me at all   Spot on

    1   2   3   4   5   **Score**   ⇨⇨⇨ ☐

Visual–spatial intelligence   **Total combined score/15** ⇨⇨⇨ ☐

Bodily–kinaesthetic intelligence

		TICK
1	I would rather drive than be a passenger	
2	I prefer it when my hands are occupied with something practical	
3	I find it difficult to sit still and relax for long periods	
4	I am well co-ordinated physically	
5	I am good at building or repairing things	
6	I enjoy hobbies which have a physical result like carpentry, wood carving, knitting, model building, gardening	
7	I enjoy physical sport or exercise	
8	I like to spend my free time outdoors	
9	I enjoy human touch and use expressive body language	
10	I would rather play than watch	

Total number of ticks/10 **Score** ⇨⇨⇨ ☐

Bodily–kinaesthetic people like to interact with the world physically. They have an ability to control their bodies and handle objects skilfully. They respond best to work that is physically active, 'hands-on' and practical. They often enjoy sports and the outdoor life.

Give yourself a score between 1 and 5 in terms of how well this paragraph describes you

Not me at all   Spot on

  1   2   3   4   5   **Score**   ⇨⇨⇨ ☐

Bodily–kinaesthetic intelligence   **Total combined score/15**   ⇨⇨⇨ ☐

Musical intelligence		TICK
1	I have a good 'ear' for music	
2	I can hold a note	
3	I sing or play a musical instrument	
4	I often remember tunes in my head	
5	I would rather listen to music on the radio than discussions	
6	I can follow a musical score	
7	I have a good sense of rhythm	
8	Music speaks to me emotionally	
9	I am very aware of an 'off' note or an instrument which is out of tune	
10	I enjoy rhymes, poetry and limericks	
Total number of ticks/10	Score	⇨ ⇨ ⇨ ☐

Musical people respond well to sound, music and rhythm. They often have a talent to interpret or produce music. They will often find it helpful or soothing to listen to music while studying or reading. Music will often 'speak' to them in terms of colours, emotions or themes, even when there are no lyrics.

Give yourself a score between 1 and 5 in terms of how well this paragraph describes you

Not me at all   Spot on

    1   2   3   4   5   **Score**   ⇨ ⇨ ⇨ ☐

Musical intelligence	**Total combined score/15**	⇨ ⇨ ⇨ ☐

Interpersonal intelligence		
		TICK
1	I would rather be in company than on my own	
2	I'm a good listener	
3	I prefer group sports like football or badminton to solo sports like swimming or running	
4	I generally talk about my problems with my friends	
5	I enjoy parties and other social events	
6	If I learn a skill I am happy to teach it to someone else	
7	I quickly tune in to the moods of other people	
8	I can express an idea best by talking about it	
9	I have a number of close friendships	
10	I am often called on to manage teams or organize social activities	
Total number of ticks/10 **Score** ⇨⇨⇨ ☐		

Interpersonal people are interested in others around them, are good listeners and communicators. They prefer to be in company, and like to share with others. They are naturally inclined towards teaching, caring or nurturing roles.

Give yourself a score between 1 and 5 in terms of how well this paragraph describes you

Not me at all   Spot on

    1   2   3   4   5   **Score**   ⇨⇨⇨ ☐

Interpersonal intelligence   **Total combined score/15** ⇨⇨⇨ ☐

	Intrapersonal intelligence	
		TICK
1	I enjoy my own company	
2	Learning and personal development are important to me	
3	I have some strong opinions	
4	Spending time alone reflecting is important to me	
5	I have a strong sense of intuition	
6	I enjoy a quiet space in order to meditate and reflect	
7	I keep a journal that records my thoughts and feelings	
8	I have a strong sense of independence	
9	I normally solve my own problems	
10	I would probably enjoy being my own boss	
	Total number of ticks/10 **Score**	⇨⇨⇨ ☐

Intrapersonal people value time spent alone and are very aware of their own personality, strengths and weaknesses. They tend to solve problems alone. They are often highly independent and self-motivated. They value the inner self, personal development and spirituality. They may be entrepreneurs or interested in becoming self-employed.

Give yourself a score between 1 and 5 in terms of how well this paragraph describes you

Not me at all   Spot on

   1   2   3   4   5   **Score**   ⇨⇨⇨ ☐

Intrapersonal intelligence   **Total combined score/15** ⇨⇨⇨ ☐

Primary intelligences	Your total
1. Linguistic intelligence Using and loving language, whether written or spoken	
2. Logical–mathematical intelligence Using or interpreting numbers, data, facts, sequences, scientific research	
3. Visual–spatial intelligence Seeing things in pictures or images, map-reading, making 3D models	
4. Bodily–kinaesthetic intelligence (sometimes known as 'physical intelligence') – the ability to control one's body and handle objects skilfully	
5. Musical intelligence Having an 'ear' for music, a talent to interpret or produce music	
6. Interpersonal intelligence Communicating with and responding to other people	
7. Intrapersonal intelligence Valuing personal growth, independence, reflection, meditation – the inner world	

Your three strongest intelligences

Interpreting your primary intelligences

What do the results mean? First of all, they should make you look again at the way you respond to people whose intelligences are very different from your own (it can be very difficult, for example, for visual–spatial people to understand what those with high linguistic intelligence are explaining in such a long-winded way. They will say 'just draw me a diagram!')

How can the results help your career choice?

It will be rare that you will see a direct correlation between one strong intelligence and one occupation, e.g. 'I should be a mathematician!' Your intelligences combine with your preferred areas of knowledge, your motivational skills, your upbringing and your personality.

Here are some pointers in relation to strong scores. In every case what you may be spotting is an opportunity to expand your natural intelligences.

Linguistic intelligence – Does your work give you opportunities to express yourself clearly in writing or in speech? Where can your organization improve its communication? How can you adapt messages so that they are better perceived by those who have strong intelligences in other areas?

Logical–mathematical intelligence – Your preferences lie with numbers, statistics, data or scientific investigation. How far is this intelligence being stretched? Do you have difficulty communicating what you see in numbers to others?

Visual–spatial intelligence – Where in your job is this intelligence used? Can you learn how to use software to design slides and presentations? Can you make signs or posters?

Bodily–kinaesthetic intelligence – What happens if your work is entirely intellectual and desk-bound? Can you translate your work into another context (e.g. move from management training to outward-bound leadership training)?

Musical intelligence – Can your musical intelligence be used in any way other than a career in music, e.g. in sounds, jingles, rhymes (perhaps in advertising copy or rhymes to help people to learn and remember things – 'an apple a day ...').

Interpersonal intelligence – Your skills in 'handling' people and relationships are much in demand in the modern workplace. Which aspects of interpersonal intelligence are strongest for you, and which need nurturing?

Intrapersonal intelligence – Do you take your inner world seriously enough, and apply reflection to your work? Some managers consciously set aside thinking time when they can reflect. Don't always take work with you on the train. Sit and think. Advice to this group might be 'Don't do something, just sit there ...'.

'MUST DO' LIST

Questions to help you to reflect on your personality and working style:

☑ What brings you to life? When or where do you become *energized*? What has a deadening effect on you?

☑ How far do you really understand your own personality? Can you define the kind of work roles where you will be most effective *and* comfortable?

☑ What barriers to career success have been caused by your problems reading people, and getting them to understand your 'take' on life?

☑ How well can you anticipate the results of any personality profiles that will be used by selectors? Are you ready to answer questions about your strengths and weaknesses?

CAREER AND PERSONALITY TESTS

Quintax is a highly valid personality questionnaire that gives useful user-friendly feedback on personality at work, leadership and team fit, innovation style and areas for development. The **Career Motivation Indicator**, from the same stable, is based on the Career Hot Buttons which appear in this book. READER OFFER – quote reference JL2011 to complete CMi at half-price (see www.sr-associates.com or telephone Stuart Robertson & Associates on 0161 877 3277).

Career Horizons is also highly recommended. This software suite provides information about your skills, learning style and personal career goals. Visit www.careerhorizons.net. READER OFFER – save 25% or more by obtaining a discount code from Stuart Mitchell & Company Ltd on 01483 423943 or email info@careerhorizons.net.

What Kind of Work Would Suit You Best?

This chapter helps you to:

❙ Discover the importance of field in career choice

❙ Understand why it's difficult to choose a career path

❙ Find a range of ways of discovering new sectors

❙ Identify subjects, fields and sectors for investigation

❙ Use lateral thinking to help you to identify new areas of work

Work is much more fun than fun.

Noël Coward

CHOICES, CHOICES

According to the New York Times in January 2010, approximately 9% of all humans who have ever lived are alive today (some sources suggest that there are more people over 50 alive today than have ever lived, which may not be far from the truth). And this 9% slice of human history has more life choices and more work choices available to it than any previous generation. Even three generations ago, the average European worker probably had about 5–10 obvious occupations to choose from. Today we have tens of thousands. What's more, since this is such a new idea in human terms, we don't have a very well developed toolkit to help us choose.

So it should surprise none of us that the big question facing career coaches is 'what is the right kind of work for me?'. An interesting question, which betrays some underlying ideas about career matching – for example, the idea that there is a single, 'right' path for each of us. The fact that it is framed as a question assumes that someone has the answer, or that the solution will jump out at us if we take the right kind of test or have the right kind of insight.

Several factors are working together here at the same time – an abundance of choices, freedom of action, a consumer-led society that believes we are entitled to a satisfied life – and even the pressure put on us by media, friends and family who tell us that we could, or should, find 'something better'. No wonder that many career changers manage a kind of long-term stress. This may be close to what Alain de Botton describes as *status anxiety*, mixed with a vague sense that there might be a perfect occupation out there, waiting, with your name on it.

FIELDS OF WORK

How do we deal with these choices? First of all, we need to learn to draw maps of what is out there. The way we have traditionally done this is to break occupations down into different categories, or sectors. Imagine an office full of filing cabinets. In those cabinets is a file for every job you can imagine. If you had to organize that information in some way, you would group jobs together into separate headings. These we call fields or sectors.

Some sectors are huge. Think of medicine – a large and very general sector. Within that large 'job family' are several smaller sectors, including nursing. But even if you choose nursing, you will soon have to decide whether you want to be a general hospital nurse, a nurse dealing with mental health, children or old people, an operating theatre nurse, or perhaps a community nurse, a nurse in a health centre or an occupational nurse in a factory environment. Qualified nurses can also find themselves acting as teachers, counsellors, managers or expert witnesses. So within any sector you can find a huge number of occupations.

WHY SECTORS ARE POWERFUL

Many careers counsellors believe that your choice of sector is one of the most powerful factors in taking you to an inspired career.

Let's take another job title: teacher. We think we know what a teacher does. But this role can appear in a number of sectors in interestingly different ways, for example:

▮ a teacher of sign language to parents of deaf children

▮ an education officer interpreting a nature reserve to the public

▮ a gallery officer making art and sculpture exciting for children

▮ a salesperson demonstrating the potential of new software

▮ a business consultant specializing in team building

▮ a motor mechanic supervising apprentices.

Sectors and funnels

Human society needs to find some way of categorizing everything, and this includes ideas and activities. This begins at school. You didn't have classes titled thinking, speaking, imagination or wisdom. Actually, you might have attended such classes if renaissance ideas about education had continued to the present day. In the Victorian age educators reclassified what was taught into much narrower boxes (and at the same time invented new subjects, including English and physics). The subjects you are taught in the classroom lead naturally to educational and career decisions. We have all got used to putting knowledge into separate boxes: music, history, French, chemistry. These boxes shape the way you imagine your adult life will be, following a simple construct: 'I'm good at science so I should be a scientist.'

This process of 'educational funnelling' is the basis of much of our early careers advice. You see a box with a label on it that looks attractive. The label shows somebody doing things which look rather like activities you have enjoyed at school, whether this involves grooming animals or handling test-tubes. You are attracted towards that box because of the idea that this sector will be like something you have already enjoyed or shown some talent in before.

This approach falls down in a number of ways. Firstly, your secondary education narrowed your studies down to no more than about a dozen subjects, but there are literally thousands of sectors of knowledge and work out there. Anyone working with school or university leavers needs to explore this thinking carefully: there are few people practising 'pure' geography, history or mathematics in the world.

Sectors and motivation

Find a job you like and you add five days to every week.
H. Jackson Browne

It's easy to choose a sector that seems 'safe'. At times of crisis you will be attracted by sectors where you can operate inside protective boundaries – your comfort zone. It's common among career changers to hear people say 'I would really like to work in a sector which inspires me, but I will find it much easier to get a job in the sector I have been working in for the last 20 years'.

Talk to people who love the field of work they have found themselves in. You will hear in their voices enthusiasm, love of detail, a willingness to share what they know with others, and a wish to encourage others to follow the path they have taken.

Once you find a sector that gives you the same 'buzz', you will approach both your job search and the work you do with a far more positive spirit. The spin-offs, both for yourself and for any organization which employs you, are important:

▮ You will be more enthusiastic at interviews – and employers love enthusiasm.

▮ You will retain what you learn and enthusiastically pass it on to colleagues.

▮ Your love of your work will communicate itself to clients and increase their loyalty.

▮ You will find it far easier to fit into an organization where others share your passion.

▮ Efficiency and productivity will come naturally to you.

▮ You will be forever interested in new ideas, new connections and increasing your learning.

Limitations of sectors 1 – Choosing too narrow a range

The problem with looking at sectors is that they are just ideas in boxes. They can be extremely helpful and practical in terms of a job search. You may end up identifying between 5 and 15 organizations in your local area in suitably attractive sectors, and you can begin a highly active and targeted programme of making speculative approaches and networking.

However, sectors can often be very restrictive. You may choose sectors that are obvious and safe. You may focus only on one area of interest and fail to ask 'what parts of me will *not* be developed if I work in this sector?'.

Let's say your interest is forestry. You like working outdoors in the wild woods. You go through the training which adds to your depth of background knowledge about forestry and conservation. You get a job. You find yourself dealing with peripheral problems such as record keeping, litter or car parks.

You find that less and less of your knowledge and enthusiasm is being tapped, and you are increasingly learning about regulations, funding and government initiatives. Possible career crisis. You find yourself saying 'I came into forestry because I love conservation and wildlife, but I've become a bureaucrat'.

I hear the same story almost every week from people in teaching, personnel, nursing, travel, university lecturing and ministry, among a wide range of sectors. 'I was attracted by the box called Nursing', they say, 'and I liked what it said on the label: caring for people, being there for patients and relatives. What am I now? A form filler.'

You can only begin to really know what's out there by being fascinated by what's out there. It can't be just an exercise. One characteristic about people who have made huge, brave career changes is that they became excited about what they didn't know – and started to do something about the gap in their knowledge. Chapter 10, designed to help you if you sense that you want to do something completely different, will also point to the importance of active exploration.

The best way to predict the future is to invent it.

Alan Kay

Limitations of sectors 2 – Not knowing what's out there

Choosing from unknown careers is like trying to plan a journey using a road atlas full of blank pages. Sector discovery helps to draw the missing maps.

If you can't find a sector that suits you, you may have to find a new angle. Work is changing so rapidly that new disciplines are being created all the time. Maybe you'll dream up an entirely new sector. Before Galileo there really wasn't a field you could describe as experimental physics. The word 'scientist' wasn't invented until the 1830s. Before Freud there wasn't a sector called psychoanalysis. In view of the range of jobs now associated with Googling, social media and online sales, it's worth remembering what business guru Kevin Kelly said in 2009 – the Web is only 5000 days old. Something that has transformed society has only been around, in human terms, for a heartbeat.

Limitations of sectors 3 – Starting with the wrong idea

A huge amount of the information we hold about sectors of work comes secondhand. We rely on out-of-date information from family, colleagues and friends. The problem is that most of this information is filtered and interpreted by someone else, and probably out of date. It doesn't give you an overview of the job.

The second problem is that what we see is weighted. When people describe jobs to you they attach value tags (safe/risky, dull/exciting, boring/cutting edge, fixed/changing). Sometimes this information is entirely on the button, providing you with really important clues about what work is actually like. At least 50% of the time, however, it's out of date, subjective or just plain wrong.

The first principle is to start with your own impulse, not with someone else's idea of what a job is like. Find out for yourself. Don't rely on the slanted, possibly jaded views of retired professionals, recruiters or friends.

And remember that *the* great question to ask about any job is 'what do you do most of the time?'.

Limitations of sectors 4 – Moving on from subjects to sectors to choices

A common place where my clients get stuck is that they identify subject areas that interest and inspire them, but they can't make a connection between a subject of interest (e.g. gardening) and a sector of work. They succumb too quickly to either/or thinking: sectors are for work or pleasure. You will hear some career counsellors say things like 'maybe you should follow this interest in your spare time'. Even more worrying is the idea 'If I do what I love for a living then I might get sick of it … better to have an ordinary job and do what I love in my own time'. All this can be a great way of keeping work separate from 'life', in other words, a new excuse for avoiding enjoyable and interesting work.

If you can't see how you can move from subjects you love to potential sectors of work, you need to do some work on ways of making connections. Exercise 9.1 shows you how.

EXERCISE 9.1 – MOVING FROM SUBJECTS TO SECTORS

Step 1: Listing the subjects that interest you

1. Begin with the subjects you are interested in. Use the House of Knowledge exercise in Chapter 6 to identify all of the subjects you have ever been interested in. Write them all down.

2. Pick your top 20 subjects. Do this by asking yourself the question 'Which subjects am I most interested in?' At this stage don't think about work, just think about the subjects you would like to know more about.

3. Transfer your top subjects on to 20 cards; use cards about the same size as a playing card, or blank postcards.

4. Review your cards by discarding anything that is essentially a repetition of something else. Combine any duplicated or very similar sectors. You may have *Product Design* and *Design* – perhaps they would be better as one card.

5. Add cards to get a total of 20. Think again: 'What would I like to know more about/study/think about/spend time discussing …?'

Step 2: Refocusing on sectors

6. Review your top 20 cards, splitting them into two columns:

Primary fields Fields I would like some contact with through work during the next 12 months	**Other fields** Fields which I found interesting, but don't need to be part of my work during the next 12 months

7. Look at the cards you have placed in the Primary sectors column, and choose your top 10.

8. Look at your top 10 carefully. Redefine any sectors that are too vague: 'Management' or 'Administration' or 'Company Director' – these are roles that can be exercised in virtually any occupational sector.

9. You have now arrived at your top 10 sectors for investigation.

10. Check: are your sectors too big? If so, they will not be helpful to you. People tend to select too wide a sector, assuming that this will lead to a wider range of opportunities. In fact, what it leads to is a vagueness which quickly communicates itself to recruiters. If necessary, convert sectors into subsectors. For example, if your sector is Marketing, ask yourself whether there are any particular sectors where you like to exercise marketing. Are you more interested in marketing products or services? Do your interests lie in advertising, direct mail, brand development or at a strategic level? Are you more interested in marketing one kind of product or service than another?

Step 3: Sector combining

11. Look at the connections between sectors. Move your cards round on a table or notice board to see what happens when you combine them. Try grouping your sectors in different ways.

12. Take three of your chosen sectors and put them in a row. Then take three more and put them in a column. Draw a $3 \times 3 \times 3$ grid of nine squares between the two. In each of your nine blank squares write down any new sectors or subsectors that come to mind. An example is shown in Figure 9.1.

	Physical fitness	Translating	Export/import
Creative writing	Writing self-help books to encourage fitness	Translating novels	Writing export guides
Safety management	Organizing safety in physical fitness programmes	Specialist translation of safety management material	Exporting best practice in safety
Ecotourism	Environmentally friendly mountain biking	Translating commercial tourism ideas into ecotourism	Importing ecotourism models from other cultures

Figure 9.1   Example $3 \times 3 \times 3$ sector grid

Step 4: Putting ideas into action

13. Now begins a key step: research. Research the key information about these sectors (entry routes, qualifications and training you need, measures for success, prospects). Talk to people actually working in these sectors to find out what the job is really like.

14. Once you have researched your top five or six sectors, come back to this exercise. You will probably find that sector exploration leads you to redefine and adapt your working list. Don't think of your sectors list as definitive or fixed; think of it as a work in progress.

EXERCISE 9.2 – THE LOTUS BLOSSOM TECHNIQUE

(Based on an idea developed by Yasuo Matsumura.)

In this technique, you place any sector idea in the centre of a blank Lotus Blossom grid (see Figure 9.2). Then think of eight parallel, related, contrasting or complementary sectors – add anything that feels exciting or useful. Write them in the empty boxes around. Each of those new sectors then becomes the centre of another 'petal'. This works well on a very big sheet of paper.

Entertainment	Media	Writing
Community advice	**Law**	Mergers & acquisitions
Resolving conflict	Negotiating	Property

Figure 9.2 One sector into eight

Each of your new connections then becomes the centre of another web of ideas, as indicated in Figure 9.3, which shows the original petal centred on 'Law' and a new petal starting with 'Resolving conflict'. Each grey cell can now be opened out to generate eight new possibilities, generating 80 from your original single thought. It is, of course, possible to open the petal out even further and create hundreds of connected ideas, but it's also productive to begin again with one key word at the heart of a new grid.

			Entertainment	Media	Journalism			
	Entertainment		Community advice	**Law**	Mergers & acquisitions		**Journalism**	
			Resolving conflict	Negotiating	Property			
				Media				
	Community advice						**Mergers & acquisitions**	
Team building	Violence at work	Counselling						
Marriage guidance	**Resolving conflict**	Personality assessment		**Negotiating**			**Property**	
Industrial relations	Risk assessment	Arbitration						

Figure 9.3   Lotus Blossom grid

WAYS OF IDENTIFYING SECTORS

Where do I begin? Identifying sectors that will interest and inspire you

Begin with yourself. Look back at your House of Knowledge in Chapter 6. What subjects, topics and themes energize you? What do you love learning or talking about? What do you want to know more about?

Prompts to thinking about sectors

Use this tried and tested prompting sequence to identify possible sectors of work:

Stage 1 – Remembering

1. Dream jobs you had as a child.

2. The most enjoyable topics you have studied.

3. Any of the sectors you've worked in, or near.

4. Sectors where your friends, family or contacts work.

5. Jobs done by friends which you find fascinating.

6. Jobs that attracted you in the paper, even if you never applied for them.

7. Particular assignments or projects you enjoyed.

Stage 2 – Three great days at work

8. Think about a time when you had a great day at work. The sort of day where everything went well and you went home energized. Write down what you were doing, what you enjoyed and what you achieved.

9. Do the same thing for two other memorable days.

Stage 3 – Imagining

10. What jobs have you ever imagined doing?

11. If you could try someone else's job for a day, what would it be?

12. If you could do any job in the world for a week and still receive your normal salary, what jobs would you try?

13. Who are your role models or champions, and what sectors are they in?

14. If you won a million pounds and you didn't need to work, what activity would you happily do for nothing?

Analysing job themes

Starting from the inside means putting together a working recipe for the kind of job that will work for you. One simple index of whether the job will work well for you is to think about the Job Themes that appeal to you most strongly – see Table 9.1.

Table 9.1   Job Themes

Job Theme	Description	How strong is your interest in doing this in your next job? 3=Strong interest 2=Mild interest 1=Weak interest 0=No interest at all
Working with and for **PEOPLE**	Your ideal work is *mainly* about working with people, e.g. helping, caring, nursing, nurturing, developing, healing, coaching, mentoring or teaching …	
Working with **FACTS**	Your ideal work is *mainly* about working with information, e.g. analysing, cataloguing,	

gathering, planning, managing projects, researching, tracking down information, working with numbers or accounts, making the most of computers ...

Working with **REAL OBJECTS**	Your ideal work is *mainly* about working with the physical world, e.g. building, shaping, cooking, craft, DIY, working with animals, plants, working outdoors, machines, vehicles, sports, physical fitness, hands-on therapies ...
Working to **INFLUENCE**	Your ideal work is *mainly* about working through other people and will involve: leadership, management, changing organizations, setting up a new business or department, inventing, re-organizing, shaping teams, driving others, influencing, persuading, motivating, selling, getting results ...
Working with **IMAGINATION**	Your ideal work is *mainly* about working with ideas or creative activity, e.g. being active in the arts, performing, creative writing, lateral thinking, business creativity, adapting ideas, coming up with new ideas, challenging assumptions ...

Working with **SYSTEMS**	Your ideal work is *mainly* about working within systems, e.g. book-keeping, quality control, continuous improvement, legal frameworks, procedures, health and safety ...

Look at your top three Job Themes from Table 9.1. The answer to the way your career puzzle comes together is clearest here. How is your career a unique interaction between these three? How can you make sure that your work feeds all three? For example, if your top three Job Themes in order are Imagination, People and Real Objects, you'll want to ensure that your work allows you a high degree of creativity generated by teams of people, the chance to invent new rules from time to time, but you'll be happiest working where you achieve results you can see and feel. Remember, your Job Theme combination is a combination unique to you, because it also draws upon your knowledge, values and experience.

Try out your Job Theme combination as a working recipe for your ideal job. Add information about your skills to the mix. Combine this information to the master sheet at Table 16.1. Using the master sheet helps you bring all your career ideas together into one place.

It's important to keep checking your results. The more you learn from this book about your ideal job, the more you need to ask questions of other people: a question along the lines of *what does this combination of information suggest to you?*

If I could do anything at all ...

If you're discussing career choices with a friend, a common question is 'What would you do if you could do anything?'. Or 'if you could do any job in the world for a month, what would it be?'. Another variation, which I prefer, is 'what would you do if all jobs paid the same?'. The interesting thing is that having taken status and money out of the picture you can focus very simply on that key question: *what would I be doing most of the time*?

Another common prompt (used in Chapter 6) is 'what would you do if you won the lottery?'. People who have won millions on the National Lottery seem to follow an interesting pattern. After playing with the money for a year or two, buying houses, holidays and cars, they then tend to get bored and look for something to do. Now that money is not the reason for working, what they choose to do is somehow even more authentic. This might mean investing in a business or starting a charitable foundation, or it might be taking up a simple trade. One lottery winner went back to his job as a staff trainer for McDonald's restaurants. So the real question is 'if you won the lottery, what would you do 2 years later when you were bored and could do anything you wanted?'.

Resources

Finally (and don't ignore this one because it seems too obvious), use books and websites about occupations and career choice as ways to add to your list of possible sectors (see the website recommendations in Appendix 3). An alternative method is to go through the Yellow Pages for your nearest city and mark any sector that interests you. Look at books about unusual occupations like *Offbeat Careers* by Vivien Donald. Many trade bodies publish guides giving entry requirements, training details and prospects. Read the careers pages of general newspapers: sections on graduate careers often contain career tips and company information useful to the full range of job seekers.

Confidence

Notice that moment of hesitation before you write down the name of a sector. Look at what's going on through your head. *I'll never get into this sector. I don't have the training. I don't know enough.* In those moments remember this: President Abraham Lincoln carried with him everywhere a newspaper clipping stating that he was a great leader. John Lennon's school report read 'certainly on the road to failure'. We all need a little more encouragement.

Pushing sector alternatives

The ability to push for alternatives is a powerful thinking skill for all aspects of life. The natural tendency of the mind is to move towards certainty and security. We often shun alternatives. A training colleague used to have a phrase for this: 'Don't confuse me with facts, my mind is made up.'

Most career changers love tests, boxes and checklists because their mind is saying 'I feed the data in here, and the answer pops out *here*'. We all love that idea of a magic button, which is why formal testing is so hit and miss in career work. It's so easy to sit back passively and wait for a computer or test to tell us the job we should do next. Most dangerous of all, in my estimation, are computer programs that sample your interests and aspirations and then give you a list of job titles. First of all, this kind of test cannot identify what really motivates and interests you. Secondly, no careers test can keep track of the huge range of jobs that are available in the workplace. Tests should only ever be used as a way of seeking alternative possibilities, and never as a way of narrowing choices.

We feel that our thinking should follow a logical sequence:

This might look a little like scientific investigation, but science is a rather slippery model for thinking. In the twentieth century scientists learned that there are few certainties and an infinite number of strange possibilities. Light appears to behave as both a particle and a wave. Heisenberg's uncertainty principle means that we can no longer say where something is and what it is doing at the same time. Quantum theory blurs notions of common sense and logic, while relativity challenges any secure notions we have about space and time.

Problems cannot be solved at the same level of awareness that created them.

Albert Einstein

On first impression, having too many alternatives seems a recipe for indecision and vagueness. One of the great tools to business creativity is the process of brainstorming, but this is often misused because the process is cut off halfway through. Brainstorming is a good way of generating a large number of ideas in a free-flowing, non-critical environment. The effect is rather like a shotgun blast – both broad and inaccurate. What any brainstorming session needs (and this will apply to your own creative thinking applied to the career process) is a secondary tool to help you to prioritize, test ideas, group ideas together and focus on the next step (see my discussion of De Bono's six thinking hats in Chapter 8).

Switching sectors: the practicalities

Building on the work of *What Color is Your Parachute?* author Dick Bolles, a few simple truths about career change:

1. It is relatively straightforward to change occupations and remain within the same sector. For example, you may remain in secondary school education but become an administrator rather than a teacher.

2. It is relatively straightforward to switch sectors but remain in the same occupation. You may want to remain an accountant, and switch from manufacturing to the hotel trade.

3. The hardest shift is to change both occupation and sector at the same time. Don't believe those negative voices that tell you this is impossible. You just need better research, and a better strategy for finding out what's really out there. Sometimes it's worth thinking about a stepping-stone approach: change one element now, and another in, say, 12 months' time, when you have gained some relevant experience.

What work I have done I have done because it has been play. If it had been work I shouldn't have done it.

Mark Twain

Jane's story

Jane had spent 10 years building up a successful computer consultancy. Her quality of life was excellent, her products were cutting edge. However, Jane recognized that there was something missing.

Jane sold her business and now runs two restaurants. When asked why she decided to switch from the field of computing solutions to the restaurant trade, she answered, 'I love food, and I love being in restaurants. But the real reason for changing jobs was that I wanted to work in a business where I can see customers enjoying themselves. My computer clients were satisfied, but the service I provided hardly ever brought a smile to their faces.'

If you want to achieve a career breakthrough it's vital that you commit some time to exploring your sectors of interest. If some of the following exercises make you feel uncomfortable or seem unconventional, then it means they're working. Sector exploration is about putting aside the rulebook and discovering new ways of thinking.

One-step-at-a-time career breakthrough

Many career and self-help books are written around the idea that we all have a hidden, 'real' self, and if we can unlock this secret then the answer to the question 'what should I do with my life?' will become crystal clear. The popular press reinforces the idea that deep down we all have a single dream job, and what we long for is an overnight transformation. That's why newspapers love stories of 'accountant becomes skydiver' or 'commando becomes nanny'.

In fact, such transformations are relatively rare. It's far more common that people progress by gradual steps and 'try on' different careers. Many of us do this quite naturally in our first 10 years of work, when it's relatively easy to change direction and experiment. We often write off this period of our life as uncertain 'drifting'.

The idea that we are more likely to make incremental than dramatic career changes was explored in depth in Herminia Ibarra's book *Working Identity*, and a new twist has been added recently in Professor Jim Bright's 'chaos theory' of careers (see www.brightandassociates.com.au) which suggests that many career decisions are unplanned and are made in response to complex, unpredictable changes in the world.

Making a huge leap in your career is not straightforward. This is particularly true if this involves a change of field (e.g. moving from marketing to photography) or a major change of lifestyle (e.g. from financial director to author). It's a risky process because it's about moving from known to unknown. And others will be only too keen to tell you how risky your idea is.

A STEP-BY-STEP GUIDE TO EXPLORING NEW SECTORS

▌ Don't ignore the power of sectors when searching for a job you'll love.

▌ Don't allow 'Yes, but' thinking to prevent further investigation of a sector that interests you.

▌ Begin by looking at the subjects you have really been interested in, often outside work.

▌ Look back at your working life. What sectors have you found most satisfying? Why?

▌ Draw up a prioritized list of sectors that appeal to you. Set out a plan to investigate more about them.

▌ Write down your top three Job Themes. If you combine those three together, what ideas do you come up with?

▌ Look for sector ideas in unexpected places which say something about you: your bookshelves, your photograph albums, articles you have clipped from newspapers.

▌ Become a future watcher. Read articles about how the world of work is changing. See how many new sectors and new job titles you can discover.

▌ Don't be put off if you can't find sectors which interest you – it just means that you need a new way of looking.

'MUST DO' LIST: 8 THINGS YOU WILL NEED TO DO TO MAKE A BIG CAREER CHANGE:

☑ Research career ideas energetically and thoroughly. Investigate them as if you were finding out for somebody else.

☑ Try about half a dozen ideas without saying 'no' or 'yes, but' too early.

☑ Talk to real people in real jobs. Find out how they got them. Use Informational Interviews (see Appendix 1) to help.

☑ Look for flexible ways to make change happen – don't believe job myths about retraining.

☑ Try things out. Take opportunities for site visits, work experience, volunteering, helping out at the weekend ....

☑ Find out how people get the jobs you're after. How will you need to shape your CV and your interview performance?

☑ When you've decided what you find exciting, tell people. Ask for their help.

☑ When you get focused, get really focused. Target the organizations, recruiters and decision makers who matter, and keep pushing.

What About a Complete Change of Career?

This chapter helps you to:

▌ Rethink the way you choose your career

▌ Explore sector combinations

▌ Map out sectors you would like to actively research

▌ Take the first steps towards a total change of career

Your imagination is your preview of life's coming attractions.
                                                    Albert Einstein

I want a complete change of career

Let's tackle head-on the whole 'change of career' idea. There is a strong case that we only have one career. This is built up through a range of experiences which include work, learning, personal development, interests and activity outside work. In fact, you will do better at interview if you talk in these terms rather than apologizing for 'changing career' or 'switching paths' or any other loaded language which implies (a) you have no idea where you're going next and (b) there's only one, conventional way of having a career.

So how do you begin if you want to add more colour, more variety to your single, integrated career path? Here's an interesting fact about the world of careers advice. People prefer to buy careers books with the words 'interview' or 'CV' or 'job search' in the title. However, when it comes to asking for help, most enquirers begin with a statement like 'I would like to find out what else I could do' or 'I have a feeling I want to do something completely different' – a question about direction of travel rather than means of transport.

People ask for help partly because of the huge ranges of choices available in life, as explored in the last chapter. Making a career change is much tougher than making a job change. It's a journey into the unfamiliar that will require new information, new ways of thinking, a strong CV and well-planned interview answers. Deciding to change career increases risk – small risks of rejection, and big risks that it will all go wrong. So, confidence and learning how to make progress without burning all of your boats are both critically important.

Many areas already touched on by this book will help you if you would like to try a very different career path. You have already looked at your constraints, examined your personality, skill set and knowledge base, and looked at the activities in life and sectors that give you a sense of fulfilment. You may already have a half-formed idea, matched by a sense of longing. That's where you begin. This chapter will take you forward so you start looking at – and acting upon – completely new options.

How do we decide on a career path?

When I have a first session with a client I want to know a few basic things – past, present and future. What has motivated this person in the past, both within work and outside it? What was the best job? The best organization? Then the focus shifts to the present – what's going on right now that makes the client ready to make a change. And so to 'what next?'. People usually begin by stating that they have no idea about what they want to do next, but they usually do. I think it was the US careers specialist Dick Knowdell who stated that everyone in the world knows exactly what job they should be doing. The problem, he says, is that half of the people haven't yet found the words to describe what they're looking for, while the other half knows exactly what they should be doing but is too frightened to say it.

The most interesting – and demanding – question you will ever have to deal with if you go to see a career coach is not 'what are you going to do next?' or even 'how are you going to get it', but 'how are you going to decide?'. Most people secretly believe that the answer will just come along if you take a test, read a book, or just sit at home long enough with the curtains closed and think really, really hard.

Let's backtrack slightly. How do we choose our career paths? As Chapter 9 reveals, we are initially funnelled into sectors of work by academic choices. It's worth looking at the influences which typically shape career choice:

> **Influences that affect the way we choose career paths**
>
> **Parental expectations** – occupational groups tend to repeat themselves in families
>
> **Parental aspirations** – pushing young people towards careers that match what parents believe to be the right kind of work
>
> **Academic subjects** – what you choose to study may seem like the key to your future
>
> **Money and status** – academic high-achievers are often pushed towards high pay, high status occupations such as law, finance or medicine
>
> **Peer pressure** – doing something cool, avoiding things that look boring

Your boss's advice – the advice of your very first boss is highly influential and often quoted as a turning point

Personal values and beliefs – the kind of work that seems worthwhile

Media influence – the jobs we see done on TV or in films or on YouTube

Teachers and lecturers – because of the effect of educational 'funnelling'

High visibility – jobs you see around you a great deal of the time

Careers advisers – particularly influential while you are also making study choices

Work-related tests – ranging from *bona fide* personality or interest inventories to something you found on the Internet

Personal inclination – your strong (or vague) sense of what might work, what you are 'supposed' to be doing or what you feel called to in life.

We understand jobs that touch our lives frequently, for example a doctor or dentist. But do you know what a systems analyst does, or a risk assessor, or a behavioural psychologist or a voice coach? In our modern economy, new types of jobs are created every day. Most will be invisible to us, and we have to rely on hunches, insider information or assumptions to choose between them.

Some jobs are more visible than others. You know what a surgeon, a barrister or a fire-fighter does. Or, you *think* you do – how much of your perception is based on television roles rather than the way people really do their jobs?

The power of the media on career choice cannot be underestimated. Television, in particular, samples the world of work in a very slanted way. Some jobs are shown frequently (doctors, nurses, pathologists, teachers, police officers, chefs and shop assistants), others rarely (prizes offered for anyone who has seen any of the following jobs portrayed within TV fiction: order pickers, people who pack chilled or frozen food, 3-D designers, furniture makers, opticians, car valeters, bookkeepers). Interestingly some jobs that never appear are also linked to national shortages, for example chiropodists and civil engineers. Some occupations in the same sector are given very different weighting – TV loves architects but tends to ignore surveyors. Headhunters are often shown, career coaches virtually never.

Editing also happens in another way. When you see a police officer portrayed on TV, either in fiction or in a documentary, what is shown? Normally an officer chasing, apprehending or cautioning a member of the public. If you talk to actual police officers you discover that even those on the 'beat' spend most of their time checking emails or completing paperwork. TV prefers the more exciting moments: the airline pilot avoiding a crash, the lawyer bringing in a surprise witness, or the ambulance crew saving a patient's life.

In fact, television shapes the way we see jobs more than anything else. We work on the assumption that viewers can tell the difference between television and reality. Worryingly, more than a few can't. The actor Johnny Briggs played the factory owner Mike Baldwin in *Coronation Street* for 30 years. Every week the actor received a handful of genuine job applications seeking work in his fictional factory. Even more worryingly, about once a week someone applied for the job of assistant manager.

Deciding what or who?

The trouble with most of the careers advice we receive as young people is that most of it revolves around the question

'What do you want to do when you grow up?' We are supposed to look thoughtful, and then come up with a job title: 'Er ... a ... Chartered Accountant!'

A more authentic decision might be about what kind of person you hope to be. So, many people, particularly those taking a more spiritual view of life choices, say that the most important thing is about who you are, not what you do. Others will say that it's self-indulgent to focus on the individual, and more practical to focus on the work that is actually available.

The answer, I believe, is like so many of the most important truths in life, a matter of holding conflicting ideas in your mind at the same time, as the career spectrum model in Figure 10.1 makes clear.

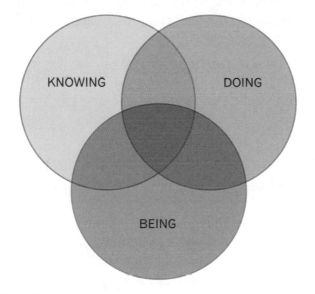

Figure 10.1 Career spectrum

The first step to a complete career change takes very little time at all. Draw a larger version of the above three circles for yourself, and within each circle write in the key words that capture what's important for you, right now, using the paragraphs below if you need a nudge.

Knowing

In Chapter 6 we revealed the way that *what you choose to know about* provides powerful clues about the kind of work that will seem meaningful. So if you are considering a complete change of career, it's worth thinking carefully about the kind of topics you would like to read or talk about while you are at work. Secondly, review all the things you know about so you have a clear idea of the underpinning knowledge you may need to demonstrate for handling competency-based interviews (see Chapter 13).

Understanding the knowledge angle of work is also an insight into your motivation, both now and in the future, because it treats each job as a learning curve. Most roles are interesting in their first few weeks or months, but whether a job is intrinsically interesting in the long run is often about how much you will continue to learn and grow.

We are what we repeatedly do.

Aristotle

Doing

Aristotle was writing about developing virtuous habits, but his words remind us of another powerful notion: *what we choose to do most of the time matters*. The activities that take up most of our waking hours have a strong influence on our effectiveness, the outcomes our work generates, and the way people see us. Remember that word 'occupation'? A job is what 'occupies' our time and attention. Skills are powerful reinforcers of self-esteem and are the best way of making our values tangible in the world by getting things done. Skills need refreshing and updating, but more than anything else they need to be used. Using only part of your skill set, or using skills you really don't value very much, can lead to long-term demotivation and cynicism.

Refer to Chapter 7 to refresh and build on your understanding of what you do regularly and well in terms of behaviours, skills and competences.

Being (and valuing)

How you exercise the skills you have is very dependent on your attitude and values, two factors which are strongly linked to personality. To perform a task well, accurately, with care, taking into account the needs of other people, to be able to meet deadlines, to be cheerful or resourceful under pressure, these are all aspects of personality that you should revisit through the various opportunities offered in this book, notably in Chapter 8.

The question of 'being' is not just about the personality you were born with, but also a big clue about values. During life we also build up a sense of what is important to us. Some of those things are clearly demonstrated through the things we choose to learn about under the 'know' heading, but others are deeper still. Think about the causes or charities you support (whether with time, money or sympathy). What issues energize you? What makes you angry?

VALUES – THE BIGGER PICTURE

We all take our values to work with us. Your values are expressed in work through the tasks and outcomes you find interesting and meaningful. Sometimes this is on a macro scale – you're interested in what your organization contributes to the world. For others values are expressed in relationships at work and the way colleagues are treated. Ultimately, you will be more motivated in work situations where the organization and your colleagues share most of your values.

What values do you express through your work?

Using Table 10.1, list the jobs you have done in the past. Think about the *values* that were expressed in each of these jobs (e.g. helping others, delivering a quality service, providing value for money, providing a good experience, etc.). Now give each job a score:

0 – no overlap with my personal values

1 – a minor overlap with my personal values

2 – a clear overlap with my personal values

3 – a strong overlap with my personal values.

Table 10.1   Values expressed In my work

Job	Values Score 0–3

Next, do the same thing for sectors or jobs you think you might be interested in, as in Table 10.2. This is a fairly good review of sectors, so worth doing anyway.

Table 10.2 Potential sectors and their values

Sectors I am interested in	Reasons why these sectors appear to match my values

Finding a values match

Thinking about how your values have matched your work leads you into thinking about your personal values. You might find more clues by looking at your House of Knowledge in Chapter 6.

What values are expressed in the things you care about most? Table 10.3, the **Values grid**, will remind you.

Table 10.3   Values grid

My personal work values	The values of my ideal employer
(Values expressed In my work – e.g. how my work helps others, the end result, how my work adds value or meets certain standards)	(e.g. how the employer treats staff and customers, attitude to quality, integrity, social and environmental responsibility …)

Values expressed in my life
(How I want to be remembered)

The bottom half of the Values grid may give you pause for thought. What would you like said in your obituary? What would you hope that people would say about you at a memorial service to celebrate your life?

CAREER CHANGE: STARTING FROM THE INSIDE OUT

What calls you?

Job: what you do to support your vocation.

Anonymous

Are you looking for a role which is more of a vocation than a job? The word 'vocation' comes from the Latin *vocare*, 'to call'. In popular usage a 'vocation' feels different to an occupation. Sometimes it's used to describe a job, either professional or voluntary, that is poorly paid but makes an important contribution to the well-being of others. Often there is a conscious sense of letting go of conventional ideas of status and advancement.

A vocation is something we feel 'called' to do – we feel a sense of commitment stronger than ordinary levels of motivation, and a sense of 'rightness' in our choice. The term can also be used to describe any occupation for which a person is specifically gifted, and usually implies that the individual's sense of calling towards the task in hand has been recognized by others. In fact, not only have we redefined what we mean by 'career' in the last 50 years, we have redefined what we mean by 'vocation', too. Now it's just as common to find someone expressing that they feel a vocation towards working with animals, being a chef or making hand-made furniture.

The biggest difference, if you're wondering whether your strong career idea is actually a vocation, is that it's *not just about you*. Most vocational choices that lead to the commitment of decades rather than weeks or months arise out of a strong sense of personal values or a sense of service – a life lived, one way or another, for others. If you feel called to the work you do there is a sense that you fit, that it feels like the right thing to do. Just to put the word back into the context of faith it comes from, the most important thing about 'calling' is not the individual being called, but the calling itself. Sometimes there's a belief that we are called to account for the way we spend our three score years and ten. Sometimes it's a belief that our calling is less important than whatever it is in the universe who calls us to be the best version of ourselves.

There is an additional and often forgotten dimension: it should be a good experience. 'Good experience' isn't the same as 'fun', but shouldn't be a million miles from it. Peter Sinclair, author of the 'After Sunday' movement, is fond of reminding people that one of the indicators that you are following a vocation is that you will probably look as if you are enjoying yourself. If the job makes you miserable, can you really be called to do it? There are an awful lot of glum-looking people holding down clergy, teaching, nursing or charity roles we would normally describe as more of a vocation than a job.

A vocation is not just a strong career impulse. It should describe an experience where commitment matches response – in other words, you're fully drawn to something you find fully satisfying. Or, as this book repeatedly points out, something you find satisfying most of the time. This isn't to say that every job should be enjoyable all the time, but work should perhaps enrich the person conducting it at least half of the working week. Even those who are clearly living out a vocation will admit that they are not 100% committed to their calling all of the time. The difference is they keep to the path, trying to be authentic to that original calling, and to live out long-term life choices even when things are difficult.

CAREER CHANGE: STARTING FROM THE OUTSIDE IN

Look again at the sector choices prompted by Chapter 9, particularly from the Job Themes discussion (Table 9.1).

Are you sure you don't know what you want to do? Begin, as suggested above, with the question *If all jobs paid the same, what would you do*? Then try on the question *Which jobs would you like to try out just for a week*?

Look again at what's out there, using Chapter 9 to assist you to map sectors of work. Try the following expanding sequence:

1. Sectors of work you know well

2. Sectors and sub-sectors that have intersected with your job

3. Sectors you have had some contact with during your career

4. Sectors you know something about through your personal interests, friends or commitments.

At this stage, try not to allow 'Yes, but' thinking to get in the way. You don't have to make a decision at this stage – all you are doing is generating ideas. Here are some other tried and tested prompts to get you to generate job ideas:

▮ Think of people you know who are doing interesting jobs. What's interesting about them?

▮ What jobs have you applied for in the past but didn't get?

▮ What jobs have you seen advertised that caught your attention for 30 seconds, even if you did nothing about them?

Go back to your House of Knowledge (see Chapter 6). The clues are all there in the topics that have called you, year after year. Somewhere in a box, in your loft or under the stairs, there's a box with the evidence: those projects that keep coming out every 2–3 years. Look, too, at the things you have chosen to study over the years.

Refer back to Exercise 9.1 to look at the way you can move from subjects that interest you generally in life to sectors of work. Use the exercise to brainstorm sector ideas.

Don't get hung up on another job myth: that if you try to turn a hobby into a living you will fall out of love with it. Plenty of people are busy being paid to do things which they would happily do for nothing in their own time. Starting with subjects means starting with enthusiasm and energy. Remember the origin of the word *enthusiast* – 'filled with God'. The apparently trivial things that fill us with happiness are often big clues about the kinds of activities which feed the soul.

You might also want to try out a few more exercises which force you to use lateral thinking to answer the question 'whatever next?' Exercises 10.1 and 10.2 are designed to do exactly that.

CAREER CHANGE: JUST DO IT

As this chapter has rehearsed, the question is not how you are going to find a new career, but how you are going to decide. Thinking things through matters. Re-imagining the possibilities of your career makes all the difference.

The next big question is *what are you going to do about it*? The second half of this book provides several prompts to activity, but let's nail down one plain fact. If you want to put off career change forever (or at least until it's too late) then keep on reflecting, analysing and mulling over. Keep on thinking that you have to make the perfect decision before you act. That will happily put change off forever.

However, if you don't want to be spending your last inactive years saying 'I wish', then do something. A great deal of psychological research (much of it summarized in Richard Wiseman's book *59 Seconds*) suggests that things are more likely to happen if you have a short-term, step-by-step plan, and if you do something about step one.

Finding out, following your enthusiasm, costs very little. You don't need to have a perfect target job to start the process of discovery – just a sense of curiosity. And here's a big clue: your breakthrough probably has a 5% likelihood of happening as a result of reading or thinking, and a 95% likelihood of arriving as a result of a person. Someone you already know, possibly. Or, even more likely, someone you meet in the next 2–3 months as a result of your active enquiries. So what's the first step? A conversation. Start with people you know, even if they seem very disconnected from the world you want to enter. Find opportunities to talk to people who love what they do for a living. Experiment with informational interviews (see Appendix 1) use Chapter 16, **Beginning It Here**, and act upon the Career Change Action Checklist given at the end of this chapter.

THE FIELD GENERATOR

EXERCISE 10.1 – USING THE FIELD GENERATOR TO MOVE FROM INTERESTS TO FIELDS

As Chapter 1 indicates, sometimes it is necessary to use provocative thinking to kick-start new ideas. The **Field Generator**, described in Figure 10.2, helps you to generate new ideas for sectors or fields. It begins with what you know and your primary areas of interest, and then moves you through a thought process to help you to generate unexpected ideas about potential sectors of work – new fields for you to wander into and explore.

If you are short of sector ideas, go back to the House of Knowledge exercise in Chapter 6. Use a highlighter pen to mark your preferred interests. Now use this information in the Field Generator.

The brain is a wonderful organ. It starts working the moment you get up in the morning and does not stop until you get to work.

Robert Frost

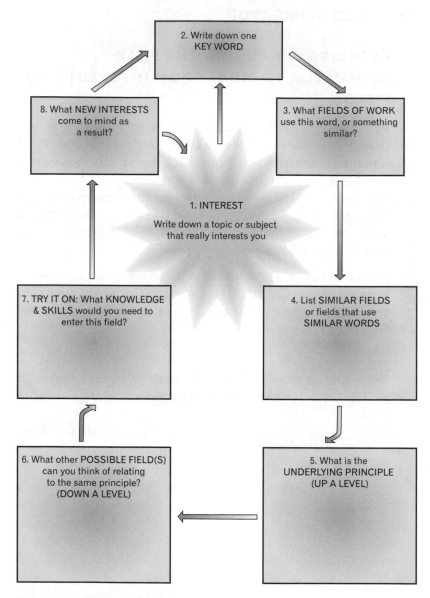

Figure 10.2   The Field Generator

How to use the Field Generator

Step 1 | Take copies of Figure 10.2, the Field Generator, and try this exercise out using as many interests as you can. This exercise works best with someone else working with you, prompting and asking questions.

Make sure you have completed the House of Knowledge exercise in Chapter 6. Pick five or six of your strongest interests.

Write one of your interests in **Box 1**, e.g. boats, sailing and the sea.

Step 2 | In **Box 2** write down a key word from your area of interest, e.g. sailing.

Step 3 | Look at your key word and in **Box 3** write down three sectors of work where this word appears, e.g. sailing instruction, sailing boat design, sailing restoration.

Step 4 | Now that you have expanded your sector a little, think of fields of work that use similar words, and write them in **Box 4**, e.g. ship building, naval architecture, merchant navy, navigation. Make a note in the margin of any new fields that you hadn't thought of before that are maybe connected in some way with your interest, e.g. outward-bound training, water safety.

Step 5 | This is where you have a chance to use a technique which in idea-building terms is called 'going up a level'.

Look at your fields in Box 4. Is there any overriding category that describes them? If you were to find these ideas together in one drawer, what label would you put on the front of the drawer? (e.g. nursing and osteopathy can be placed within the general category of 'medicine' or 'physiology'). This may take a while to work out, or you may think of several alternatives. The answer will be unique to you. In this case you might come up with weather, racing, healthy competition, low technology, getting away from it all, being captain of my own boat ....

What is the underlying 'big idea'? Write down your final answer in **Box 5**, e.g. healthy competition might be your preferred underlying principle here.

Step 6 | In Box 5 we moved up a level to the underlying principle. In **Box 6** we come down a level at a different point.

In this case you might come up with something totally unconnected to sailing arising from 'healthy competition', e.g. sports coaching, teaching kids about diet and exercise, or teaching fund-raising skills to charity staff, or selling ethical financial products. Write down any ideas that appeal to you, making sure you don't try to exclude them at this stage by misguided thinking about what is 'practical'. You may discover sectors or new interests here that could one day become part of your House of Knowledge.

Step 7 | Underline one of the fields or ideas generated in Box 6, and write it in **Box 7**. It's probably best to begin with one that has surprised you most (e.g. in this case you might have come up with teaching fund-raising skills to charity staff).

Write down what you feel to be the key skills and knowledge that you would need to work in this sector. Begin by putting down what you already know, and add more by putting yourself mentally into the shoes of someone working in this area. The only way to build up an accurate picture is to find out. Ask someone already working in this sector, or do some desk research.

If this step was productive and interesting, go back to Box 6 and do the same again with any other interesting sectors.

Step 8 | **Box 8** allows you to record any new areas of interest that the exercise might have brought up, e.g. coaching. Take a new copy of the Field Generator and put this new interest in Box 1, and begin again.

A completed Field Generator is shown in Figure 10.3.

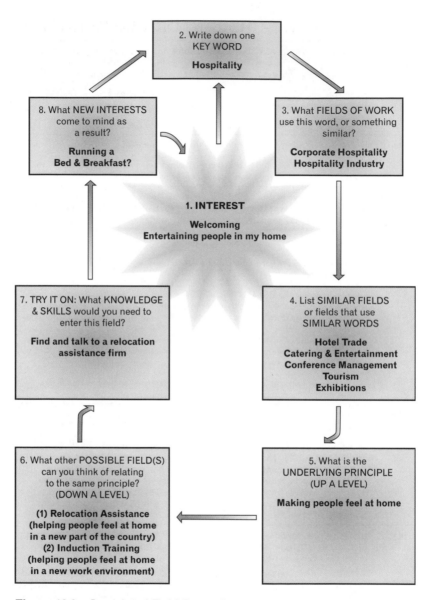

Figure 10.3 Completed Field Generator

EXERCISE 10.2 – DISCONTINUOUS THINKING

This process is great for times when you are completely stuck for ideas, and works well alongside the Field Generator. Discontinuous thinking is about provoking your mind into making new connective pathways. It's the driving force behind Edward de Bono's concept of provocative thinking, and also one of the characteristics of Roger Van Oech's delightfully off-the-wall book *A Whack on the Side of the Head*.

There are few rules with this kind of exercise. One of the principles behind it is that you think about something else entirely, and then allow some kind of connection or comparison between your thought process and your main problem. Here are some ideas that might work particularly well with sectors:

1. *Try a provocative statement which sounds deliberately illogical or nonsensical*. For example, 'a sector which is about persuading and influencing but avoids people'. This might take you into ways of translating your interpersonal skills into text-based or alternative contexts, e.g. writing to influence, finding great words for websites, writing other people's speeches, designing models for negotiation and conflict management that can be communicated by distance learning. Another one might be 'building houses that nobody will live in' – you might apply your construction skills to buildings used for housing animals or equipment; you might start building models rather than sketching things out in words; you might create 'virtual' libraries, supermarkets or conference centres on the Internet.

2. *Try turning your sector upside down*. For example, you may be interested in child development because you are interested in the way young people grow. Turning that upside down might lead you to thinking about the way older people degenerate. This may be a sector which interests you in itself, or it may help you to refocus on your chosen sector, e.g. by looking at the effects of head injury in young people.

'MUST DO' LIST

Your checklist for beginning a career change TODAY

KNOWING	1)	Review what you enjoy knowing about (try the House of Knowledge in Chapter 6).
	2)	Review your preferred Job Themes (see Table 9.1).
	3)	Look seriously at the things you have chosen to learn about in the past.
	4)	Use the exercises in this book, including the Field Generator, to translate these ideas into potential sectors for investigation.
DOING	5)	Review your skills using either the first impression list in Table 7.1 or any of the more detailed skill exercises in Chapter 7.
	6)	Consider using the JLA Skill Cards to identify your motivated skills.
BEING	7)	Look at the values and preferences expressed in your jigsaw job (Exercise 5.1).
	8)	List your top three Career Hot Buttons (see Chapter 5).
	9)	Review your personality by looking at Chapter 8.
	10)	Complete the values exercises in this chapter.
NEXT STEPS	11)	Put together the above information on one sheet of A4 (the master sheet in Table 16.1 provides a useful template). Now STOP reflecting and move into action steps, namely:
	12)	Show your results to friends and colleagues. Ask for ideas and connections.
	13)	Talk to people about what you think you might be looking for – use the Two-Breath Message in Chapter 13.
	14)	Write down five potential target fields. They don't need to be perfect.
	15)	Use the REVEAL method from the end of this book to generate meetings with interesting people.

Creative Job Search Strategies

CHAPTER 11

This chapter helps you to:

■ Debunk job-hunting myths

■ Discover the hidden job market

■ Anticipate employer risk aversion

■ Research before you search

■ Build and improve your personal networks

An idea is nothing more nor less than a new combination of old evidence.

James Webb Young

WHY DO WE KEEP MAKING THE SAME MISTAKES?

No matter what electronic tools are available to us, no matter that candidates get good advice from a range of sources, no matter what kind of opportunities are readily available, it seems that we keep making the same mistakes when we try to change jobs.

Banging your head against a brick wall

How many of the following dead-end strategies are you currently adopting?

▪ Chasing jobs in declining sectors (rather than seeking out the sectors and organizations that are going against the tide)

▪ Pursuing only advertised positions (when you are easily up against hundreds of others)

▪ Relying on the Internet to do your job searching for you

▪ Applying for jobs you don't really want 'just for the experience' (and yet getting knocked back by rejection)

▪ 'Lowering your sights' when things go wrong

▪ Using up all your best contacts in the first three weeks and then complaining because you don't know anybody

▪ Sending out a CV which pushes you into the 'same old same old' but still hoping for a change of career?

MYTH-CRACKING

One of my discoveries when I moved from training recruiters to assisting career builders was that there really are some fairly well-kept secrets about the way people get jobs. It's also true that people restrict their job-hunting strategy within limits defined by **job-hunting myths**.

If you've been waiting for the moment when you felt you got your money's worth from this book, this may be it. Job-hunting myths are explored and debunked in Table 11.1.

Table 11.1 Job hunting: myth or fact?

What your mother/careers teacher/best friends told you	Job market reality
Jobs are filled by people applying for published vacancies.	About 20–30% of jobs are filled in this way (less in executive markets).
It's easier to get a job when you have one already.	True to a point: employers like to bet on certainties, not outsiders, so they want a recent track record.

	If you have 'problems' with your CV, you need to have a good narrative ready to cover gaps, changes of direction, 'unemployment' (is it really unemployment if you are learning or extending your skills?).
It's who you know, not what you know.	Making connections will increase your chance of being seen. Employers buy experience and potential, so at interview they will be far more impressed with what you can do than who you know, unless it's the kind of job where you're supposed to bring contacts and clients with you.
Qualifications count.	Employers often have a blinkered view of what qualifications they need. The key question is: what is the standard for the job or industry? If yours are a little light, don't over-highlight them on your CV, and stress the intellectual standards you have achieved through your work experience. If you have constantly turned your back on opportunities to extend your knowledge and training, you need to have a pretty good reason.
You'll have to retrain.	Believing that you will have to spend endless time or money retraining is often the reason why people fail to take the first step. Fewer jobs than you think require you to retrain. Find out about the range of routes people follow to break into new sectors.

Send as many CVs out as you can.	Do you know how many employment agencies push out CVs every day?
	How much time do you think a busy manager will give to a speculative CV where there is no obvious connection to the company's needs? Five seconds? Speculative letters and CVs *do* work (far better with employers than with recruitment consultants) and give you access to the hidden job market, but only if they are extremely well targeted and followed up by personal contact.
Sometimes you have to push yourself forward.	'Sometimes'? It's the idea of 'pushing' that puts people off, as if you are advertising something shoddy. Don't claim to be what you are not, but in everything you do, present the best version of yourself, and a clear message of what you can do for others. Try it as a way of life, not just job search.
Only pushy people get jobs through networking.	Not true. Networking works for everyone as long as they do it positively and honestly. See below for more on networking.
A job's a job. Think of the money. Good jobs are hard to find.	OK, red card. Go back to Chapter 1. Do not pass Go. Do not collect £200.

THE HIDDEN JOB MARKET

Insanity is doing the same thing over and over and expecting a different result.

Eva May Brown

The majority of jobs are not advertised. If you only ever respond to job advertisements, you'll never know about them. This is the hidden job market. Many job hunters are unaware of it; most don't know how to break into it.

You can look at the hidden job market in two ways: right or left brain.

First of all, food for the imagination. If you want to slow down your job search and limit your options (maybe somebody is paying you to fail?) then act on the negative myths in Table 11.1 and limit your job search to advertised positions. You'll miss out on most newly created jobs, all positions filled by word of mouth, and most jobs with small, energetic companies. You'll miss out on all those companies that are just on the edge of thinking about creating a new job. You'll never have a chance to be recommended by a friend or colleague.

Secondly, for all you people who need to see the numbers, Table 11.2 records the way that people in the UK find jobs. The information presented is based on a UK survey of workers who had been with their employer for 3 months or less at the time of interview.

Table 11.2 How people find jobs

Method	Men	Women
Reply to an advertisement	24.2%	31.6%
Hearing from someone who worked there	31.3%	25.3%
Direct application	14.1%	15.6%
Private employment agency or business	10.3%	9.4%
Job centre	9.0%	7.3%
Some other way	10.7%	10.3%

UK Labour market 2003 — www.statistics.gov.uk

This 2003 review is the most up-to-date UK picture available. Surprisingly, there is relatively little research available internationally on the ways people find work. Surveys in different countries do, however, tend to indicate that around a third of workers find jobs through word of mouth connections, and direct approaches are also surprisingly effective.

Using job boards and the Internet

Don't exclude any job search method – use everything in your toolbox. Although job boards may help, the Internet is not the magic tool it seems. The Web can be a great source of information, but statistically it is one of the least effective job search methods. The Internet of course also offers the benefits of social media. This is such an important topic that it gets its own chapter which also covers electronic job search – Chapter 12, **Using Social Media**.

EMPLOYER SAFETY HABITS

Here's another section that in itself probably justifies the cover price of this book: when it comes to finding and filling jobs, employers and job seekers use totally opposite strategies. Table 11.3 illustrates how employers prefer to recruit, and why.

Table 11.3 Employer risk aversion

Employer's preference	Risk level to the employer	Employer thinking
Almost family Somebody we already know: an internal appointment is ideal, or someone already doing consultancy or temp work for us.	Virtually risk free	We know exactly what we're getting.
Known quantity Maybe someone working for a competitor, someone whose reputation we know even if we haven't met the individual yet.	Very low	A clear track record. This person has done well elsewhere and will do the same for us.
A friend of a friend In other words, someone who is known and trusted by someone we know and trust, or someone who comes highly recommended by a trusted colleague.	Low	We have a pretty good idea of what we will be getting. Fred always recommends good people.
Achiever Someone who may be known to us at a distance, and comes with clear evidence of past success – ideally in terms of a portfolio of work, a fistful of testimonials, excellent and highly specific projects with their names all over them.	Relatively low	Again, clear evidence of past achievement. We can measure what we'll be getting for our money.

Employer's preference	Risk level to the employer	Employer thinking
Competence-based recruitment We've accurately assessed what a successful post holder must know and the skills required by the job, and we are going to test or interview to identify specific competences.	Controlled	We're using a careful filter, trying to predict workplace performance. We would still like to know what candidates are like in terms of personality and team fit.
Unsolicited application This is much more than yet another CV sent out on a 'spray and pray' basis. A well-aimed direct application can sometimes prompt an employer to do something about a new job, or solve an old problem.	Moderately high (but potentially low risk if it's the right person)	We are now talking to strangers, but sometimes it's nice to be surprised by the right people. We're more impressed by people who know something about us already, particularly if we have a problem right now. In fact, if we get to talk to this person and like what we see, we'll reclassify them as 'achievers' or even 'friends'.
Attractive agency candidate OK, we'll talk to an employment agency or recruitment consultant at this point, because they know where to resource people who have done well in the past, and they can screen for us. They can	Risk increasing	Agencies don't always know as much as they should do about the actual requirements of the job, and they sometimes pigeon-hole candidates. However, they are very good at giving feedback about how an employer is likely to react to a CV.

Employer's preference	Risk level to the employer	Employer thinking
sometimes head-hunt people directly.		
Response to specific advertising Who knows if we'll get the right people? *And* we run the risk of buying advertising space without being sure of a result.	High	It's going to be tough to filter out the ones who know what they're doing. Who do we interview? It feels like a lottery.
Response to general recruitment advertising Oh dear. Here we go – hundreds of hopefuls to be filtered out.	Sky high	Nobody reads the skill or qualification requirements, nobody filters these people, and they're all desperate to get a job.

Table 11.4 shows the mirrored position for the job seeker, outlining job seeker assumptions and comparing them with the market reality.

MAKING GOOD USE OF RECRUITMENT CONSULTANTS

It's vital to remember that although most recruitment consultants keep a bank of potentially suitable applicants, they are largely vacancy driven. That means that they are most interested in you if you are a quick fit for a vacancy that needs filling immediately. However, recruitment consultancies do have an extremely good feel for the market, and where they deal with specialist fields, the information they can give you can be priceless.

Table 11.4 Job seeker thinking

Activity	Job seeker's thinking	Market reality
Response to advertising Hours spent filling in application forms, drafting a letter of application, sprucing up the CV. A quiet prayer or a philosophical shrug as the envelope goes in the post, then the waiting begins. It's useful to remember that someone will be short listing, probably into three piles: *No, Possible* and *Yes.* Have you done everything you can do to get on to the *Yes* pile?	**My big chance** Great, a chance to show off my CV, list my skills. The more information I can give, the more they'll be impressed. Now all I have to do is put a stamp on the envelope and cross my fingers.	**Small chance** How many other applications hit the desk in the same post? How differentiated is your message? How do you convince the employer that you are worth talking to in person – particularly in comparison with internal or recommended candidates? You might improve the odds if you follow up your application with a telephone call. Many advisers say you should *always* ring to confirm that your application has been seen.

Unsolicited application

This is much more than yet another CV sent out on a 'spray and pray' basis. A well-aimed direct application can sometimes prompt an employer to do something about a new job, or solve an old problem.

Keep shooting ...

and I'll hit something eventually. At least it gets me noticed.

Long shot ...

if you're firing with a shotgun, but effective if you use a sniper rifle – is the recipient going to be intrigued, pushed to action or irritated at yet another piece of junk mail? It depends on how well targeted your CV is, what the accompanying message has to say, and whether you press the right buttons by knowing something about the needs of the company.

This method is more effectively used in conjunction with personal contact. If someone already knows why you are interesting, your CV gets read.

If this method works you may end up in a shortlist of one – pretty good odds.

Table 11.4 *Contd.*

Activity	Job seeker's thinking	Market reality
Recruitment consultant or employment agency Do your homework – find out which consultants are regularly placing staff in your sector.	**Guiding hands** At last, my chances are in the hands of a recruitment professional, somebody who will help me to develop my career and find me a job. They have all the unadvertised vacancies, don't they?	**Check your assumptions** Agencies make money by placing obvious skills into obvious jobs, not by being career coaches. They receive far more speculative approaches than they can handle. However, an agency interview *can* help you to get a feel for your market worth and check your message to potential employers. Good agencies set up interviews using strong personal contact and recommend you. Poor agencies simply distribute unsolicited CVs. Good agencies will give you focused feedback on your potential. Poor agencies will over-promise and under-deliver. See Chapter 13 for further tips on talking to recruitment consultants.

Achiever

In your job, what would be the equivalent of a 'portfolio of work'? How can you present tangible evidence of what you have achieved: brochures, articles, testimonials, records of projects, etc.?

My chance to shine

This will really impress them.

And it might – as long as what you have to offer matches what the employer needs. The achievement you demonstrate should be a close match to the employer's shopping list, otherwise your prized portfolio is irrelevant.

Collect evidence

It's all too easy to make claims about yourself, but you need to back them up with measurable facts. Your CV, and what you say to support your application, and your words at interview, are all *assertions* which you need to support by *evidence*.

Keep good records of what you have done: copies of documents, client feedback, affidavits, good appraisals. The more objective the evidence, the lower the perceived risk for the employer.

Table 11.4 *Contd.*

Activity	Job seeker's thinking	Market reality
Competence-based recruitment If you are interviewed, be very clear what you have achieved and how you did it. Even if there is no formal testing, use evidence of achievement to demonstrate the same arguments.	**A chance to demonstrate what I can do ...** but daunting for many job seekers who are unfamiliar with competence-based interviewing.	**Focus ...** on what you know, your skills and your achievements. Be prepared to come up with a range of achievement stories (use the skill clips technique in Chapter 7). Listen for the language that the selector is using so you know which competences are being sought.
Known quantity I get interviewed because of the work I have done in the industry.	**A way in** Keep your eyes and ears open for these opportunities, and make sure people are aware of the contribution you have made as a 'fringe' member of an organization.	**How do you get to be a known quantity?** Simple. Shine. Get to be good at your job and let others know it. Keep a record of your achievements. Write articles or circulate good ideas. Talk with energy to customers, suppliers and partner organizations.

A friend of a friend

What I need is someone who can put me on the inside track.

Who, me? I don't have friends like that

I don't know anybody connected/at the right level/in this field/of that age group, etc. Besides, I'd feel awkward approaching them, because it feels like I'm asking for special treatment, or a favour. I might even look desperate. I will feel terrible if they say they don't have time to see me, and they probably won't be able to offer me any real help. So perhaps it's best if I don't ask …

(See this chapter's section on building a personal web).

Look around you

Yes, you. Who do you know (not necessarily in work) who admires what you do, and would be happy to recommend you to others? Have you enlisted help from these people as career coaches, dummy interviewers, idea factories?

Look around you at family, friends, associates, and find out which ones have pushed opportunities towards others like this. Life has its natural match-makers and fixers, and they love to be known for their contacts and good judgement.

Table 11.4 *Contd.*

Activity	Job seeker's thinking	Market reality
Almost family I'm happy approaching this kind of organization. They feel comfortable talking to me because they already know what I am like.	**Old school tie?** This old boy network stuff is unfair and, in any case, the internal candidate's got a head start. Anyway, how can I possibly get myself known that well to every company I apply to? Beware of the problems that can arise from informal conversations: the company may not be clear that you are looking for a post, or the conversations may continue endlessly without a clear decision.	**Becoming close means becoming wanted** This is *not* about old boy (or girl) networks – those often produce dreadful appointments. Your research into the *right* fields and companies will get you known as an enthusiast. Work experience, consultancy or simply keeping in touch by sending in good ideas are all strategies that can move you into the target's bull's eye. If you're not comfortable getting close to these people, you probably don't want to work with them anyway. See below for advice on 'Networking for softies', and also see the REVEAL method in Appendix 1.

Furthermore, a good recruitment consultant will have got to his or her position by knowing a lot of decision makers. A good strategy is to identify about 15–20 recruitment consultants dealing with the kinds of jobs you are after. Find the name of the individual consultant handling this kind of job, and send in a speculative email with a brief CV. Follow up within 2 days or so with a telephone call, and ask for the opportunity to meet the consultant. Recruitment consultants like to be valued for their industry knowledge, and will often respond well to you if they feel they can learn something from you about organizations or sectors you've worked in.

Many consultants ask you to email in your documents. Remember that an email is remembered for only a few minutes, and your attachment may not be opened. Send a posted version of your CV in as well, with a short, crisp covering letter.

You will also be asked to register, usually online. That's fine, but remember that most recruitment consultants admit that they only refer to their database of candidates if they are bored or desperate. Remember that most recruitment consultants are strongly people-oriented. They like to influence, persuade, encourage and sell. So the key to making the most of a recruitment consultant is for you to establish a good working relationship. You will only do this by having at least one good conversation ideally face-to-face. If your consultant really understands what you're looking for, remembers you and believes you will be enthusiastic at interview, chances are you'll get short-listed.

A good recruitment consultant will also tell you what you are worth in the marketplace, and what hurdles you will have to jump if you want to change sector. Many recruitment consultants have strong views about CV construction, so the best question to ask isn't 'what do you think of my CV?' but *what does my CV say to you?*' If you recognize and like what you hear, your CV is working.

BEGINNING A CREATIVE JOB SEARCH

A creative, multi-strategy job search will draw upon most or all of the following activities:

I Make applications in response to vacancies advertised in a range of media.

I Scrutinise all job ads, whether paper or electronic, to identify likely employers and useful agencies, and approach them directly.

I Approach companies in your chosen fields on a speculative basis with a strong covering letter matching four or five of your key areas of experience to the employer's needs.

I Talk to recruitment consultants who regularly advertise jobs in your sector.

I Make other, speculative approaches to recruitment consultants who you believe may be able to help you, or those you have been recommended to contact.

I Follow up recommendations to talk to people and organizations – but do your homework first to make the most of opportunities.

I Conduct informational interviews (see below) to deepen your understanding of sectors and improve your contacts.

I Undertake personal networking to increase your visibility.

I Ask for meetings with decision makers and people who are at the heart of great networks.

I Register with appropriate job boards.

I Monitor job boards operated by employers and agencies.

I Maintain a strong online presence through appropriate use of social media.

I Join online discussion groups and forums.

I Undertake temporary or project work which increases your visibility to decision makers.

I Encourage an employer to create a new job where one does not already exist.

The key to a successful job search is to combine methods effectively and by doing so, increase their power. Review your activity and ask yourself how many of the above methods you are using, and why you are avoiding key elements in a multi-strategy job search, and you will reap the following benefits:

▎ You will consciously target the hidden job market.

▎ You will anticipate employer risk thinking.

▎ You will be choosing a different strategy to the majority of job seekers.

▎ You will broadcast confidence.

▎ You will be remembered for what you can do for your next employer.

Not networking

Let's begin with the truth. Career changers, whether recent graduates or experienced executives, hate one activity: networking. They say 'it's pushy' or 'it's not me', 'it exploits people and loses you friends' or even 'it makes me look desperate'. We should respect these suspicions. Anyone who suggests networking without addressing those issues is trying to get you to buy a jacket that doesn't fit, isn't your colour, and is something you'll never wear after you take it home.

Networking is something we all do unconsciously. If you move to a new town and want to find a good childminder, dentist or plumber, you ask around without worrying what that looks or sounds like. Networking has been done a huge disservice by people and organizations who exploit human networks for commercial advantage. You know who they are: those people who want to sell you things you don't really want, and use friendship or family connections to make you feel guilty enough to buy something.

Networking books will tell you about 'working the room' and giving your business card to as many people as you can. That's another huge misunderstanding. Anyone who thinks that networking is about exploiting people has misunderstood the whole concept. True networking is about a fair exchange of helpful information and ideas.

Networking for softies

How can we tap the power of the network economy to assist our career development and job search? Firstly, it's vital to recognize that networking is **not** about getting a job. It's about expanding your range. It's about creating new possibilities. It's about learning more about other jobs, other fields. It's about identifying key people and decision makers.

Most important of all, it's about **what you put in**. The process was once described in the 1950s by US careers writer Bernard Haldane as a 'chain of helpfulness'. It begins not with the question 'who do I know that I can exploit?', but with 'who do I know that can tell me something interesting?'. It may even begin 'who do I know that I can help?'. Personal webs are connections of people. This doesn't mean trashing friendships for the sake of a quick fix. Networks are *social* networks – they work best when we take a genuine interest in others. The best personal webs are a pool of freely shared knowledge; everyone puts something in, everyone has a chance to take different things out. Begin with what you can add – this 'what do I know that would be helpful to others?'. It can be something quite ordinary or modest, such as useful Web pages, book recommendations, telling people about cheap travel deals or free resources. A chain of helpfulness begins with what you are prepared to give, not what you want to take.

Be kind to yourself, and network like a true softie. Never put yourself in the situation where you are ringing someone and saying 'you don't know me, but ...'. Start with people you know really well – who are they? – the people you can ring up *without having to compose an opening statement in your head.*

In difficult calls the telephone feels heavy as lead – for this kind of call it should feel feather-light. The kind of people you can take out for coffee and say 'this is going to come out all wrong, but can I try this out with you?'. Ask them to help you with something and arrange an actual meeting – learn the habit of speaking to people face-to-face because it will make all the difference in the long run. Ask them about anything you like, but learn the skills of *asking rather than telling* – find out about the work they do, how they got into it, what overlaps exist between their world and yours. Thank your friend for their time, but don't say goodbye until you've asked the number one all-time breakthrough networking question:

Who else should I be talking to?

Degrees of separation

The theory of **six degrees of separation** was popularized by the American playwright John Guare. The idea is that anyone can reach anyone else in the world in six jumps or less. Person A leads you to B, and eventually to your 'target'. You begin by talking to someone who is connected, no matter how tangentially, with the person you're after. Often it's quicker than that. I once saw this explained to a room of MBA students. When the speaker asked for a random example, someone called out 'Nelson Mandela!'. 'What would be the first step if you wanted to speak to Mr Mandela?' A hand shot up near the back: 'Er … my uncle knows him.' You never know who people know. Unless you ask.

I use the example of someone who has been into space as a genuine example. In my life I have been within half a mile of two famous astronauts (Yuri Gagarin, when I was in my pram and he was guest of honour in Manchester, and Neil Armstrong when he spoke in Tatton Park in Cheshire some 40 years later). I regularly ask large audiences 'Who's met someone who has been into space?'. The first time I asked, a woman in the second row put her hand up, and told me afterwards that it was one of the most amazing discussions of her life. You could probably fit everyone who has been into space into a small coach, but in the average audience one person in 80 or so has talked to someone who has been up there. Even the most extraordinary people are not that far away.

Try finding out what you have in common with the people you talk to, and ask what you can add: what contacts, information, ideas do you have? If others can help you, ask for their assistance honestly. Once you get someone to talk to you, *never* leave them feeling that they haven't helped.

How the numbers work

Networking isn't about the number of people you talk to but the connections that develop between them. If 4 people are acquaintances, there are 12 one-to-one relationships among them. If you simply add one more person to the group, you get 20 relationships. Six people means 30 connections, and 7 makes 42. As your personal web goes beyond 10, the number of possible interactions explodes.

We're talking about the difference between mailing lists and interest groups. A mailing list may be 1000 separate, unconnected people. An interest group 1000 strong can overturn national policy. Just look at the way a handful of farmers and truck drivers brought the UK to a standstill over fuel prices in the year 2000.

Following the maze

It's easy to feel sceptical about networking, even if it is for softies. Questions like 'does it work?', 'how long does it take?', and 'is there something else I can do instead?' arise frequently. Yes, yes and yes. To answer the last question first – yes, there is always an alternative to talking to real people. It's called an average, dull, low-octane job search.

As for questions one and two, talk to people who have been made redundant in the last 2–3 years and have gone on to find interesting work. Most people you talk to will tell you that a breakthrough conversation brought the opportunity to light. The problem is, just as businesses don't really know how to generate word-of-mouth business, you can't ever predict which activity is going to bring in a result. It's like working your way through a maze. The treasure could be there at the first turn, around the next corner, or a long way, deep into the maze. You can't know in advance, so you have to trust and keep going. Keep asking 'who else should I be talking to?'. Every maze has a centre. The more turns you take, the closer you get. Networking is like that – the more you do, the clearer the process becomes, and you see what the end result might look like.

Be assured: things will happen along the way. For example, you will fall over jobs. You may not want the jobs that are mentioned, but do alert others in your network to your discoveries it's a really good way of putting something back into the system. Secondly, simply because you are talking to people who share your values and interests, you are going to meet some very interesting people, some of whom may become life-long friends.

When I speak to large audiences, at some stage I make sure that everyone in the room has a conversation with a stranger. The conversation begins with 'this is why I am here and this is what I am looking for'. It's sad that out of 300 people half a dozen will sneak out at this point, claiming an urgent appointment. Sad because out of 140-plus conversations I know that most will be useful, some fascinating, and at some time later the same day someone from the room will track me down and say 'I had a conversation today which may have changed my life'. The fact that it happens on every occasion means that it just happens – you just need to keep asking.

Three predictions

Here are three calculated predictions. The first is the fact that you already know at least one person who can help, really help. When we begin networking for softies we tend to start by scanning the far horizon – people some way off who you know only vaguely. These people will be great contacts, and soon, but first of all you need to take some baby steps. Who do you know who is close by? There's a simple test – you're looking for the kind of person you could pick up the phone and talk to without having to plan what you're going to say.

The second prediction is that you will probably find a job through someone you know already, or someone you meet in the next 3 months. Play the game backwards. Imagine it is 6 months down the line and you have found your unusual and absorbing job, and think about how you got it.

The third prediction draws on the exciting work of Swiss careers expert Daniel Porot, who says that the best results come from the third level of networking. The first level covers the people you know well. The second level describes people you know vaguely and the people you get introduced to. The third level is composed of people you don't know at all right now. Why does the third level work? Possibly because it puts you in front of people who have no assumptions about you. Not only that, but by the time you get to the rich territory of the third level you've got pretty good at the process.

Informational interviews

There are many versions of this idea in print; an early version appeared in *What Color is Your Parachute?* and the idea is also systematized in Daniel Porot's PIE Method. The principle is straightforward: find someone who knows about a field or occupation in detail, and ask to see them for a short interview during which you ask a series of key questions about entry to the field, rewards and pitfalls, and – most importantly – the names of other people who can give you further assistance.

The important thing to realize is that the technique is about *research, not job search.*

This activity is critically important if you want to access the hidden job market. It helps you to find out the roles and fields which are a great match for your skills and experience, and then helps you to identify target organizations. You may also find that you fall over jobs before they become vacancies. This strategy is so important that it is outlined in detail in Appendix 1: Informational Interviews – The REVEAL Method.

Networking Secrets from Gael & Stuart Lindenfield, authors of *Confident Networking for Career Success* (Piatkus, 2010)

1. Research your target
   The more knowledge you have about the other person, their world, its challenges and interests you may have in common, the more confident you will feel. At the very least do a quick search on Google or LinkedIn. If you have enough time make contact with people who have connections in common to find out even more information. You may well find someone who will offer to open the door for you and give you a glowing introduction at the same time.

2. Clarify your appeal
   Gain clarity not just about why you want to meet them but why they might be pleased to meet you! Make a list of at least three areas of knowledge or skill that you have which could be of value to your target. For example: knowledge of relevant research; experience of a new market; a specific skill which could help with a project your contact has championed.

3. Rehearse your key lines
   Confidence is built on experience. But, like an actor you can fake that experience! Scripting and editing

some of your 'lines' will enable you to be more brief and articulate. This is especially important if the person you are meeting is a high level contact and you have little time to make an impact. Your voice will have more resonance if you practise taking a deep slow breath before you start to talk. And, if you rehearse taking pauses before important points as all good orators do, you will be very much less likely to use those give-away 'Ums and Ah's'.

Using your research to guide you, compose a few meaningful conversation openers with instant appeal. You could for example mention a mutual contact, or make reference to something that you know is of particular interest to them personally. Prepare a punchy and positive self-introduction, highlighting in a discreet way one factor which will be of interest (e.g. 'I'm a Financial Analyst specializing in performance measurement').

4. Prepare for difficult questions
Plan assertive answers to questions that might floor you. For example, if you are in 'transition', and are worried about being asked what you are doing now, confidently state what you are (even if you're thinking of a career change) and say what you are evaluating and exploring.

Speak your 'lines' out loud in front of a mirror or, better still, in front of a supportive and assertive colleague or friend. Rehearse again and again until you find yourself speaking in a natural and easy-going tone. Remember, confident networking is simply a skill. It may be one that is easier for extrovert people to learn, but even the shyest among us can perfect it with practice.

Gael Lindenfield is author of 21 personal development books; Stuart Lindenfield is Head of Transitions Practice at Reed Consulting and runs networking workshops.

Managing your personal web

It's possible to build up a personal web of between 60 and 100 useful, curious and interesting people within about 3 months. Some principles that will help:

1. Learn how to conduct informational interviews.

2. Start the easy way. Begin with people you know, asking them the question 'Who do you know who works in ...'.

3. Get people to introduce you to other people (see Appendix 1).

4. Build slowly and methodically. Put time aside each week.

5. Use electronic tools will help you track and build on your contacts (see Chapter 12), but keep a good, accessible record of who you are trying to reach, and the people who might call you (not just networking connections but employers and recruiters). Anyone in your network may contact you at any time, so it pays to keep a notebook or a printed list of people you have approached in the last month within easy reach wherever you are. There's nothing worse than somebody returning your call only to discover that you can't remember who they are.

6. Ask yourself all the time: What can I add to this network? How can I be helpful? Be remembered as a source of information, a person who brings others together.

EXERCISE 11.1 – BEGIN YOUR PERSONAL WEB

First of all, decide what record-keeping system you are going to use so that you can build up a personal web methodically. You'll need full contact information, and be able to cross-link records and keep a note of the areas you discuss. Finally, you'll need a diary reminder of any action or follow-up agreed.

Can't think of anyone? Start with categories rather than names. Draw a 2-inch circle on a piece of paper. This represents family and close friends. Who else do you know really well? Draw a larger circle around it: put in the names of any clubs or organizations you belong to. Think of courses you have attended. Who are your suppliers of professional services – how can they help? Next, draw an even larger circle to take in business contacts, past or present staff, customers, advisers, anyone who has ever helped you or you have helped. Then ask yourself – who do they know?

'MUST DO' LIST

☑ Base your job search on reality, not urban myths.

☑ Focus on the hidden job market.

☑ Take account of employer risk aversion in your job search strategy.

☑ Use every job-seeking strategy in the box. Combining them improves their effectiveness and shortens your job search.

☑ Start your networking today – think of two friends you can approach.

Can I Find a Job Using Social Media?

CHAPTER 12

This chapter looks at:

▌ The value, and necessity, of having an online presence

▌ How to use social media as part of an active networking plan

▌ The classic errors people make online

▌ Adding an electronic dimension to your job search

Live in fragments no longer. Only connect …

E.M. Forster, *Howards End*

WHY THE INTERNET WON'T SAVE YOUR CAREER

In the twenty-first century, job seekers have been making the same mistakes that career changers made in the 1980s and 1990s. We're still essentially passive, waiting for the right opportunity to come along, waiting for the phone to ring, waiting for someone else to take control of our career. In the past passive behaviour was about putting your future in the hands of agencies, your boss, HR, and firing off lots of application forms. Now we sit at our desks and pray to St Google.

In previous recessions redundant workers had to stay at home in case the phone rang. This ironically meant that sales of home furnishings and home entertainment systems could sometimes do well even in a slump. When more recent downturns came along the prediction was that behaviours would be very different – because everyone owns a mobile phone and is contactable anywhere, so everyone would be out and about.

This prediction failed to take account of preferred behaviours. Faced with a job search, most people instinctively decide that they should spend most of their time sitting in front of a screen. Why? It feels productive, firing off messages, looking at job boards, investigating companies, and Tweeting away at the same time. More than anything else, because in employment most of us spend a lot of time looking at screens, it *looks like work*.

Seven years ago I helped out at a job workshop in the suburbs of San Francisco. It was a salutary lesson to see that even in a relatively buoyant, hi-tech economy there were career changers expressing the same worries and facing the same problems as the jobless all over the world – 'there are no jobs out there', 'I don't do well at interviews', and 'it's who you know, not what you know'. However, outplacement colleagues in California give their clients a strict rule – use your PC outside working hours only. The thinking is simple. The Web is a fantastic research tool, but a poor tool for communication. A Tweet is forgotten in microseconds, and email in 2 minutes, a telephone call forgotten after half an hour, but a good face-to-face meeting (followed up by a thank you note) can be remembered for 6 months or more. You, as the Americans say, do the math.

So, the first step in a creative career process, as the last chapter made clear, is sometimes to go against your instincts. Nothing new there. Talk to anyone who has made a career breakthrough and they will tell you that at some stage they had to adopt new ways of thinking, and new behaviours. Otherwise, all we do is seek repeated negative experiences – 'I know this doesn't work but I might just try it again a few hundred times to be sure'.

In a tough market an average strategy gives you below average results.

HOW USING SOCIAL MEDIA CAN GIVE YOU AN EDGE

However – and it is a very big however – you need to use the full range of tools available to you. You'll often hear the suggestion 'it's not what you know, but who you know', and as Chapter 11 reveals, that idea is often used as a great excuse not to find anyone to get to know.

If you want to make a difficult career change (and difficult could simply be about the state of the market) then you really are making life an uphill struggle if you don't focus on the one activity that is likely to make the biggest difference – creating contacts. The great advantage of social media is that you can make more contacts, at greater speed, and if you use the right tools your contacts will update themselves so you no longer have to track people down or wonder who they are working for this year.

Why bother? While some are happy to update Twitter all day, others fail to see the point, or just see an embarrassing over-supply of trivial information. There are two main reasons you may discover a need for a balanced use of social media. The first is about visibility. How are people going to find you and recommend you? If they do find you online, will you like what they see? If you're looking for a job as a senior manager and all that can be found about you via Google is something about your weekend hobby or your last holiday, how does this help you get a job or win customers?

The second reason is all about people. Making a big life change is about relationships – finding stuff out, talking to people who can give you ideas and encouragement, making connections. Yes, your relationship needs to be with people, not with Google, but the best way to find and contact the right people now is to use online networks – creating your own, building on other people's connections, joining in online communities. Not to do so is to be the equivalent of the 1980s job seeker who refused to use the phone to follow up on opportunities – if you limit the tools you use, you will still get a result, but it takes so much longer.

So, take another look at social media tools. We all know people who have the latest electronic gadgets – the 'early adopters' in marketing terminology. You don't have to become one. All that matters is that you use the standard electronic tools and use them thoughtfully and frequently enough to maintain your visibility.

HOW CAN SOCIAL MEDIA HELP MY JOB SEARCH?

The first thing, of course, is to look at your online presence with a critical eye. Is your main focus of work clear, at a glance? Have you said the right things about your background and experience? Get someone to look at your online information, and ask them to summarize what they see.

Users of LinkedIn and similar sites take advantage of two ways of getting strapline messages across. The first is your job title, or a summary phrase that captures the kind of work you do. Look at this as carefully as you would examine the first sentence of your CV – does it help the busy user understand what kind of work you do?

Secondly, you will have some kind of 'status bar', which is essentially a quick update of what you are doing. Sometimes this is linked to your Twitter account. People are often unsure about the best thing to write if you're looking for a job. You might fall into one of two categories:

1. You are currently employed and thinking about making a change (you might not want your employer to know that you're looking)

2. You are looking for a job, or contracts, and you don't want to sound desperate about it.

Either way, use your online profile to make yourself stand out. If you are in a job, update your status bar with news of current projects, areas of research, things you want to know more about. In some sectors this will be enough to attract enquiries, possibly even approaches from recruiters, although you can't rely on this until you have extended your visibility. Don't forget that you can always send direct messages to online contacts – don't confuse private requests for help with online 'broadcasts' which everyone can see.

Make regular updates to your status. Think about ways of keeping your message varied and interesting. Demonstrate enthusiasm, for example: 'Reading everything I can get my hands on about healthcare reform ....' or 'Just read a fascinating paper on new construction technology.' Show not just your interest, but the fact that you are keeping up to date on current issues. Mention conferences you have attended (or conference summaries if you can't get there in person), books you have read, sites or people who have inspired you. Bookmark interesting pages so you can send out recommendations on a drip feed basis – one a day, for example, rather than a whole burst in one evening. Most importantly of all, don't waste the opportunities presented by your status bar to say that you are unemployed or finding it difficult to find work. A phrase such as 'Qualified procurement specialist' is great, condensing experience and credibility into three words, but by adding 'looking for next great opportunity!' or similar often sounds like quiet desperation. You can, however, be clear, focused and unemotional, e.g. 'seeking full time employment as an HR Manager in the East Midlands area'. Questions of tone are difficult to get right – ask the opinion of someone you trust who can give you objective advice *before* you publish.

Don't confuse a business-focused page with social chat. If you want to look like a serious, committed candidate don't fill online space with update on your cat, your love life or favourite recipes. Use a separate account in Twitter or Facebook to do that. Avoid any hint of desperation you would not put in a CV profile, e.g. 'would appreciate any help you can give me', 'getting tired of rejections', 'been looking for some time now' or 'will consider anything'. Worse still, don't leave your LinkedIn page or similar unattended, otherwise anyone looking will see a 'last amended' date which shows you've changed nothing for several months. If you don't update, people assume you have found a position or lost interest. Most advisers will tell you to update something every couple of days. It only takes 5 minutes to update the whole of your online presence every 24 hours – there is a wide range of software that will help you connect everything together and update all your online material at one go. If you're not going to update your profile every few days as a job hunter, you'll be better off not using the status bar at all. Put what you're doing in your summary statement so it stays the same and doesn't look like you've neglected it.

It's sometimes hard to think of updates when all you can really say is 'I am still here and still looking'. You can talk about the fact that you are 'researching opportunities', 'talking to interesting people', 'actively networking' or 'eager to broaden my range of contacts'. A key sub-message is the fact that you are doing something for yourself rather than waiting for the market to come to you. This is why it rarely works simply to send your CV to a colleague and say 'would you kindly email this to everyone you think might be interested?'. To do so has already passed the buck in terms of relationship building and turned you back into a passive career changer.

KEEP GOOD RECORDS

Use an electronic diary and address book to keep the details. Record the 'hooks', i.e. factors that you have in common.

Record personal information you discover about your contact that you might need for future conversations – for example the name of your contact's partner or children. Most important of all, use a system that remembers the connections for you. Beyond 40 or so connections your memory will fail. When you're thinking 'who was that designer Bill mentioned?', a programme such as Microsoft Outlook allows you to record connections and how you made them.

TIPS TO MAKE THE MOST OF ELECTRONIC MEDIA

▌ Keep abreast of developments – join relevant online discussion groups and forums, and be seen to be asking questions and making contributions.

▌ Maintain a Web presence. In the past, job seekers were advised to have their own Web page, but this probably only makes sense if you are offering some kind of product or service. However, you do need some kind of professional shop window somewhere on the Web setting out who you are and what you do. LinkedIn is an ideal tool for this purpose as you can present most elements of your CV there. Keep it up to date.

▌ Create networks – as soon as you have about 30 or so people visibly connected to you for professional reasons, that shows you are serious about using the Web for work purposes.

▌ Think about how people are going to find you using the Web. Try Googling yourself and see how long it takes. You will discover that having an article, a review or similar online usually does the trick – as long as your email address is then available.

▌ Think in terms of attracting interest rather than just chasing jobs. Becoming a content producer instead of just a consumer attracts job opportunities to your doorstep – for example, launch a blog that showcases your expertise and interests. Review books or events, contribute to online discussions, recommend people and organizations.

▮ Use voicemail both on your home number and mobile, and check your voicemails regularly. It's worrying how often key messages are left unheard.

▮ Use the tools your contacts and colleagues are using – whether it's Facebook, MySpace, LinkedIn, Twitter or other channels, work out the cultural norm for the people you are trying to reach.

▮ Some people don't want to use social media because it gives away sensitive personal information. Firstly, *never* put your CV randomly online where anyone can find it, and *never* put in a CV or anywhere online information that could be used for identity theft (don't publish your home address, date of birth, details of family members, etc., and exercise the normal extreme caution you would use when giving out banking details and credit card numbers on the Internet). Some security advisers recommend that you should create your own social network profile before someone else does using your name.

▮ That said, don't get too precious about privacy. The principle of the Web is open access to information. If you don't have any kind of electronic footprint it makes it very difficult for someone to track you down – and they will give up very quickly.

▮ Finally, having set things in motion, keep on top of your inbox. Even a hint that you don't regularly pick up your emails or use the Web as a research tool will indicate to most employers that you're past your sell by date. However you do it, it's vital that you create time to pick up and respond to email traffic at least once a day – what's the point of being out there making an impression if you can't reap the side benefits?

LOOK FOR PEOPLE, NOT JOBS

However you look for a job, you are more likely to find something through people than any other method. The same applies to an electronic job search. Although your ultimate aim is to get face-to-face meetings, and then interviews, you have to find some means of initial contact. Fortunately, most of the people you need to reach can be contacted online. However, you need to learn how to approach them. An email out of the blue is likely to be ignored, so how do you use electronic communication to reach decision makers?

Focus on one organization you are interested in. Start to look for named individuals – the people you know will have an actual need. This usually means someone who does not work in HR. Once you know who you are interested in, see if that person has a blog or Twitter account you can follow. Find out what they are interested in, and who they are talking to. Try to become part of the same online communities as the people you want to work with – ask questions (about the sector, not about jobs) and post useful information. Once you know something about a decision maker, you are in a much better position to make a direct approach. Before you do so ask yourself the most important question: 'Is there any method I can use which is better than email?'

Ask around – who do you know who works there, has worked there, been a consultant, supplier or adviser to that organization? Word of mouth referral will always get you in the door quickest. Having a strong enough message may mean that you are able to make a direct approach by telephone.

If that doesn't work, try looking through your electronic address book on LinkedIn or its equivalent – who do you know that has a connection with someone in or near your target organization? If you see a connection, pick up the phone and ask for an introduction. If you really can't make that happen, ask for an electronic introduction. And if that really isn't possible, consider making a direct approach by email. When you do so, remember the principles of any job search letter – keep it short and focused, and spell out just two or three reasons why that person might want to see you. You're after a face-to-face meeting at this stage, not a job offer.

THINK ABOUT WHO WILL BE FOLLOWING YOU

In order to follow you, someone needs to be able to find you. Having a page set up on one of the social networking sites is usually the easiest way, and because someone needs to know they have found the right person, make sure you include up-to-date information about your location, specialisms and work history. Many commentators recommend that you build a strong personal brand on the leading social networks, which isn't just about content but also about connections – your page should show that you are in touch with the right organizations, discussion groups and professional bodies. It takes no more than half an hour or so to research which online forums are right for you. Not only does this help when people are checking up on you, but also makes you visible to people searching for qualified candidates.

While positive information online will always help, anything negative will slow you down like a lead weight. Don't say anything online, even in emails that might be copied or forwarded outside your control, which conveys a negative message about your previous employer, former colleagues, how you have been treated, unhelpful recruiters, or how and why you have been rejected. You never know who is checking out your online presence and history.

Similarly, take great care about the amount of information you really want to be spread across the Web. If you want to live on the wild side, either use an online name or make sure that your on-screen confessions, conversations and photographs are visible only to trusted friends. Many employers and recruiters use the Internet for background checking. If you insist on putting embarrassing photographs of yourself in a state of undress or inebriation, you might as well bring them with you to the job interview – it's called *public domain* for a reason.

TWITTER – CAN YOU GET A JOB IN 140 CHARACTERS?

If you believe this year's buzz, Twitter is the new job tool. There are, certainly, great job sites broadcasting through Twitter. Its main uses are, however, still research and a means of following and connecting directly with key staff at organizations you want to work for.

If you are going to use Twitter as a job search tool, set up an account specially for the purpose. Before you follow anyone on Twitter, it's vital that you have a completed profile which shows, at a glance, who you are. This means a short biography, some well-chosen statements about your expertise, your approximate location, and a link to a site that recruiters can go to for more information (a blog or your LinkedIn profile). You also need a photograph or an appropriate image – *not* a cartoon or a photo of you as a toddler.

Some social media experts argue that to get jobs on Twitter you need to have thousands of followers, but if you already have that kind of presence you can pretty much do anything you want. For most people it's about having a co-ordinated way of reaching out through all forms of social media, and simple ways for people to find out about you and get in touch. However, don't overlook the simplicity of tweeting 'just got laid off, looking for a job in HR' because that alone may be enough to get your some offers of help. Don't get locked into electronic correspondence – try to turn those offers into direct (i.e. private, offline) messages and then actual conversations.

Whatever you do on Twitter, it seems that three strategies help:

1. Present a simple, understandable picture of who you are and what you do – keep it clear and simple.

2. Be consistent in your use of Twitter – become known for what you say and the way you use Twitter, and stick to it.

3. Engage with your network. Interact with the people you follow, share and pass on ideas, react to news, and keep the 'social' aspect of online networking.

Tips for searching job boards

▌ Don't try to search every single job board out there – have a broad selection of specific job boards for your role, your sector and a good selection of the national newspapers.

▌ Don't register with every job board – only select those that regularly contain jobs of interest.

▌ Search on some of the job board aggregators like Indeed or Twitter job search to expand your reach.

▌ When searching initially keep the search quite broad and then narrow each search criteria in turn.

▌ Don't just search on your old job title – jobs have different names in different organizations.

▌ Read the search tips – each job board will have different search options, and it helps to explore the advance search features.

▌ Once successful do remember to remove yourself off the job boards and make a note of those that were the most useful for future reference.

▌ Be careful with sites which charge to show you job ads – the adverts can sometimes be found on other job boards or company sites simply by searching on Google.

USE JOB BOARDS, BUT DON'T OVER-RELY ON THEM

It makes sense to ensure that you are registered with job boards that (a) handle enough traffic so that jobs relevant to you come up every week or (b) specialize in your field. Upload a good quality electronic CV, and make sure that you use the key words that a database will be searching for.

You will also find that you can use electronic job boards in unconventional ways – to identify recruitment agencies that regularly handle vacancies in your sector, for example, or search by location to find organizations on your doorstep.

You will also find it useful to look at employer job boards – where you may come across jobs you don't see advertised elsewhere. In general, job boards work best for workers whose skills can be communicated quickly in key words (e.g. computer programmers). They are best used as part of a multi-strategy approach: use job boards to work out salary levels, to spot employers and to identify recruitment consultants you can telephone. Appendix 3 contains a list of websites useful for online job hunting and career development – and you can find an expanded and updated list at www.johnleescareers.com.

'TO DO' LIST: ONLINE JOB SEARCH AND JOB APPLICATIONS

1. Be proactive. Every month new employers switch to online recruiting, so don't leave online applications out of the mix. But don't use online job search instead of other methods, or as an excuse for not speaking to real people.

2. Remember the range of resources online: vacancy listings, CV databases, Internet-based career centres, self-assessment tools useful in career search, search engines to help you to find companies and organizations, trade associations and professional bodies, as well as news and information services.

3. Check sites regularly and learn how to use the relevant search criteria.

4. Don't define your search too early, too soon. Use broad categories at first, then use search tools to refine the listings.

5. Electronic job applications, like conventional applications, need a brief covering letter. Format this as neatly as a printed letter, and cover the essentials: what the job is, why you are applying for it, what you have to offer.

6. Compose a CV in plain text ('Text Only') form in a word-processing package. Ignore all text effects except for capital letters. Do not use tabs or columns. Once you have a clear layout you can then copy and paste your CV on to a jobsite.

7. Make your electronic CV concise: be exact, be interesting and communicate your strengths. Do not clutter your online CV with unnecessary detail – think about someone searching for key words rather than a whole CV.

8. Set up more than one CV – think about the different kinds of employer that may be hunting for you online.

9. Renew your CV every month or so. If you do this, the database will usually treat your document as a new CV and put it to the top of the electronic pile.

10. Plan an electronic campaign using a range of social media tools, but have at least one 'base' where people can find your online profile easily. In the business world LinkedIn probably works best for this purpose.

Interviews and How to Survive Them

This chapter helps you with:

▮ Getting yourself shortlisted

▮ Alternative thinking to win you the interview

▮ Responding to job adverts

▮ Thinking the other side of the desk – the interviewer's mindset

▮ Dealing with interview anxiety

▮ Spotting buying signals

GETTING TO INTERVIEW STAGE

There are many books on interview techniques and strategies. The purpose of this chapter is to show you what is going on at the heart of a recruitment interview, and to offer you a few key pointers to success.

A senior colleague once told me that getting a job offer is a matter of luck. He was right up to a point. Luck is a mixture of pure chance (the roll of the dice) and the law of averages. You can't do much about chance, but you can improve the averages. Everything you do should be aimed at improving your odds. Everything that you communicate in your **message** is intended to achieve one result: to get you a meeting. What gets you an interview? To answer that, you have to begin to see life through the eyes of a recruiter.

ALTERNATIVE THINKING TO HELP YOU WIN INTERVIEWS

Refuse to play by lottery rules

Negative-minded friends and fellow career changers will tell you that even getting an interview is like playing the lottery: the odds are stacked against you. In that situation, do you keep on using the same strategy in the hope that you will be lucky? Think about all the things you could do to *guarantee* that you wouldn't get in front of a decision maker: inappropriate CV, lack of preparation, and so on. What would your chances of success be? Now think of fixing just one of those things. Do the odds improve?

Get an interview through someone you know

It sounds obvious, but it's the key to success. Employers prefer to buy things they know, and that includes people. If you come even mildly recommended, your chances of a favourable decision are much higher. Being visible to a decision maker may put you in a shortlist of one.

10 WAYS TO SHORTEN THE ODDS WHEN APPLYING TO ADVERTISED VACANCIES

You may face 200 to 1 odds of getting an interview if you apply to an advertisement. You can, however, improve the odds with these strategies:

1. Find out as much as you can about the job – Ideally by talking to someone who knows the organization well, but using *every* resource available to you, particularly the company website.

2. Make the most of initial telephone contact – If you get a chance to ask questions in advance by telephone, think about the way you present yourself and the questions you are going to ask. Don't ask questions you could discover by a fleeting glance at the website.

3. Work out the key result areas in the job – If the company doesn't say, ask. If the company doesn't know, write a draft job description and find out if it's anywhere near right.

4. Make your message clear and distinctive – The key is a short covering letter listing your relevant areas of experience and achievements as bullet points, supported by a strong CV. Think of the first page of your CV as an A4 poster offering at least half a dozen pieces of evidence that match you to the job.

5. Produce a quality CV – This sounds like kindergarten stuff, but in fact a high proportion of CVs are poorly laid out, contain errors of spelling or grammar, or miss out key information. Recruit help from a friend who knows how to lay a document out attractively on a page, using white space and different layouts for effect. Never send in a document that contains tightly packed paragraphs in a small font size. It won't be read.

6. Avoid negative messages – Don't start your covering letter 'I was made redundant in June ...' or with any other negative material. The job is hard enough without giving a recruiter reasons to reject you.

7. Prepare for screening by Human Resources – Someone in HR who may not even be working in your department could have the job of screening your application. Be clear about job titles and job reference numbers, and in your covering letter offer details that match all requirements shown as 'essential' in the job description. Pick up words and phrases used in the job advertisement: remember that applications are often read at great speed. If sending your CV by email (see Chapter 12) make sure your CV is in a commonly accessible format.

8. Offer a clear match to everything in the job advertisement – see the **£10 note concept** later in this chapter.

9. Think APPROPRIATE in terms of everything you present, including yourself – If you get an interview, remember that YOU are the message. What are you saying in terms of your dress, your behaviour, your history, your defensiveness when you answer questions?

10. Work out who makes the decision – Especially if the decision maker is also going to be your boss – the interview will give you big clues about your future working relationship. If you haven't yet met your boss, how can you decide whether you want the job?

READING THE CLUES

When you are putting yourself forward for any kind of job, even a job that doesn't exist yet, you need to be a detective. You need to read the clues. It's sad how many people go into an interview well prepared to discuss their own virtues, but with very little idea how they will suit the job. Many plan to use the interview to find out more about the job. Don't wait that long. The clues are there in front of you in any information you can lay your hands on about the job or the organization.

Key result areas

Consider the overall **purpose** of the role and key result areas (KRAs). Why does the job exist at all? It costs an employer a great deal of money to put somebody behind a desk or out on the road: anything between 1.25 and 2 times salary (including all the real costs of hire, including recruitment, training, National Insurance and overheads). See Table 13.1 for issues that you can explore before the interview *and* during it. Recruiters will tell you that employers buy experience. What clues does the advertisement or job profile give about past experience that an employer would like to see repeated?

Table 13.1 Asking questions about key result areas in a job

1. **What is the purpose of the job?**
   Why is the job there at all? What headache, problem or opportunity does it address?

2. **How big is the job?**
   Is this a big job? Does it have a lot of leverage?

3. **How does the job fit into the organization?**
   How will my work depend on/affect others?

4. **Who does the job report to?**
   Who takes the flak? Who is my direct boss? What is his/her boss like?

5. **What specific skills or knowledge are required?**
   Will I be out of my depth? What will I need to learn quickly?

6. **What are the main problems to be solved, and how variable (or consistent) are they?**
   What can go wrong? What skills will I need to fix problems? How did previous post holders survive?

7. **What or who controls the job holder's freedom to act or make decisions?**
   Do I need permission for every action I take? Do I need to be a self-starter?

8. **What end results does the job exist to achieve? How is performance measured?**
   What are the key results? How will they be measured?

9. **What kind of people have done well/badly in this job in the past?**
   Who thrives, who survives, who sinks?

10. **What kind of results really matter?**
    A probing question which you can put to the decision maker: find the right words to suit you, but try something along the lines of 'in 6 months' time you might be sitting in your garden or on a train, thinking about this appointment. How will you know if you have been successful? What will have happened or changed?'

Problems and opportunities

Where is the company going? Is it in a shrinking market and fighting its corner, or in a growth market and exploiting new opportunities? Look around for background information, using business-related search engines. Recruiters love to talk about their company's successes, and you can prompt this by knowing something about new products or services or brands in development, takeover plans or geographical growth.

Company culture

Every organization has its own personality. Some companies are naturally conservative and cautious, others dynamic. Some companies expect their employees to work long hours, others judge people by results. Many twenty-first century companies expect their employees to be up to date with this week's trends or technological advances. Try to work out the real values of the organization, not just the ones they boast about. You will learn a lot about company culture from websites and press articles, but even more by finding someone who can tell you the inside story – someone who works there already, has worked their recently or knows the organization well.

INTERVIEW PREPARATION

There is a mental and a practical side to interview preparation: thinking the right way, then doing the right things. Preparation of every kind is the key. Don't be passive when it comes to interviews: 'I'll just turn up and see what they ask me.' You wouldn't approach your bank for a loan or go into a business presentation like that. You'd prepare materials, evidence and presentation statements, you'd anticipate questions. Your career matters even more.

Avoiding interview stress

You can't. Stress is a necessary part of the process. The important thing is to use the energy that comes out of a stressful situation to your advantage, allowing it to make you more responsive, more creative. Make sure that panic doesn't lead you into a little safety corner called 'I can't do any more', which is another way of failing to anticipate and plan.

The word anxiety has its roots in 'choking'. When you're anxious, you feel you're in a narrow, confined space. You refuse to see openings and ways out. Narrowness is for bigots, people who want to withdraw from the bright light of creation into their shells. Stress is often the mind finding it hard to cope with possible outcomes. Look at your anxiety sideways, upside-down, whatever it takes to find something in it, paradoxically, that you enjoy (it may be excitement or uncertainty). That way you become far more open to possibilities, and to letting the process look after itself. In hindsight, most of the things you worry about in relation to jobs matter very little in the long run.

Your mindset

The prospect of hanging, said the writer Samuel Johnson, concentrates the mind wonderfully. Interviews can do the same. You can easily generate a particular mindset that shapes the whole experience, as in Figure 13.1. Next read through Table 13.2 to see how many myths you have created around job interviews, and what they are really about.

It's interesting to observe a recruitment interview and then ask the participants to say how it went. Interviewees are usually poor judges of their own performance. In an interview you suffer from information overload – there's just too much going on. The person who makes the picture dark or light is almost entirely *you*. You can look at the same questions, the same reactions, in terms of light or shadow. Is the glass half full or half empty? You can learn something from every interview experience.

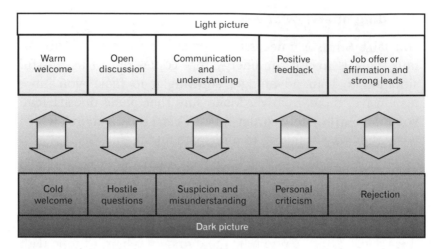

Light picture				
Warm welcome	Open discussion	Communication and understanding	Positive feedback	Job offer or affirmation and strong leads
Cold welcome	Hostile questions	Suspicion and misunderstanding	Personal criticism	Rejection
Dark picture				

Figure 13.1   Alternative ways of seeing the interview process

Table 13.2   Interviews: the essential truths

Preparation	There is no such thing as enough preparation. Do what you can, but try to do at least four times more than you think is enough.
Dress code	If you dress like a banker, you may be employed as a banker and paid a banker's salary. If you dress like a new age traveller …. Read the signals, and try to look like you're already on the payroll; it's one time in life when conformity really matters. Dump your coat with the receptionist, maybe even your briefcase – it helps to reinforce the feeling that you already work there.
Behaviour	Behaviour, like dress, sends a huge message. If you wanted to wear a sandwich board into the interview, would it say 'Employ me, I'll fit in' or 'Born to be wild. Please subsidise'? Here again, remember that selectors love to minimize risk.

Decision makers	There's little point strutting your stuff in front of someone who has no influence over the appointment decision.
Openings and closings	... should be clear and positive. Think about what you're going to say. Research suggests that interviewers are most influenced by what you say at the very beginning and very end of the interview.
Prejudice	... which simply means 'prejudging'. We all do it. If your interviewer is unreasonably prejudiced against you for some reason that has nothing to do with the job (age, skin colour, politics), do you really want to work there anyway?
CV	If your CV lets you down at interview, that's because you haven't really thought about what it's saying. It should, essentially, suggest that you are the answer to an employer's wish list. If you're using interview time to recover from CV failure, you really have set yourself an uphill battle.
Qualifications	There are well over 20,000 accredited qualifications in the UK. How do employers tell one from another? On the whole, they can't. The employer who wants a 'relevant degree' may just feel flattered if surrounded by fawning graduates. Focus on the needs of the job itself in terms of experience and know-how.

The solo interview

You've heard of the Zen idea of one hand clapping? Let me introduce to you the concept of interviewer-free interviewing.

Find time, on your own, to reflect on the interview. Think of it as a time management exercise: a short window of opportunity for you to impress. Look at the requirements of the job, known or guessed. Now have a conversation with the best part of yourself, not the negative voice that's whispering 'You can't *do* this!', but your better half, the one that's prepared to have a go. The solo interview both anticipates questions and places the job within a much larger pattern. You'll know what the big questions are, but Table 13.3 offers some prompts.

Table 13.3   Questions to prompt your interview preparation

▮ What in my past makes me a good choice?

▮ How would this job be a great opportunity to use my skills/experience/gifts?

▮ How would this job be a good stepping stone?

▮ How does it fit into my life plan?

▮ Who will I help if I do this job?

▮ How does this job/company fit my personal and work values?

▮ Since employers buy experience, which parts of my past are going to be in my window display?

▮ Which of my past achievements are most relevant here?

▮ What presentation statements do I need to rehearse/improve?

▮ Why do I want this job?

▮ What problems will I solve in the job?

▮ What special combination of skills do I have that no-one else can offer?

▮ What will it *feel* like to do this job? In the first week? The first month? After a year?

▮ How will I know if I am successful?

▮ Which parts of the job will be really me?

▮ Will this job make me happier than I am now? How would others tell?

Get your message straight

Too many job changers try to win a job by pitching an unclear or untargeted message. Your message is contained in everything you send out (letters, CV, emails) and everything you say. It's what you say when someone asks you at a party 'what are you going to do next?'. Think of it as a highly concentrated burst of data.

When people are recovering from being treated badly by a past employer, feeling desperate enough to take anything, or they don't know what they are looking for, their message can become a series of negatives. You'll get sympathy, but you won't get past the first interview stage.

You will quickly learn that decision makers want to try to sum you up pretty quickly, and they are really only interested in their problems, not yours. Therefore it helps to prepare strong presentation statements (see Chapter 7). It's also vitally important to both job search and networking that you have a short, coherent message that sums up what you are about.

Your Two-Breath Message

Learn to compose a short, two-breath message. Something that sums up who you are and where you want to get to. Two sentences which sound something like this:

Your Two-Breath Message

'I want to do a job that allows me to do A and B and C ... in an organization that's doing X and Y and Z.'

The A and B and C are your motivated skills – the things you do best. X, Y and Z describe the key ingredients in the mix as far as your next employer is concerned. You might be talking about what the organization actually produces or the services it provides. You might also talk about the style (high-tech, customer-focused ...) and culture of the organization (private, public, blue chip, privately owned ...).

Employers, recruitment consultants and networking contacts respond well to this kind of message because it is clear, succinct, memorable and packed with enthusiasm. What's more, people respond in a completely different way compared to simply asking about job opportunities. It's a bit like the TV show 'Ready Steady Cook' – you dump the ingredients in front of someone and ask for a good recipe. They say things like 'You know, you really should talk to my friend Rashid …' or 'Have you thought about talking to Acme Industries …' or, best of all, 'That sounds to me like …' – when they identify a sector or field you haven't yet fallen across.

This kind of message is also great for interviews (especially when you meet the question 'tell me about yourself' or 'why do you want this job?') and very handy when someone at a barbecue or party says 'what would you like to do, ideally?'

SHINING AT THE INTERVIEW

At interview, be yourself, but the best half of yourself.

John Courtis

What on earth are they going to ask?

Prepare well, do your homework about the organization and the job, plan for interview questions, and you can shine at interview. Others will be trying to 'wing it' without thinking the activity through. Begin by putting yourself on the other side of the desk and adopting the interviewer's point of view. Starting with the key result areas of the job, what questions are almost certain to come up?

See the **Key Checklists** in Chapter 17 for more details of difficult interview questions, and see the relevant chapters in *Job Interviews: Top Answers to Tough Questions* and *Why You? – CV Messages to Win Jobs*.

Questions focused on skills

Supply *evidence* of your skills. Even relatively sophisticated competence-based interviews are essentially saying 'You say you have skill X. Tell me when you used this skill successfully.' Work out the skills that will make a real difference to the job, and match them to the skills that you know you exercise with ease and enthusiasm.

The £10 note concept

No, this isn't advice on bribery and corruption, but a way of getting you to read the clues. Think of the job as a £10 note torn in half:

Look at that ragged edge where the bank note has been torn. That's what the job should look like to you: a series of connections. Each connection is a clue to the way a post holder might be successful, a piece of information about a key result area.

Now think of yourself as the other half of that bank note. That's the mental image you should have in mind, so you can communicate this to the employer, and everything you do in the interview should be saying, for example, 'I understand that you need problem-solving skills. I'm good at coming up with solutions to problems under pressure. This is when I did it.'

Minimum qualifications

Employers are clear about the qualifications they *think* are needed for the job. How far are these requirements justified by the job itself? How many are there just to filter out candidates, or to massage a manager's ego? If you lack the named qualifications, demonstrate how your experience compensates, and is maybe even more up to date or relevant than paper qualifications. As with any apparent hurdle: address the problem directly, don't avoid it.

Your weak points

How will you cope in a crisis or under pressure? It's difficult for an interviewer to gauge this at interview. Some will try to put you under stress during the interview. Better interviewers will ask you about times in the past when you overcame challenges while working to strict deadlines, or times when everything went wrong and you found some way of coping.

Interpreting interview language

Listen for verbal clues: the snippets of information the interviewer gives you about the job, the questions that are asked – all these things give you huge clues about the job, but also about the language you should use. If the questions are all about targets and performance, match your language.

Listen for checklists

Be aware of the structure of an interview. Some interviewers want to jump straight in with a question of the 'Tell me about yourself' variety (technically, a high-order, open question). Others will have a game of two halves in mind: a first half where they go through a checklist of the things they want to know, and a second half where they probe things more deeply and get a chance to discover some background. If you sense a 'checklist' approach, don't go into too much detail with each answer, since it irritates the interviewer. You can always give a brief answer and then offer more detail if invited.

Hiring winners

Employers are geared to a continuous process of success. So naturally they want to hire winners. Recruiting organizations are happy to talk about potential, but the primary question is: 'Where's the evidence of past achievement?' Essentially what a recruiting employer is looking for is a win/win: both parties get something good out of the deal. Once an employer has decided you are the one, then an interview turns much more into a negotiation: 'If I offer you X, then you will achieve Y ...'.

Looking at the big picture, recruiters are likely to spot winners by asking questions that all fit, ultimately, within a six-point structure, as shown in Table 13.1.

Table 13.4   The six-point structure at the heart of all interview questions

1. **What brought you to us?** Why did you apply? What is your career plan?

2. **What do you have to offer?** What do you bring to the party? What solutions do you have to offer which match our problems?

3. **How well do you understand us?** Have you worked out how we tick as an organization? Have you worked out the key result areas of the job?

4. **Who are you?** What kind of person are you? Are you like us? Will you fit in? What will you add to a team?

5. **Why *you*?** – rather than someone else with the same general profile? What puts you ahead of the pack? What's your unique selling point?

6. **What will it take to bring you on board?** What will you cost us? How do we have to motivate and develop you to retain you in the future?

COMPETENCY-BASED SELECTION PROCEDURES

Currently employers are eager to measure competencies as well as skills. A 'competency' is in fact a combination of know-how, skills, attitude and demonstrated behaviours – all directed towards outcomes which actively assist an employer. A competency is not just about what you do, but how you do it, and to what level.

Prepare by looking carefully at any information you can find about competencies which are considered essential or useful for the job. You may be given a written statement listing the competencies and inviting you to give detailed information about times when you have used them. Alternatively, you may have to make an educated guess (from the job description and information about the organization) at the five or six top competencies for the role.

A strategy used by a number of employers now is to give you a list of up to 20 competencies, and to ask you to write a written statement against each one. If you do so, look back on this information carefully when you plan your interview performance. Ideally, have one or two ideas up your sleeve of things that you have not mentioned in writing.

If you are not asked for written evidence, don't make the mistake of thinking that competency-based questions won't come up. They will usually be flagged by the introductory words 'Tell me about a time when …'. Look at what you believe to be the main competencies required by the role and plan short, upbeat examples of what you have actually done, and when, and what the end results were.

THE FINISHING LINE – THE END OF THE INTERVIEW

Timeframe

Listen for a change of tense. Most interviews begin by looking at your past. Indeed, some careers counsellors say that's exactly the problem with a CV – it's a historical document. If that's all it is, then it's an obituary. It only talks about your past. To address the needs of the job, address the future. Try to encourage the employer to see you in the job. Suggest ideas and possibilities for the company: it weaves you into the fabric of the company's future.

Buying signals

We all demonstrate buying signals, and some people are trained to spot them. If a market trader is trying to sell you something, he watches your buying signals carefully: you might try a garment on for size, explain its virtues to a friend or check how much cash is in your wallet. A less obvious buying signal is that you ask questions about the product: Is there a guarantee? How long will the battery last? Interest is a powerful buying signal.

The first, but perhaps least obvious, buying signal in an interview is when the interviewer starts to talk about the present, and then the future. Stay with that, encourage it. The stronger the image in the interviewer's mind of you sitting in a real office at a real desk, the greater the chance it will become reality.

Other buying signals? An obvious one is when the interview turns to point 6 in Table 13.4: how much will you cost? No-one discusses terms unless they are interested. This is *not* the time to say how little you would settle for. Bring the discussion back to key result areas, to the value you can add to the organization. Ask the employer what he had in mind when he decided to advertise the vacancy or start seeing people. Only as a last resort should you mention what you are actually looking for, because you're in danger of setting far too low a limit. If you absolutely have to mention a figure, base it on hard knowledge of what others in similar positions are earning, or aspire to, and then add a bit. Remember that employers are buyers, and buyers always feel happier if they can knock you down from your initial price.

Never, ever, fall into the trap of answering the question 'how much do you need?'. You should aim to be paid what you are worth to an employing organization, in relation to the value you add, the professionalism you deliver and the size of the problems you can solve. The final factor is what the market will bear, but at this stage of the process – at this stage only – you have the upper hand. They want you. They are falling in love with you. And just for a fleeting moment you have some leverage.

Closing with enthusiasm

The first and last things you say at interview will probably be remembered more than anything else you say, so think particularly about what you say as the interview closes. Always have some good, detailed questions you can ask about the job and the organization (see below). This might be a time to get across one or two key messages (see Exercise 13.2). You might also ask for the job. Failing that, the question 'is there anything else I need to tell you that would help you come to an appointment decision?' might take the employer into buying mode.

Questions *you* should ask as the interview closes

When asked 'do you have any questions for us?' too many candidates politely say 'no, you've covered everything in great detail, thank you'. Wrong answer! Say this, and the interviewer feels you have little real interest in the job. Questions will arise from the interview, but prepare three or four good ones in advance. Good ones come in two types: questions that show you have thought carefully about key result areas, and questions about the future of the job that help the interviewer to picture you in the post. The main thing is to show interest and enthusiasm. Before you ask any questions at the end of the interview, **say something positive** about the role. Then your question sounds like *your* buying signal: you like the job so much you want to know more.

You won't get the chance to ask more than a couple of questions at the end of an interview. If one or two pop up during the meeting, take your cue from the interviewer as to the topic. Your main chance is, however, at the end, and the main purpose of your questions is message reinforcement, not information gathering. You want to leave a final positive impression about your awareness of the role and your strong interest in it. You can decide later whether you want the job; for now, make only positive noises.

A couple of danger areas remain. Avoid asking questions about selection criteria: they so often sound as if you are asking for special treatment or believe that the interviewer doesn't know what he's doing. And don't ask anything you could have discovered by spending 5 minutes looking at the company website.

REJECTION

It's trite to say that you shouldn't feel 'rejected' if turned down by an employer. Recover in your own time, and try not to take it personally: people are rejected for all kinds of arbitrary reasons. In any job search you will receive more rejections than acceptances. You will hear the word 'no' more often than you hear the word 'yes'. This is a neutral statistical fact which *has nothing to do with you*. Even the very best sales people in the world work on the basis that they need to hear the word 'no' at least three times before they get a 'yes'. The problem is that when it is 'no' to you, it can knock you off balance. Be careful not to use it as evidence to support 'Yes, but' thinking: 'I knew I was unemployable ...'.

INTERVIEWS WITH RECRUITMENT CONSULTANTS

Recruitment consultants are, of course, professional selectors who make a living finding workers to fill particular vacancies for client employers. Remember that the recruitment consultant will not make the final selection decision, but is a gatekeeper between you and the decision maker. You are dealing with an **intermediary**, i.e. someone who is both a broker and barrier. If a recruitment consultant is talking to you, it is likely to be because they hope to place you in a role. Few recruiters will give you an interview otherwise, unless they are hungry for information about your market sector. Some pointers:

▮ The consultant acts as the employer's eyes and ears, but will see things in an even sharper perspective: if there's something unacceptable about your dress code, interview behaviour, CV or qualifications, the consultant will be highly attuned to it. The reason is simple: a recruitment consultant wants to put forward a **safe bet**.

▮ Therefore, you need to know what buttons you are pressing in terms of safety, reliability or energy and enthusiasm. Get the recruiter to describe to you what he or she is really looking for, and respond to that.

▮ Finally, it really pays to encourage your consultant to switch from gatekeeper to lifelong friend. Ask for professional advice on your interview technique or the state of the market. Be flexible and available. Don't let your doubts about recruitment consultancies or agencies influence this one interview or decision. Agencies need a flow of enthusiastic, committed candidates. Just as you will show an employer how your presence in the workplace will solve problems, be a problem solver to any intermediaries.

EXERCISE 13.1 – TEMPORARY TERRORISM

Just for a few moments, imagine the worst. You face an interviewer with a huge overdraft and an even bigger headache. She's having a bad day, and will look at everything you have put forward in a bad light. Be that person just for a few moments. What's the worst question you could ask yourself, knowing your own weaknesses? What's the second worst question? What areas of preparation are you weakest on?

Where do you think your skills are inadequate? Where do you lack evidence of achievement?

Prepare for that interview, and the real one will be a dream. But now it's vital to remember how easy it was to see the whole thing negatively. Why is it that you are happier seeing the interview as a nightmare? Why are you more prepared to believe a poor self-image than a positive one? If it's all about anticipation, what happens if you tell yourself how brilliant you will be? Sounds corny, but try it. Self-confidence is just as powerful a career change tool as skills, experience or knowledge.

EXERCISE 13.2 – SHOPPING LIST

Find a vacancy that interests you, perhaps through a published advertisement. Ring or write for a job description.

Take an A4 piece of paper and divide it into two vertical columns. Interrogating the job description, write out the employer's **shopping list**, everything the recruiter is looking for, using the following checklist:

▌ List all the 'wanted' elements: qualifications, experience, know-how, etc.

▌ Work out what's essential, and what's desirable.

▌ Now use your own industry knowledge to work out all the stuff between the lines: the unstated assumptions.

▌ Finally, try to think yourself in the interviewer's shoes. If you were interviewing, what would you really be looking for? What achievements would you recognize?

Now, in the right-hand column, write in your matching claims *and* evidence. Think in both terms – you should be able to say what you can do, and give an example of an achievement that substantiates your claim. Go back to skill clips and presentation statements in Chapter 7.

EXERCISE 13.3 – THE POLITICIAN'S TRICK

Listen to a seasoned politician being interviewed on the radio. One thing you may notice is that, no matter what questions are asked, the minister always manages to make three or four strong points about government policy. The questions just provide an opportunity: the airtime is being used as a way of getting a particular message across.

You can use the same technique. **Step 1**: look at the *key result areas* in a job, and ask yourself 'What *three points* is it vital that I make during this interview?' **Step 2**: write them down, and rehearse a clear, concise way of talking about them. **Step 3**: make sure you get those three points across at interview. Why three points? Politicians know that their listeners can only hold a few ideas in mind at one time. Interviewers are much the same.

'MUST DO' LIST

☑ Practise being a detective, picking up vital clues about the employer's needs.

☑ Don't go to any interview without exploring the purpose of the job, and key result areas.

☑ Think of yourself as a product which solves the employer's problems.

☑ Learn how to spot buying signals during the interview.

☑ Try anticipating an employer's risk aversion in your interview preparation.

☑ What strategies are you going to use to ensure that at interview you are *the best you there is*?

☑ Prepare for the worst and best interview questions. See *Job Interviews: Top Answers To Tough Questions* by John Lees and Matthew Deluca (McGraw-Hill, 2008).

☑ Use the interview checklists in Chapter 17.

How to Love the Job You've Got

This chapter looks at ways to:

▌ Learn to use tools from your career transition to apply to the rest of your working life

▌ Acquire job survival skills

▌ Turn your next job into a success

▌ Manage and negotiate your future

Furious activity is no substitute for understanding.

H.H. Williams

CHANGING THE WAY YOU THINK OF YOUR CAREER

This chapter introduces you to the idea of managing your career, but for a great deal more information see *Take Control of Your Career* (McGraw-Hill, 2006).

Most of us have inherited a strong idea of a career. We think of it as progression up a ladder of growth and success. This model has been put under considerable pressure in the past 25 years, and has been stretched to breaking point during the last recession in the UK where redundancy has become increasingly part of our everyday experience. The latest recession has been unusual in that it has hit across all sectors and regions, and as a result has probably had more impact on the nation's understanding of work stability and career management than any economic events since the early 1980s.

Fewer people than ever have a 'job for life'. Where our parents' generation enjoyed high job security in return for company loyalty, workers of the twenty-first century work under a psychological contract under which employers do not guarantee employment, and employees have to take responsibility for their own career development and their own employability. For some this has meant reinventing themselves and their skills, and also seriously rethinking working relationships, looking at work as a series of projects rather than as long-term relationships. Hence the rise of terms like 'giganomics' – when work feels more like a 'gig' or a one-off task, your focus is on multiple clients rather than a single employer.

What is career management?

All too often we think that career management is about having a career *plan*: a clear timetable for how you will move from one rung of the ladder to the next. So many career changers believe 'I am the only person in the world who doesn't have a career plan'. In fact, very few people have their lives planned out that precisely. We usually start with a problem such as 'I need a job' or 'I hate my job' and then look around for some kind of action. Most career 'plans' look something like Figure 14.1.

This is the way we are taught to fix life problems, by using A–Z thinking: I have a problem, I fix the problem. This is why so many of us make a job change by taking the first vaguely suitable job that comes along, almost as if you are going to plan a holiday by picking on the first flight you find on a departures board at the airport. A great strategy for a spontaneous adventure, but perhaps not the best way of deciding how to spend most of your waking life.

Figure 14.1 A conventional career strategy

The difficulty is that we don't fix the problem, we fix the symptoms. And sometimes this means that people actually take their problem with them. Anyone who is seriously thinking 'I need to change jobs' should ask themselves 'can I fix the job I've got?'. We need to look properly at ideas before making decisions.

Should I have a career plan?

I have come to believe that career management isn't about having a step-by-step plan for your whole life. It's more about being able to respond to the here and now: to recognize the opportunities that life offers.

The problem is that we use the idea 'I should plan my career' as a way of avoiding the issue. It seems too big a project. Naturally we also beat ourselves up for not doing it. As Chapter 1 shows, we have no difficulty at all finding reasons not to have a great career. And so it follows that we will find any avoidance strategy to avoid a career review. Why? Maybe because you'll have to ask yourself difficult questions. Maybe because you instinctively know that something needs changing, and a review will require activity. Avoidance strategies usually come out of a reluctance to change, even if this means moving from an uncomfortable position. The status quo is very attractive, and you will even adopt a language that locks you into it: *Don't rock the boat … Better the devil you know … The grass is always greener …* .

At least begin by looking at your major areas of dissatisfaction, and allow yourself to imagine (without any commitment) what is possible to fix where you are. Sometimes this might mean changing the rules, using some lateral thinking or surprising your boss with a radical thought. But aren't these the skills that your employer expects you to use anyway?

CONDUCTING YOUR OWN CAREER REVIEW

Here are some pointers to conducting a career review for yourself. This takes time, a little imagination and some fairly robust strategies to cope with 'Yes, but' thinking.

Past performance

Look at your work history. Understand and accept what has happened in your past. You don't have to repeat mistakes or experiences. Use the tools contained in this book to assess all the things you have to offer: your know-how, your skills, your achievements, your attitude to work. Focus on your strengths, and work out your wish list of how you'd like your job to be.

Where are you now?

Look at your current job as objectively as you can. What's the real problem? What are the opportunities? If push comes to shove, what can you *really* change? Review your progress and update your 'message' every 3 months. This means keeping a personal portfolio of work you have done, problems you have overcome, where you have added value to your organization and made a difference. This will provide the basis for you to assess your skills, achievements, development needs and future opportunities. It will also enable you to know your true worth and marketability.

Self-review regularly: at least once a year, fill one side of A4 with a review of

▮ your progress this year

▮ your main achievements

▮ how you think your boss sees you

▮ your learning plan

▮ how you are stocking your lifeboat in case this ship sinks.

Improve your offer

Learn new skills or become more proficient at old ones. Read widely and keep up to date with the changing environment and both the demands and opportunities it creates. Don't restrict networking and informational interviews to times when you are undertaking job search. Seek out people who can give you cutting-edge ideas, tell you about interesting projects and keep you informed about industry developments.

Don't get so bogged down in your job that you miss learning opportunities. Make sure you go to conferences and exhibitions and industry seminars, even if this is in your own time.

Communicate your achievements

Make your successes known. This doesn't mean point-scoring or bragging, but making sure that key people know how you have added value to the organization. Be willing to share information about *how* you achieved your results so that others can learn from you. Understand what is expected from you, by whom and when. Remember that if your boss changes, then the expectations are likely to change too. Your attitude towards change will say much about you, especially when others are fighting against it.

Be ready, almost at the drop of a hat, to communicate:

▌ your key successes this year

▌ your top motivated skills and preferred working contexts

▌ at least three suggestions of ways you could work more effectively and create new opportunities for your employer.

Become 'politically aware'

Organizational survivors are often not those with the best skills, but those who are most keenly tuned to office politics. Make sure you are seen as an innovator, as a key player, not as dead wood. Understand what your boss really wants in life, and help to provide it. Be very careful around new bosses: re-establish your presence just as if you were starting a new job.

Look for win/win

We work to become, not to acquire.

Elbert G. Hubbard

Planning ahead doesn't mean knowing all the moves, but is about having a set of personal objectives: a wish list. This will relate to the skills you want to use and develop, your learning, and the scope and size of your job. Organizations find it difficult to interpret personal wish lists until they are communicated in terms that are attractive: your offer. Show how both parties gain: win/win. But don't assume that the employer sees a win just because you do. Good salespeople will tell you that win/win really means 'This is how I see that I win/This is how you see that you win'.

Get more out of appraisals

Try the **suggestion box** concept. This doesn't mean the traditional box in the works canteen which gets a half-baked idea once in a blue moon. Go to your next appraisal with two things – a summary of what has gone well in the last 6 months, and a positive suggestion that will assist your career development and help the needs of your employer in the half-year ahead.

Managers get worn down by conventional appraisals because they are faced with problems that they find very difficult to solve. If you go into an appraisal with a positive offer couched in win/win language, it's much more difficult for an employer to say 'no'.

Watch out for panic signals

It's surprising how quickly people move from moderate satisfaction to 'I hate this job'. It's equally surprising how often a client who tells me 'I need to be out of here today' can switch to positive ideas about fixing the job from the inside. Still, it's true that we can outgrow jobs. It's no bad thing to leave an organization when you have done as much as you can.

One other key point about retention: research data show that people leave managers, not organizations. Ask yourself: is it the job, the organization or the person? And the next question has to be 'What can I fix?'. You may find that your organization is happy to change your job or transfer you to a new manager. You may be more of an asset than the person making your life miserable.

Act positive

Acting positively isn't about walking round with a fixed grin, flattering the boss or supporting junk ideas. But it does mean that people in your team should think about you as the kind of person who will give things a go, take on board new ideas or go the extra mile. You don't have to undergo a personality transplant: just listen for all of those 'Yes, but' reactions, and don't act on them. Be willing to look at new ideas, and don't get caught up in a culture of office cynicism. It's all too easy to say 'It'll never work', and easier still to act on it.

Being positive doesn't mean being a doormat, either: have your own agenda, and put forward ideas that will work for you as well as for your organization. Usually these will be relatively short-term in nature, and will relate to things which are top of the organizational agenda.

NEGOTIATE YOUR FUTURE

The early twenty-first century is an odd time to be in work. It's a time of major redundancies and stock market uncertainty, but also huge skill shortages and retention problems. Which means that skills are still being sought, projects undertaken, goals achieved – but not necessarily in the jobs or organizations that you imagined they would be. One of the ways you can become more objective about your 'offer' is to think of yourself as an external supplier, a one-person Plc.

Use the 'You Plc' exercise at the end of this chapter to work out the value that you currently offer your employer, and how you can adapt or improve in the future.

When job seeking you should only negotiate pay when the employer has decided he or she can't live without you. Similarly the best time to renegotiate your salary is when your employer is most aware of your 'offer', most aware of the value you bring to an organization. See Figure 14.2 for tips.

DON'T be tempted to talk about what you 'need'. Talk about the value you add.

DON'T jump in with a figure too soon. Spell out your 'offer' first.

DON'T guess on what the job is worth. Find out the upper and lower points of the salary typically paid for this kind of job. Rehearse all the reasons why you should be paid in the top 25% of this band.

DON'T hold a gun to your employer's head like 'I am getting offers from ...' or 'I'll be forced to look for another job'. Do that and you have no offer, just a threat.

DON'T focus just on the past: describe what you can do in the future.

....

DO focus on what you are bringing to the deal, remembering to explain in 'win' language which means something to your employer.

DO – if the employer won't move on the money – ask for an early review date, or an enhanced bonus, or some other way of improving the package quickly.

DO look at alternatives. If you can't get a pay rise, can you use your position of leverage to make the job more interesting?

DO negotiate like a pro. Remember the 'salami' technique. Work out the difference between what you want and what the employer will offer. Divide it by 12, then say 'We're talking about a difference of £XX per month. You must pay more than that in photocopying/coffee/stamps ...'.

DO look, act and sound like a person already doing the job you want to be promoted into.

Figure 14.2 Tips on getting a pay rise or promotion

EXERCISE 14.1 – 'YOU PLC' IN 8 STEPS

When you are marketing yourself to employers, it's sometimes useful to think of yourself as a one-person corporation: 'You Plc'. This is an idea championed in William Bridges' famous book *Creating You & Co.*, and adapted here as a tool for helping you to undertake your own career review. Take a blank piece of paper. Look at what sets you ahead of the competition by answering these questions:

1. What is the **main** service you provide to your current organization (e.g. problem solving, contributing new ideas, coaching, managing relationships)?

2. How does this activity match the needs of the organization?

3. What results have you achieved?

4. What do you have to offer which is a better solution to your organization's needs than similar services from other people? (Think of other potential suppliers, internal or external.)

5. What do you think is the main service you have to offer your own or another organization in **future**?

6. How can you improve, update and communicate your offer more effectively?

7. What new results do you think you can achieve?

8. Why do you think that your future service will be a better solution for an organization's needs than others can provide? (Again, include both internal and external suppliers.)

EXERCISE 14.2 – TIME BALANCE

How would you like your time to be balanced in your ideal job?

Using Table 14.1, consider your present (or recent) job and your ideal job. Give each of the following a percentage score so that your total equals 100:

Table 14.1   Time balance

Present job		Ideal job
	Working independently Working on my own without distraction. Working things out, being given space to sort out a problem or finish a piece of work, writing something, having time to reflect …	
	Having own area of responsibility within a team Being responsible for own results	

	but having colleagues around. Having ready access to the ideas and encouragement of other people ...	
	Working 1:1 Explaining, persuading, influencing, selling, coaching, managing, teaching ...	
	Attending meetings Meeting to deal with agendas, share information and make collective decisions ...	
	Working in active teams Group problem solving, planning brainstorming ideas, reviewing, getting things done, training, motivating ...	
	Extending your network Telephoning new contacts, networking, meeting plenty of new people, going to conferences, seminars ...	
	Working with an audience Public speaking, performing, entertaining, giving talks, informing larger groups ...	
	Other Define this yourself:	
100%	**Total**	**100%**

'MUST DO' LIST

☑ Prepare yourself to take control of your career, because no-one else will.

☑ Decide now how you can remotivate yourself to undertake a personal career review regularly.

☑ Find a coach or mentor. If your employer doesn't offer one, recruit your own – even if it's just to look at problems and help you to suggest solutions.

☑ Start a file or notebook to record activities, achievements and contacts. Make the first sheet your wish list of how you would like your work to be.

☑ Make a diary date 3 months ahead to update your review.

☑ Look at your life/work balance. What are your priorities? What would you like to change?

For further discussion on

▌ planning your career

▌ avoiding career traps and career limiting actions

▌ renegotiating your job

▌ understanding and shaping the way your organization sees you

▌ rethinking your life/work balance

see John Lees' *Take Control of Your Career* (McGraw-Hill, 2006)

Portfolio Careers and Beyond

This chapter looks at:

▮ Continuous change: refreshing your career

▮ New choices in working arrangements

▮ Temporary, interim and flexible working arrangements

▮ Building a portfolio career

Built to last now means built to change.
                                    Stan Davis and Christopher Meyer

CAREER REFRESHMENT

This is a book that acknowledges the importance of work. Finding the right kind of work can feed you. However, the job you love now may not be a job you want to do forever. Our motivations for work and our sense of the rewards we get out of it change as we grow older. Careers need refreshing from time to time. We are becoming increasingly attuned to the idea that we will probably change career paths several times during a working lifetime. In other words, your long-term focus may not just be on getting a job you'll love, but on getting a series of jobs you'll love, and perhaps doing some of those jobs at the same time.

Things to come

Charles Handy predicted that in the twenty-first century more than 50% of jobs would be something other than 'proper' full-time jobs: part-time, flexi-hours, fixed-term contract, temporary, self-employed or some other variation. He hasn't got it far wrong. There has been huge attention to flexible working, which of course means different things to employers and workers. You may want to leave work early to go to a night class, or bank flexitime so you can regularly take long weekends. Your employer might want you to be part of the 24/7 economy.

It's something of a cliché to say that work is changing fast. The key question is how we anticipate these changes, and how we make sense of them. One of the strongest ways of flexing in response to the marketplace is to rethink the nature of work itself, and to become increasingly open to the idea of becoming a portfolio worker.

PORTFOLIO CAREERS

Pipe dream or possibility?

You may have heard of the 'portfolio' career, but what is it, and does it really exist? The answer is an unequivocal 'yes'. The term is used to describe a deliberate choice, mixing and matching different kinds of work to find the ideal balance, which will be about time, flexibility and travel, but also about the kind of work you do. A marketing specialist works for 2 days a week at corporate rates, subsiding her work as a lecturer. Some hold down three or four appointments simultaneously; for example, an HR consultant who also works as a board member of a health trust, a non-executive director of a publishing company and a charity trustee.

One driving factor here is the decline of the well-funded company pension scheme, a feature of the late twentieth century marketplace that encouraged both long service and early retirement. Problems in funding such schemes mean that many of us have to work longer to fund our retirement, but as we become increasingly more responsible for our own pension fund, there is also less pressure for people to stick to traditional working models. If it seems likely that we will have to work longer into old age, then we may want to prepare for the journey ahead by thinking about the kind of skills we would like to use.

Is portfolio working a middle-aged luxury?

It may be true that portfolio careers are available largely to older workers. This is partly because it's more important for younger people to establish a track record in permanent work, and possibly because older workers have sometimes resolved financial needs or moved beyond them. However, repeated surveys point to the growth of self-employment, and this means that increasingly we are getting used to the idea of not having a regular pay cheque. Financial security, of course, is a factor, simply because you can cope with a variable income. If your income has always been variable, adding different kinds of work to the mix is far from threatening. So we have the self-employed joiner who also buys and sells antiques, the part-time HR specialist who works as a freelance book editor, and the lecturer who runs her own business as an equal opportunities trainer. Even though few of these people would automatically recognize themselves as 'portfolio workers', they are living examples of a new, pragmatic and highly inventive method of working.

In recent years portfolio working has become something that far more people think about. In the early 1990s only about 10% of executive career changers I was working with were interested in portfolio working. Today it's more like 50% of men and women in this client group over the age of 50. Younger people, too, are adopting the approach – sometimes out of necessity – as Barrie Hopson and Katie Ledger make clear in their book *And What Do You Do?: 10 Steps to Creating a Portfolio Career*.

What kind of people benefit from this new working method? People who enjoy variety and change. People who become dispirited by the constraints of a conventional career, which may mean doing the same thing for ever. People of all ages who want to take more control over the way they spend their working week, but who wisely want to mix conventional and free-thinking methods, predictable income streams with creative possibilities. One of the exciting things about portfolio work is that it maintains an air of unpredictability: you never know what kind of project or enquiry is coming in next, and you may be doing an entirely different mix of work in 12 months' time.

Be aware that the market rarely offers you these opportunities on a plate. You also need to think about how you will communicate this job mix if you are applying for a full-time permanent position at some time in the future. Having said that, portfolio careers often offer a high degree of work satisfaction simply because you are managing your time so that you spend more of it doing a job you love.

'Yes, but' thinking (again)

Your friends and colleagues may not immediately recognize what you are trying to do, and wonder why you aren't applying for a 'proper' job. They may tell you that you are 'playing' at work or operating on the edge of the 'real world', ignoring the fact that many of your colleagues and friends are already doing the same thing. One of the great advantages of portfolio work is that you are in a very strong position to introduce new services and strategies as the market changes, and you're far less at the whim of a single organization. After several years of corporate downsizing, this degree of control may make all the difference.

You will need to draw heavily on two of the major themes of this book. The first is to dig deep in terms of creative approaches: what could you actually do? What kinds of work could you mix? The second is that you will have to work hard at communicating what you do: explaining your distinctive work mix, and actively seeking out people who can help you to find customers and other kinds of contact. Ultimately, if you plan it right, the work will find you, but that means you have to invest a great deal of time and energy initially into making a great range of contacts (see Chapter 11 for more tips on networking).

RETHINKING YOUR WORKING LIFE

You may already be on your way to a multi-dimensional career because you have already started to explore some of the unconventional methods of working that are now available. You may be already committed to portfolio working, or you want to consider the alternatives. These are set out below, along with the typical advantages and disadvantages experienced by workers who have tried them.

Temporary or contract work

Temporary work is often provided by recruitment agencies, and there seems to be no field of work where temps are not engaged, from van driving to financial management. It's best if you can take temporary work for a positive reason: seek opportunities that will expand your knowledge or skills, or extend your range of contacts. Be aware that there is a high chance of being retained in a permanent job just because you are already a known quantity. However, do be careful that agencies don't have a narrow picture of what you can do. They will assume that you will want to do what you have done in the past. Seek refreshment by asking for different kinds of work assignment. When you are in the temporary role, try to negotiate access to the learning opportunities and new contacts that are on offer to your permanent colleagues.

For: You can quickly acquire new skills and a wide range of work experience. This is often a good way of gaining experience in new fields of work.

Against: You may not get access to training and career development opportunities. It's also a difficult route if you want to change careers, as temping agencies are all too keen to pigeon-hole you.

Interim

Interim work is essentially a form of short-term contract for more experienced managers. These roles are typically filled by senior staff with experience of managing companies or functions. An employer hires them in to cover a staff shortage or, more likely, to deal with a particular project or workload. Interim assignments can last for anything from 2 weeks to 2 years, but it's more common that a company is seeking professional expertise over something like a 3–6 month period. Unlike a consultant, your role is not just to make recommendations, but to implement them. There is now a wide range of interim management consultancies in the UK, and if you are thinking of working in this field, investigate what they have to offer. However, the best course of action is to talk to someone who is currently undertaking an interim assignment. Remember, too, that your most likely source of interim work is with an employer you already know.

For: Allows you to gain experience of different work cultures without getting locked in to the company payroll. Offers a great deal of flexibility for those who want to work for part of the year and take extended breaks. Can improve your skills and quickly give you experience of a wide range of organizations.

Against: You have to consider this as a career step rather than a fill-in move, since you may need to devote considerable energy to securing your next interim role while you are currently working in your present one. You may also have to work some distance away from home. Once you have undertaken two or three interim assignments you may find it difficult to get back into permanent employment because you are now considered a 'career' interim manager.

Part-time or flexitime

You may want to choose part-time or flexible working hours for a variety of reasons: family responsibilities, easing the pain of daily travel, or perhaps because you are allowing yourself time and energy to do something else with your life (learning a new skill, taking a qualification, starting up a fledgling business ...). Remember that a great many part-time jobs are negotiated rather than advertised. Employers find it difficult to attract candidates to part-time positions, so they are often filled by word of mouth. Alternatively, a job that is first conceived as a full-time position may be renegotiated as a part-time position or job share (see below).

For: Helps to preserve life/work balance and allow you to do some of the other things you want to do in life.

Against: You will probably put in more hours than you are paid for, and you may be underexposed in the company and so not have a sufficiently high profile with decision makers, and so fail to gain career development opportunities. You may find that you do not have the opportunities for promotion and career development offered to your full-time colleagues.

Job sharing

With the rise in flexible working, a great many employers have become tuned in to the idea of a job share. This has some benefits for organizations (two people tend to put in slightly more overall effort than one) and clear benefits for candidates who only want to work certain hours or on certain days of the week. A parent staying at home 2 days a week, for example, can save significantly on child-care costs.

If you want to take an active strategy rather than hoping that something will come along, it's a good idea to find someone else to be your job-share partner, and make a joint application for a job. You may have to explain what a job-share is and how it works (so take the time to interview someone who is already working in a job-share), but many employers who have equal opportunities policies will take your application seriously, and you may be providing a creative solution to their problem.

For: A good stepping stone towards portfolio working, and a move that can free up some time for other activities.

Against: It is often difficult to persuade an employer to agree to a job share unless you (and your job-share colleague) are already working for the organization. Job-share workers often find that they are overlooked in promotion, and if your job-share partner moves on or retires you may find it difficult to find someone else to fill the role. You may find it difficult to move up the career ladder after a job share.

Short-term or fixed-term arrangements

Employers offer short-term or fixed-term contracts for various reasons, but usually the intention is to control payroll costs. However, many people hired on short-term contracts are retained in permanent roles (employers prefer to hire staff they already know – see Chapter 11).

For: Ensures you keep your offer fresh and clear to your employer, and allows you to gain a range of experience in different organizations.

Against: Uncertainty, meaning that a lot of time towards the end of your contract will need to go into getting your next role.

Mixed mode: employed and self-employed

At the end of the tax year many people complete tax returns which record their income both from PAYE employment and from self-employed activities. They may work as a part-time lecturer or writer, or possibly they obtain an income from renovating furniture or making hand-made clothes. They may have more than one employer. They may have an income from renting out a second property. You don't have to be restricted by either/or thinking. Investigate alternative careers by trying out something different one day a week or at a weekend. Others start businesses on a part-time basis, phasing one kind of work in and another out as a business starts to become successful.

For: This really is often the first step towards portfolio working.

Against: You may have to invest in your own training costs or overheads, so you may incur costs and suffer a variable income during the initial phase. You may find it difficult to cope with fluctuations in workload and income, and you may feel isolated being outside the conventional workplace.

Negotiating the right working arrangement for you

Don't begin by giving an employer a reason to exclude you from the recruitment process. If you start by saying 'I am only interested in a job that is part-time/interim/short-term ...' you are giving a recruiter a reason to end the conversation. The golden rule is to begin with the needs of the organization, not your working restrictions. In other words, find out what the employer needs, get them to realize what you have to offer, and if you are both happy with the result you may have the opportunity to negotiate something different. Some employers would rather have the right person on a part-time basis than not have anyone at all. Others may be attracted by your idea of doing the job on a consultancy basis. If they want you, things become negotiable, including working conditions. There are, of course, exceptions, particularly with highly structured organizations. Even local authorities, however, are positive if approached by a job-share 'couple' (see 'Job sharing' above).

'MUST DO' LIST: BEGINNING A PORTFOLIO CAREER

☑ Describe your ideal portfolio career. Write down what you would be doing during a typical month.

☑ Focus on the steps you would need to take to make it happen.

☑ Spot the escape route: talk to people who have left your profession recently.

☑ Don't think just in terms of a single job you'll love. Think of career pathways, clusters, patterns, etc.

☑ Be better informed about key changes in the way people work, and the impact of new technology and new working methods.

☑ Think again about what you recognize as a career and a 'proper' job.

☑ Investigate the different routes others have taken towards portfolio careers.

☑ Talk to people who have made the journey before you. Talk to people who have successfully reinvented the work they do. Use the REVEAL method of informational interviews (see Appendix 1).

☑ Ignore the job myths. Find out for yourself.

☑ Weigh up the real pros and cons of change. How can you minimize the risk and maximize your return?

☑ Watch out (here as much as anywhere) for the overwhelming, crippling power of 'Yes, but' thinking.

☑ Unsure whether self-employment would suit you? Look at Checklist K in Chapter 17.

☑ Distinguish dream from reality. If a new career or enterprise interests you, find out what you will be doing most of the time.

The reality may not be as glamorous as you think. If you are head over heels in love with an idea, speak to at least one person who is thinking of getting out of that line of business. Find out why, then match that with a balancing conversation with someone who loves their new career. Decide for yourself by matching what you hear to your own career drivers.

Beginning It Here

CHAPTER 16

This chapter helps you to:

❚ Plan the stages of career change using ADEPT, your five-point action plan for getting a job you'll love

❚ Help yourself during career transition

❚ Recruit a support team

❚ Understand the different kind of advisers in the marketplace who might help you

❚ Know what to look for in a good career coach

If you can fall in love with what you are going to do for a living, you've got it made.

George Burns

THE ADEPT MODEL

Much of this book has been dedicated to idea building, finding ways of coaching your brain to see new possibilities for your career. Reflection, imagining and planning all need to translate into activity.

Figure 16.1 takes you through all five stages of the ADEPT model, and shows how you can move from the reflection to action.

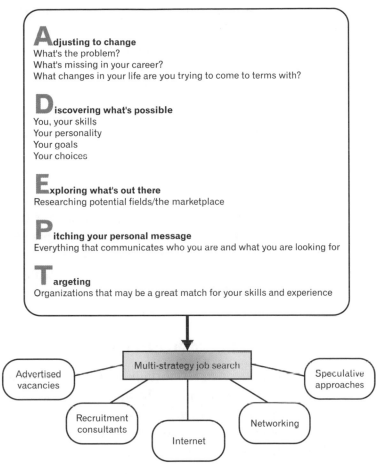

Figure 16.1   Career planning using the ADEPT model

Using the **ADEPT** model to make changes

The first step of the model, **A**djusting to change, is about your starting point: your mindset, constraints, and understanding what gets in the way of finding a job you'll love. Look at what you are putting in the way of your own progress.

Next you can move on to **D**iscovering what you have to offer by working through the exercises in this book, particularly those looking at skills, achievements and the best way to present them.

Before long you'll be itching to get to grips with something even more tangible, so the **E**xploring stage means finding out what's really out there. Put research before job search – follow your curiosity and get information from real people holding down real jobs, not secondhand information.

The next step is **P**itching your message, but to do this you need to know (a) what you are selling and (b) who you are selling to. Look again at the Two-Breath Message in Chapter 13, and rehearse short, positive presentation statements to back up your main pitch.

Finally, set real **T**argets in terms of job search. Make sure you use a multi-strategy job search (as outlined in Chapter 11) – include all the elements of the mix, particularly direct, speculative approaches to companies who are not advertising, and both face-to-face and online networking.

GETTING HELP – LIMITATIONS OF DIY

There is a great deal you can do to help yourself as the different exercises in this book have shown. Most importantly, before you ask anyone to help you, set out a basic list of what you have done, what you have learned and where you have worked. Add, if you can, a list of your skills and achievements.

Trying to coach yourself, you will probably hit one or two classic problems. The first is that you get 'stuck' somewhere. You've done the exercises, but you still can't see the wood for the trees. The second is that you need someone to see things that you can't see, and ask questions you can't ask yourself. Working with someone who can help you to brainstorm possibilities and suggest alternatives is important. And because career transition is as much about confidence as anything else, it's often vital to find people who will help you to see the best version of yourself, and help you to build up a positive picture of your skills, know-how and successes.

Recruit a support team

Few things are achievable without the right tools and the right people, yet all too many people try to break out of their career box alone. Get support. First of all, have experimental, 'what if?' conversations with as many people as you can who can give you a different perspective (but make sure the feedback is at least objective, and preferably upbeat). Secondly – and do this before you finish this book – build a support team.

Find **two** other people who will help. They don't need to be in the same situation as you, but they do need to be curious about people, jobs and the world. One other person will do, at a push, but a coach/pupil relationship often happens when there are only two people. With a trio meeting together regularly you get two perspectives on everything that's said. The conversation doesn't need to be just about you – you can help each other in turn. You'll often find that a trio discussion over a bottle of wine works very nicely.

Recruit the two members of your trio carefully. They should be people who can:

▌ support you in the ups and downs of career transition

▌ give you honest, objective advice about your skills, and help you to see the evidence you use to back them up

▌ give you ideas for exploration and connections with other people who can help

▌ use 'yellow hat' thinking (see Table 8.3) to support your ideas. If you say 'I'm thinking of becoming an astronaut', they will be the sort of people who will say 'How would that work for you? What would be the spin-offs? What first step could you take? How can you get to speak to someone who's been into space ...?'

Warning: if you hear a friend say 'Yes, but, in the real world ...' or 'It's not that simple ...' or even 'That won't work', don't invite them to be part of this process. There are thousands of people out there who will be all too happy to pour cold water on your ideas. Career success is as much about motivation as it is about strategy. Choose people who will give you positive, encouraging messages.

Record and build

As you come to the end of this book, you will have discovered a great deal of information. It may be hard at this stage to see the wood for the trees. Table 16.1 gives you an example of one method of combining information on a single sheet of paper. Write down the key ingredients, and then let the idea mull. Stick the sheet on a fridge or wardrobe door so you see it every day. Let your unconscious brain make connections for you. Show it to friends, colleagues, your support group. This master sheet is a great way of focusing on your strengths and building ideas for your future.

RECRUITMENT AGENCIES

There is a wide range of organizations which charge employers a fee for placing workers in jobs. They have different names, depending on the level of staff they place. At one end of the range you will find **employment** or **staffing agencies**. Agencies at this level tend to deal largely with temporary or contract work. Agencies working at higher levels tend to call themselves **recruitment** or **selection consultancies**, while those operating at the most senior end call themselves **selection** and/or **search consultancies** (also known as 'headhunters'). Chapters 11 and 13 give you more detail about making the most of recruitment consultants.

In the UK recruitment consultancies, whatever their label, are not allowed to charge a fee to job seekers for finding them work. They can, however, charge a fee for a separate service such as producing a CV for you, but when they do this they should give you clear written terms of business when asking for your money.

Table 16.1 Master sheet

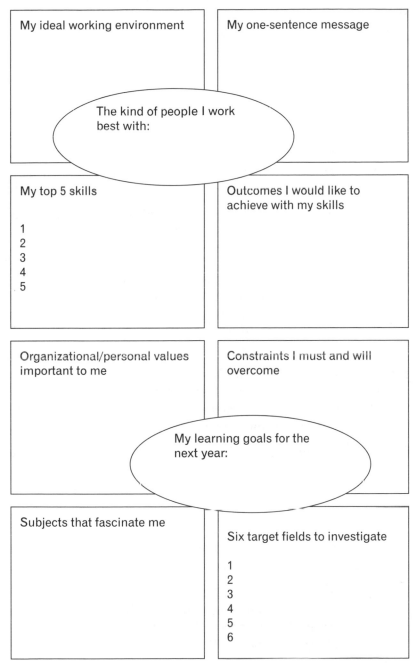

Often a recruitment consultant can give you feedback on your CV, and on your overall 'message'. Again, take this advice with some caution and get a second opinion. Every recruiter has pet likes and dislikes when it comes to CVs, which usually relate to *the kind of candidates that they place most often.*

GETTING CAREERS ADVICE

Advice is what we ask for when we already know the answer but wish we didn't.

Erica Jong

People who can advise you on career choices come in different forms. The range of people who work in career guidance in the UK looks like this:

▮ **Advisers helping young people** – full-time or part-time specialists can be found working in schools, colleges and universities. University careers services will give advice to current students and graduates but also, in some cases, people who have studied elsewhere.

▮ **Government-funded advice** for adults is available from a range of sources. Regional organizations offer advice and guidance to adults funded through the **nextstep** programme. Advice is free, but your time with a coach may be very limited.

▮ **Online free advice** is available from a range of sites but notably from www.careersadvice.direct.gov.uk – which includes the opportunity for a telephone session with an actual career coach.

▮ Independent **career coaches and consultants** are now fairly widespread, mainly in the major cities. Some are small coaching firms, others larger operations whose charges approach those of outplacement firms.

▮ **Outplacement** consultancies provide a service that is almost universally paid for by employers, usually when they are making staff redundant. Outplacement consultancies sometimes offer support to individuals paying for themselves, but the costs tend to be high.

■ **CV writing services** can be expensive, but helpful if you find it difficult to communicate your strengths in writing or if you don't have the IT skills to present a well-crafted document. The limitations on this service are that you can end up with a glossy, professional CV that is clearly not written by you, and sometimes that you don't get a CV that really communicates your message. It's generally best to write your own, and get help if you are stuck.

HOW TO TRACK DOWN AN EFFECTIVE CAREER COACH

Smaller careers consultancies used to be relatively rare, but since the downturn many people who used to work as recruitment specialists or life coaches have moved into the sector (which is why it's a good idea to find out something about the background and length of experience of the people you are working with). Consultants often work alone or in small organizations. A good career coach will offer you a mix of guidance and coaching – i.e. information, feedback, and advice which helps you to rethink what you are doing.

Some tips for finding the right career coach:

■ Ask around – word of mouth is often the best way. Ask people who have made a career change themselves.

■ Be aware that many individual consultants are not exclusively career specialists. They may also work in coaching, training, personal development or recruitment. Some careers specialists are also qualified occupational psychologists. It's worth networking in all these fields to find the right person.

■ Many personnel, recruitment or outplacement specialists are aware of someone in their region who offers career coaching services.

■ Most advisers working in this sector do not have specific careers guidance qualifications but most are highly experienced with backgrounds which include occupational psychology, HR, coaching or recruitment.

Warnings

There are careers consultancies out there who are prepared to take very large amounts of money off you. Sometimes they will provide an excellent service, but you may be able to achieve similar results by supporting yourself some of the way and then finding a career coach with more modest charges who can help you with the parts you find difficult.

Be cautious when dealing with any firm that promises to market you – this can be very expensive and you may lose control over the people you are trying to reach and influence. Similarly, some career firms promise you access to thousands of 'hidden' vacancies. This is the El Dorado of careers advice. No-one can guarantee you access to hidden vacancies, or tell you how many there are – by definition, they are hidden, not accessible in a predictable or measurable way. A professional career coach shouldn't take over the task for you, but give *you* the tools to develop and control your own career.

Charges

If your budget is very tight, see what is on offer from your local adult guidance provider or, if you are a graduate, your university careers service. You may be offered free assistance, or asked to pay a modest charge. The main limitations of such support are that you are not always advised by consultants with a great deal of business experience, and you may be offered only a relatively limited amount of time.

Private sector career consultancies' rates vary considerably. The larger the firm, the more likely it is that you will be sold a 'package' of meetings and support. You need to be sure from the outset that you need everything that is on offer, and that you feel confident that your money is going to be invested in the right kind of help, particularly if you need a lot of support working out what kind of work you want to do, and if you want to move into a completely new sector. A typical package fee ranges from £400 to £1000, but I have known fees as high as £15,000 to be quoted. You will usually have to pay VAT on top.

Career coaches working on their own tend to have far lower overheads and lower fee levels. They may offer you a fee package, but will also often work on an hourly basis. Rates vary, in my experience, from £50 to £100 per hour outside London, and from £70 to £200 per hour in London. Cost, whether low or high, does not necessarily indicate value.

What to ask

One approach is to ask about success rates, but you may find that figures quoted about the time it takes to get a job, or the number of people assisted in the past, are not particularly helpful. In reality, everyone has a different set of needs. Some people just need a little job search coaching, while others need several months of exploring. The 'Must do' list at the end of this chapter provides a list of useful questions.

The really important thing is to talk to a consultant and work out whether he or she can help you. You may get a brief introductory session to discover this. Other consultants will wish to charge for this session, but don't let that put you off: an hour with an experienced consultant should provide you with a wide range of questions, ideas and insights, and so should be worth paying for.

'MUST DO' LIST: KEY QUESTIONS TO ASK A CAREER COACH

☑ What is the hourly charge? Is there VAT on top?

☑ Am I committed to a programme of meetings? How much flexibility and choice do I have about the programme?

☑ How long does it normally take to the point where I have a fairly clear picture of what I have to offer, and where I want to be?

☑ Do you offer a free introductory session? If not, what information about your working style do you provide in advance? What kind of work are we likely to cover in a paid first session?

☑ Are you going to use any tests? If you are using ability, interest or psychometric tests are you qualified by the British Psychological Society to conduct these tests?

☑ Do you follow a Code of Practice?

☑ What happens if you feel you really can't help me? Or if *I* feel you can't help me?

☑ How do sessions work? Do you support clients by email or telephone?

☑ And, possibly the most important question: What strategies do you use to help people who have *no idea what they want to do next*?

Key Checklists

Exploration is rather hollow if it doesn't take you anywhere. This chapter provides a wide range of activity tools for getting the job you'll love.

A – What kind of career is right for you?

B – Designing a winning CV

C – What to put on the first page of your CV

D – What to put in your CV

E – What NOT to do with your CV

F – The essentials of a great covering letter

G – Preparing for an interview

H – Tough interview questions to prepare for (and what to say)

I – Questions to ask prospective employers

J – Advice for older jobseekers

K – Is self-employment right for you?

A – WHAT KIND OF CAREER IS RIGHT FOR YOU?

1. Do you want to work *mainly* with **things**, **people**, **information** or **concepts**?

2. Think about your **career drivers** – do you want to catalogue the world, change the world, help the world, sell the world ...?

3. How much **independence** do you want to have about the way you work and make decisions? If you find it difficult to take instructions or you want to go your own way, maybe self-employment beckons.

4. Look for organizations that reflect your feelings about **rules**. Are you happier working within a clear set of guidelines, or in a completely open-ended way?

5. What activities, products or ideas seem **meaningful** to you? You don't need to be inspired by biscuit technology or soap powder, but if you find any serious discussion about them just absurd, keep looking.

6. What kind of work have you **chosen** to do, either in your leisure time or as a volunteer? Often the work we *choose* to do without financial constraint is a great clue to our best work.

7. What kind of companies or products reflect your **personal beliefs** about life, other people, spirituality, the planet, etc.?

8. Look at the **skills** you *really* enjoy using, when you are impossible to distract and rarely bored. Where could you use them?

9. What subjects *really* **interest** you? How can you translate your interests into fields of work?

10. Ask. **Find out**. Don't use your career as a lab experiment. Talk to people about the jobs they do. Learn from the mistakes others have made. Get careers advice.

B – DESIGNING A WINNING CV

1. There are many different ways of setting out a CV. The most important thing to remember is that your CV will be read, on average, in under 20 seconds.

2. This means that the first page of your CV does most of the work. See Checklist C for more details about the content of the first page.

3. The example CV on pages 282–3 gives you an idea for setting out the first page of your CV in blocks of information. In this case the blocks are as follows:

   ▮ your contact details

   ▮ a profile which summarizes who you are and what you're looking for

   ▮ your key achievements and experience

   ▮ your most important professional and academic qualifications

   ▮ a quick summary of your career to date.

4. Think about whether you need a profile at the beginning of your CV. In general, if you are happy to stay in the sector you're in and just want the next big job along, you may not need a profile but you can start with your most recent (or current) job. However, if you want to make a career change you will probably need a profile to make sure the reader interprets your history the right way. It says pretty much what you would say if you were in the room handing the document over.

   (See *Why You? – CV Messages To Win Jobs* for research on what HR specialists and recruiters want to see in CVs, and help on deciding what kind of CV format will suit you best.)

C – WHAT TO PUT ON THE FIRST PAGE OF YOUR CV

1. Remember your CV will be screened into a 'yes' or 'no' pile. Do everything you can on page 1 to end up in the 'yes' pile.

2. A reader will probably have made a decision about you before getting to the end of your first page. Make sure any **key information** is here.

3. Think of the first page of your CV as a **one-page advertisement**, which should be strong enough to stand alone.

4. Don't put anything on the front page that strikes a negative note, such as difficulties you had with a past employer, or a failed course.

5. Include your contact details at the top of page 1. Include an email address, and make sure it is businesslike. 'PleasureAddict@slaphead.com' may convey the wrong impression.

6. Use summary words such as 'qualified' or 'graduate' to get your message across in the profile.

7. Don't include **empty adjectives**. Almost everyone is creative, dynamic, enthusiastic …. Focus on what you can do well.

8. Include any **key qualifications** on page 1 if you know this is an important benchmark for an employer.

9. Match your key achievements and experience to the top five or six items required by the job.

10. What do you say about yourself in the first 20 words? Think carefully about what you include in your **profile**, particularly if you use a job title to summarize what you do.

D – WHAT TO PUT IN YOUR CV (see example CV)

1. Remember – a CV only has one function: to get you an interview.

2. Make your CV immediately interesting.

3. Keep it **concise**. It isn't your life story.

4. Your CV should make **claims** about who you are and what you can do, and then provide evidence to back up those claims.

5. **Translate** what you know and can do into terms that will appeal to a recruiter – talk about solving problems, making a difference, etc.

6. Try to say something interesting about your **academic history** – relate it to an employer's needs rather than regurgitating the syllabus, e.g. if you led a seminar or gave a talk, write about your facilitation or presentation skills.

7. It's all very well being the best thing since sliced bread. **Be specific**: try to express **achievements** in terms of awards, money, time or percentages.

8. If you recently qualified, don't go overboard about your qualifications – make sure you include information on page 1 about your work skills.

9. Include something under 'interests' that is neither bland nor run of the mill. Include interests that make you appear a rounded person, and those that have some relevance to the job. Make sure you can talk enthusiastically about any interest you mention.

10. Take some time to make the layout attractive, with plenty of white space. Don't print text so small it's painful to read.

E – WHAT NOT TO DO WITH YOUR CV

1. **Don't** put any information on page 1 unless it says something important about you that might get you an interview.

2. **Don't** provide huge amounts of detail about jobs you did more than 10 years ago.

3. **Don't** put yourself down, or try irony or humour. It rarely reads the way you want it to.

4. **Don't** give the names and addresses of referees – you can provide them if they are requested, but you should brief your referees carefully about who they may be talking to, and what the potential job is all about.

5. **Don't** use obscure abbreviations or jargon.

6. **Don't** include your age or your date of birth.

7. **Don't** disclose your salary unless you think this is going to be specifically helpful to an employer – it's generally best to deal with this at interview or, if you have to, in a covering letter.

8. **Don't** include non-essential personal information, e.g. height, weight, names of your children, or your religious or political beliefs.

9. **Don't** send out poor photocopies. Ideally, print your CV out on good-quality paper each time.

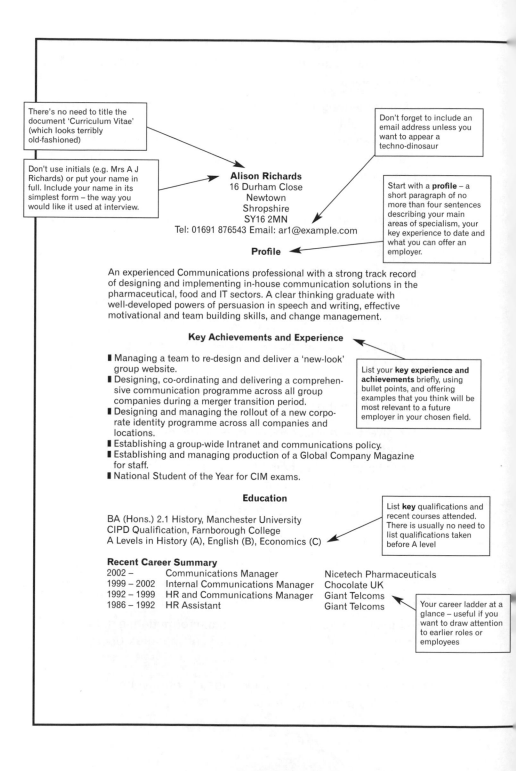

There's no need to title the document 'Curriculum Vitae' (which looks terribly old-fashioned)

Don't forget to include an email address unless you want to appear a techno-dinosaur

Don't use initials (e.g. Mrs A J Richards) or put your name in full. Include your name in its simplest form – the way you would like it used at interview.

Alison Richards
16 Durham Close
Newtown
Shropshire
SY16 2MN
Tel: 01691 876543 Email: ar1@example.com

Start with a **profile** – a short paragraph of no more than four sentences describing your main areas of specialism, your key experience to date and what you can offer an employer.

Profile

An experienced Communications professional with a strong track record of designing and implementing in-house communication solutions in the pharmaceutical, food and IT sectors. A clear thinking graduate with well-developed powers of persuasion in speech and writing, effective motivational and team building skills, and change management.

Key Achievements and Experience

■ Managing a team to re-design and deliver a 'new-look' group website.
■ Designing, co-ordinating and delivering a comprehensive communication programme across all group companies during a merger transition period.
■ Designing and managing the rollout of a new corporate identity programme across all companies and locations.
■ Establishing a group-wide Intranet and communications policy.
■ Establishing and managing production of a Global Company Magazine for staff.
■ National Student of the Year for CIM exams.

List your **key experience and achievements** briefly, using bullet points, and offering examples that you think will be most relevant to a future employer in your chosen field.

Education

BA (Hons.) 2.1 History, Manchester University
CIPD Qualification, Farnborough College
A Levels in History (A), English (B), Economics (C)

List **key** qualifications and recent courses attended. There is usually no need to list qualifications taken before A level

Recent Career Summary
2002 –   Communications Manager   Nicetech Pharmaceuticals
1999 – 2002   Internal Communications Manager   Chocolate UK
1992 – 1999   HR and Communications Manager   Giant Telcoms
1986 – 1992   HR Assistant   Giant Telcoms

Your career ladder at a glance – useful if you want to draw attention to earlier roles or employees

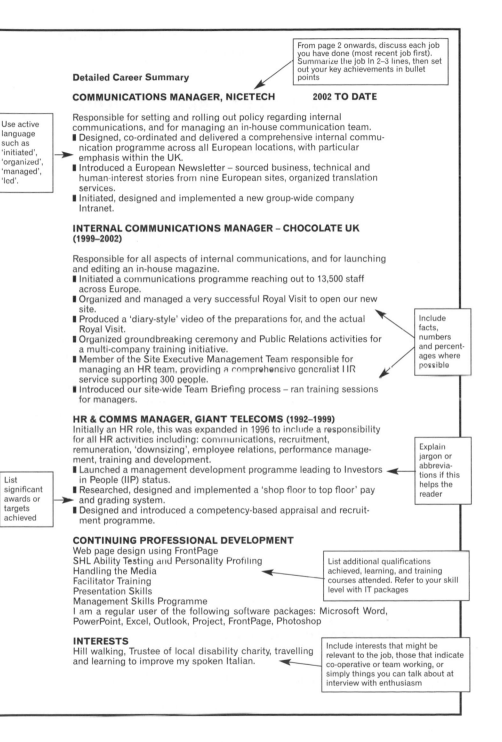

From page 2 onwards, discuss each job you have done (most recent job first). Summarize the job in 2–3 lines, then set out your key achievements in bullet points

Detailed Career Summary

COMMUNICATIONS MANAGER, NICETECH   2002 TO DATE

Use active language such as 'initiated', 'organized', 'managed', 'led'.

Responsible for setting and rolling out policy regarding internal communications, and for managing an in-house communication team.
▌ Designed, co-ordinated and delivered a comprehensive internal communication programme across all European locations, with particular emphasis within the UK.
▌ Introduced a European Newsletter – sourced business, technical and human-interest stories from nine European sites, organized translation services.
▌ Initiated, designed and implemented a new group-wide company Intranet.

INTERNAL COMMUNICATIONS MANAGER – CHOCOLATE UK (1999–2002)

Responsible for all aspects of internal communications, and for launching and editing an in-house magazine.
▌ Initiated a communications programme reaching out to 13,500 staff across Europe.
▌ Organized and managed a very successful Royal Visit to open our new site.
▌ Produced a 'diary-style' video of the preparations for, and the actual Royal Visit.
▌ Organized groundbreaking ceremony and Public Relations activities for a multi-company training initiative.
▌ Member of the Site Executive Management Team responsible for managing an HR team, providing a comprehensive generalist HR service supporting 300 people.
▌ Introduced our site-wide Team Briefing process – ran training sessions for managers.

Include facts, numbers and percentages where possible

HR & COMMS MANAGER, GIANT TELECOMS (1992–1999)
Initially an HR role, this was expanded in 1996 to include a responsibility for all HR activities including: communications, recruitment, remuneration, 'downsizing', employee relations, performance management, training and development.
▌ Launched a management development programme leading to Investors in People (IIP) status.
▌ Researched, designed and implemented a 'shop floor to top floor' pay and grading system.
▌ Designed and introduced a competency-based appraisal and recruitment programme.

Explain jargon or abbreviations if this helps the reader

List significant awards or targets achieved

CONTINUING PROFESSIONAL DEVELOPMENT
Web page design using FrontPage
SHL Ability Testing and Personality Profiling
Handling the Media
Facilitator Training
Presentation Skills
Management Skills Programme
I am a regular user of the following software packages: Microsoft Word, PowerPoint, Excel, Outlook, Project, FrontPage, Photoshop

List additional qualifications achieved, learning, and training courses attended. Refer to your skill level with IT packages

INTERESTS
Hill walking, Trustee of local disability charity, travelling and learning to improve my spoken Italian.

Include interests that might be relevant to the job, those that indicate co-operative or team working, or simply things you can talk about at interview with enthusiasm

10. **Don't** include your reasons for leaving jobs, but be prepared to discuss this at interview in a positive way.

F – THE ESSENTIALS OF A GREAT COVERING LETTER

1. The only function of this letter is to get your CV read, and to get you a meeting. Think of your letter like the first page of your CV, as a one-page **advertisement** for you. Make your letter **brief, enthusiastic and interesting**.

2. Ensure that **everything** in the reader's name, job title and address is correct.

3. Try not to begin every sentence and paragraph with 'I'. Focus on the **reader** of the letter and his or her perspective.

4. **Research** – refer to the problems, opportunities and headaches that your target company is facing. Work out the main three or four requirements of the job, and provide matching evidence.

5. Indicate in brief paragraphs **what** you are applying for, **who** you are, **why** you are interested, and **what** you have to offer. Don't oversell. State briefly why you are a good **match** for the job.

6. Refer the reader to your enclosed CV. Discuss three or four of your top **achievements** which match the job, using different terms to the way you have expressed them in your CV.

7. Don't put anything in your covering letter that gives the reader an excuse to put the letter aside, e.g. apologizing for your lack of a particular requirement, or mentioning your age, or referring to negative aspects such as why you left your last job.

8. If your letter is a **speculative** approach (i.e. to a company that isn't currently advertising a job), try to ensure that your letter is read by a **named decision maker**.

9. Think carefully what **action** you are asking for. If you are seeking a meeting, ask for one.

10. **Telephone to check** that your letter has been received by the intended recipient. Ask one relevant question, or mention one reason why you might be able to help the employer, and try to sound relaxed about the process.

G – PREPARING FOR AN INTERVIEW

1. **Plan** carefully. Do you know where you are going and how to get there? Who are you seeing?

2. Make sure you know the **names** of the people who will be interviewing you. Practise saying them if they are difficult to pronounce.

3. There's no such thing as enough **preparation** for an interview. Find out everything you can about the company and what it makes or does. Look for current news – show you are up to date.

4. Why does this job exist? What problems will it solve? What are the **key result areas**?

5. Remember: **employers buy experience**. Think about what **evidence of achievement** you can talk about in the interview; rehearse your success stories.

6. Work out what is **appropriate** in terms of everything you present, including yourself. Look the part, and you will feel it. Dress as if you are already doing the job.

7. Second guess the **employer's 'shopping list'** from the job details. What skills, qualities and experience do you have to match?

8. Be your own worst interview nightmare. What is the most **difficult question** you might have to face? Practise the answer. Practise again.

9. **Be upbeat**. Employers latch on to negative messages, so don't give them any.

10. **Prepare for rejection**. On balance you will be rejected more times than accepted. Even if you don't get the job, you can learn a huge amount about your perceived market value.

Remember, there's a job out there for you somewhere – even in a tough market, a well-planned job search pays off.

H – TOUGH INTERVIEW QUESTIONS TO PREPARE FOR (AND WHAT TO SAY)

1. **'Tell us about yourself.'** Prepare for the worst – a classic opener that can really throw you. Have a *brief* summary statement up your sleeve.

2. **'Where do you see yourself in 5 years' time?'** If your answer doesn't ring true for you, it won't for anyone else. Talk about career plans, and what you want to learn and achieve in the future.

3. **'Why do you want this job?'** Have a clear answer to this (even if, privately, you're not sure – you only have to decide when the job offer is in your hand).

4. **'What kind of person are you?'** Handle questions about personality carefully. Rather than say 'I'm an ideas person', talk about a time when you changed things with a good idea.

5. **'Why did you leave … ?'** Employers will probe for reasons for job change. If you are currently out of work, they will probe this, too. Rehearse short, simple, positive 'stories' to cover these points. This is *not* telling lies, just a simple, positive summary. (See Chapter 7 on presentation statements.)

6. **'How will you cope in a crisis?'** Have a couple of good examples of past triumphs up your sleeve.

7. **'How will you …'** questions are beginning to create a **future** which includes *you* – so welcome them. Describe what you would do within the organization as if you are there already. Create the right picture, and the employer will find it difficult to imagine life without you.

8. **'Why are you looking for a job right now?'** Rehearse a brief, upbeat answer that covers redundancy or unemployment. Don't bleat on about how difficult the market is, or how many rejections you've received.

9. **'What do you need to earn?'** Wrong question. Focus on the value you can add to the employer, not your basic needs. Find out what the company is willing to pay, or work out what similar employers pay for good people.

10. **'What are your weaknesses?'** Remember that the recruiter gives far more weight to negative information. Switch the subject to your strengths as soon as possible.

I – QUESTIONS TO ASK PROSPECTIVE EMPLOYERS

1. **Read between the lines** – what does the job description fail to tell you?

2. Make sure you communicate real **interest**, e.g. 'What are the company's biggest problems/headaches/opportunities?'

3. 'Where does the company plan to be in 12 months?' Try to work out what time with the company will do for your CV.

4. Try to find out how you will be **measured** once you begin the job – are there any set targets? Is there a formal appraisal system?

5. What **learning opportunities** (courses, qualifications, training) does the job offer?

6. What **variety** is there in the job?

7. What kind of **support** will you get? Is there a formal mentoring or coaching programme?

8. Find out what you can about **standards** and **expectations**. What will you need to achieve in the first 3 months?

9. Watch out for **buying signals** – usually when the conversation switches from past to future.

10. Wait until you're offered the job until you negotiate any part of the deal.

J – ADVICE FOR OLDER JOBSEEKERS

1. Don't draw attention to your age by giving emphasis to the year you started work, or by highlighting out-of-date terminology, organization names or qualifications.

2. For the same reason, it's generally not a good idea to refer to the ages of your adult **children** (they may be older than the person interviewing you!).

3. Finally, it may not be useful to indicate the year you obtained your **qualifications**. It may seem like ancient history to the recruiter.

4. Make your CV focus on **what you have achieved** and **what you have to offer**, not on your age.

5. Include an **email address**. Employers often assume that older workers are not IT literate.

6. Remember that employers buy experience. Demonstrate how your **know-how** and **maturity** will be a benefit.

7. Don't focus on the bad news stories. Look at the high proportion of men and women in your age group who do find work, and build on their **success strategies**.

8. Try not to reminisce ('in my day …'). **Talk about the future**. Show flexibility and a willingness to learn.

9. Explore the possibilities of a **portfolio career** (see Chapter 15).

10. **Don't** apologize for your age or lack of recent relevant experience, and do not convey desperation.

K – IS SELF-EMPLOYMENT RIGHT FOR YOU?

1. Work out what draws you towards self-employment (e.g. freedom of action, being your own boss, performing tasks you enjoy and working with stimulating people …).

2. Look seriously at how many of these drivers you could achieve in a conventional job (e.g. running your own profit centre within a larger organization).

3. Then work out what pushes you away (e.g. having to sell your services, uncertain income, lack of contact with co-workers …). Look at ways of fixing these negatives, e.g. by working in partnership with others, or moving into an existing business.

4. Look before you leap. Find people who have made a similar move.

5. If it's a competitive field, find people to talk to in other parts of the country.

6. Think hard about how you are going to promote yourself. How will people find you?

7. Plan ahead for isolation – recruit friends and mentors to support you, and network with people doing the same kind of work to swap stories and exchange ideas.

8. Focus on your offering – what product or service will you offer? How will it be different (cheaper, better, quicker, smarter) than others available?

9. Don't get hung up on the frills. It's great fun equipping your office, printing your own business cards and setting up your own website, but none of this matters as much as your first piece of work. Look hard at where the business is going to come from.

10. Pin down your first three clients. If you have three customers lined up who will pay for your services, no questions asked, you probably have a business. Don't get hooked on the business idea: look for an income stream.

(For a detailed overview of whether self-employment will suit you, try the free **Self-Employment Inventory** at www.johnleescareers.com.)

PASS IT ON

Once you've found what you're looking for, give it away.

Interestingly, in a world which offers getting and spending as the path to happiness, recent research suggests very strongly that we are more likely to feel happy by giving something to someone else than we are by receiving.

Once you have learned some of the solutions to your own career problems, what will you do with that information? With luck and a little application you'll move towards a job you love doing. When you discover anything, you can hold it to yourself or you can pass it on.

The only true reason for career breakthrough is that we become equipped to improve the working lives of those around us. That may sound madly altruistic, but skills discovery is hollow if it's only about me. First of all we discover our talents – the solo instrument we play. The exploration continues until we hear the other instruments as well and understand our role in the orchestra. The final step is to help others to begin to hear the music.

Informational Interviews: The REVEAL Method

The REVEAL method is a form of informational interviewing, a method for finding out more about a field of work. To do this you are going to identify key individuals who will love to talk about their industry sector. You will add to your personal knowledge, increase your network and learn how jobs 'feel' from the inside.

The principle is *research before job search*. You are not making a once-and-for-all career decision or trying to get a subversive job interview. You are simply finding out vital pieces of information to move your career transition forward:

▪ What kinds of roles exist?

▪ What organizations are out there?

▪ Would I find the job interesting?

▪ How do people get into this field or occupation?

Informational interviews are most definitely not about job search, at least not directly. Think about the way you would react if someone contacted you at work and asked to see you. If the caller said 'I'd appreciate your help in identifying jobs in your organization', you'd feel pretty uncomfortable. You don't know the caller, so why should you recommend this person for a post? *Think about what your contact can actually deliver.* Most people are happy talking about themselves and the job they do, and usually happy to give you information and contacts if the meeting goes well. Don't even ask questions that are partly about job search ('I'd like your advice on my CV' or 'I'd appreciate an early tip-off if any jobs are advertised'). If the interview goes well, this will probably be offered anyway.

WHAT DO *REVEAL* INTERVIEWS ACHIEVE?

▮ You get to put smart business clothes on and see people in their place of work, which boosts your confidence.

▮ You get to meet real people in real jobs. Your understanding about career routes, job roles and employers moves from desk research to field research. You learn about entry routes to careers, about organizational structures and cultures, and you get a real 'feel' for a large number of employers.

▮ You get to spend time inside organizations, which gives you a huge amount of material to draw upon at interview.

▮ People remember you, and make connections on your behalf.

▮ You are often talking to decision makers, so you get some real insights about the evidence to use in an actual job interview.

▮ It's a process that helps you to decide which career path to take, because you've seen a job from the inside.

▮ If you're tracking down people who are passionate about a field of work that calls you strongly, you will probably end up with some very interesting new contacts and friends.

▮ You fall over jobs. It's true. You fall over jobs in the hidden job market. Ironically, the indirect route which is not focused on job search often turns out to be the number one strategy for getting at the hidden job market.

HOW TO GET MEETINGS

Think of the toughest way of doing it. It's possible to work your way through the Yellow Pages or to turn up at the reception and demand a meeting, but it's an uphill struggle. If you approach an organization as a stranger, the first question in the contact's mind is 'what am I being sold?' (followed swiftly by 'is this someone asking for a job?'). If you think of informational interviews as hard-nosed networking, you've found the perfect excuse not to do them.

Begin with people you know

Get this step right and you never have to make a terrifying phone call. Begin with people who you can approach without any hesitation – practise on family, friends and colleagues while you build confidence. Can't think of anyone? Use the technique outlined in Exercise 11.1. Don't miss out your family. Often we never ask those near and dear to us who it is they know. Even people who never think about networking usually have about 100 people within their immediate contact circle. You can begin with relaxed questions about how they got into the careers they are in, but don't forget to ask two things even at this stage: (1) 'who do you know who works in ... ?' and (2) 'any ideas about who I should be talking to next?' (see the advice given in Chapter 11).

At this stage, what you're after is the names of **three initial contacts** who can help with your main career questions. However, knowing a name is not enough. It looks like your only option is cold calling, but you know how hard it is to begin a conversation 'You don't know me, but ...'.

How to avoid cold calling

At the beginning of every conversation say something like this: 'What I am hoping to do is to get to speak to six or seven people who can give me some real insights'. That way, when you get to the end of the conversation and say 'that was really helpful. Who else should I be talking to?' your colleague will probably already have thought of a name. Next move on to questions about sectors, about entry routes, about potential growth areas.

The mistake at this stage is simply to walk away with a list of names. If you do, you're back to cold calling. You need names plus introductions. So, while you are still in the room, try this: 'I hate ringing people cold. Would you be kind enough to telephone ahead for me, just to say who I am and what the conversation will be about?' That way the person you want to reach expects your call and knows what it's about. Try it. When you telephone your next contact to make an appointment, all you need do is mention the person who recommended you to call. This should be a good enough memory prompt ('Sure – Bill called me about you'). Look for personal connections between one contact and the next ('Bill tells me you're a keen fell walker …'). Next, offer a quick reminder about why you want a discussion. Ask for a face-to-face meeting. Some contacts may try to get you to settle for a phone call. Be honest: say that you learn much more by visiting people in their own organizations. Say that you'd like to ask a short number of key questions. Ask for 11 minutes of the person's time. '5 minutes' or '15 minutes' is too vague.

CONDUCTING A REVEAL INTERVIEW

When you get to the meeting

When you get a face-to-face meeting, you're ready to use the REVEAL method, as set out in Table A.1. The first few times you use the method it's probably wise to stick to this structure (although find a way of wording the questions which works for you; don't use the script parrot-fashion). Later on you can develop your own questions.

Table A.1 The REVEAL method of informational interviewing

Stages of REVEAL	Notes
Recap	**Key statement:**
	'I am here because ...'
	Remind the listener of who introduced you, why you asked for the meeting and what you want to get out of it. It always helps to say that you have been recommended to speak to your contact.
	Make it clear that you will be asking for referrals at the end of the conversation. You might say at the outset that your plan is to talk to a dozen people who know what's going on in a particular sector. At the end of the interview you can then happily ask for further contacts.
Explore	**Key statement and question:**
	'I'm here to find out as much as I can about .... What do you find most interesting/challenging about working in this sector?'
	This is your chance to ask key questions about the industry or sector being explored.
Vision	**Key questions:**
	'What changes can you see in this sector in the next 2 years? What kind of person will do well in this changing sector?'
	This should give you some useful data on anticipated changes, and the ideal skills profile of successful candidates. It may also flag up magazines you should be reading, and exhibitions and conferences you should be attending.
Entry routes	**Key question:**
	'How do people normally get into this line of work?'
	Probe the conventional *and* unconventional ways of

getting work in this sector. There are usually non-standard routes into most careers.

Action	**Key question:** 'What should I do to find out more?' Make sure your interview ends with concrete results: ideas for new connections, other organizations, sources of research.
Links	**Key statement and questions:** 'Thanks very much for your time today. As I mentioned before, I'm keen to talk to a number of people in this field. Who else should I be talking to? Can you please recommend two or three other people who can give me an equally useful perspective?' This is an issue you have flagged up earlier in the process. Show how appreciative you are, otherwise your request sounds a little like 'is there anyone I can talk to more useful than you?' If no names are forthcoming, probe for: 1. Names of organizations 2. Names of network conveners, e.g. branch Chairs of trade associations 3. (If nothing else is forthcoming) the names of good recruitment consultants dealing with this field. And finally, ALWAYS ask your contact to phone ahead to the next round of contacts, so once again you can avoid having to begin a conversation 'you don't know me, but …'.

What if I am invited to consider a job?

Don't let the meeting become a job interview – that's a breach of trust. If a specific position enters the discussion, say you'd like to go away and prepare for a proper interview. Offer a time when you are free within the next few days. Ask for full details of the job and prepare thoroughly, even if you are in a shortlist of one. That way you come back fully prepared, matching your selling points to the key requirements of the job.

Building on each interview

From your three initial contacts you can easily get to speak to 30–40 people in 2–3 months. For some people these conversations are the start of lifelong friendships.

First of all, decide what record-keeping system you are going to use so that you can build up a personal web methodically. You'll need to retain telephone and fax numbers as well as addresses, both real and email. You'll also need to be able to cross-link records, and keep a note of the areas you discuss, and a diary reminder of any action or follow-up you have agreed.

'MUST DO' LIST: GROUND RULES OF THE REVEAL METHOD

- ☑ Use the structure. Be confident.

- ☑ Don't exceed the time limit unless it is at the other person's insistence.

- ☑ Don't ask to be shown round the building or site, but warmly accept the offer if it is made.

- ☑ Don't offer your CV or ask about specific job openings (but have a CV to hand in case it is asked for).

- ☑ Be prepared for the question 'and what about you?' This is a good chance to try out your Two-Breath Message (see Chapter 13).

☑ Don't neglect the critical final step of asking for three other contacts. It's very easy to walk out of a meeting missing one of the main reasons for the interview.

☑ If the conversation isn't generating contact names of individuals, remember you can ask for (a) names of organizations or (b) names of good recruitment consultants in this sector.

☑ Keep a record of each interview, who you have seen and all connections made.

☑ Send a thank you card afterwards: it's an unexpected gesture, and you will be remembered. Recipients are often touched by the gesture and keep your card for a long time. Put your name and email address somewhere discreetly on the card.

☑ Remember that some people will turn down your request for a meeting. Think carefully about whether this is the result of what you have done, or simply because the contact was too busy or indifferent to give you a meeting. Approached the right way through an intermediate contact, about four out of five requests lead to informational interviews.

☑ If all else fails at any stage, fall back on your last ditch question: **'who else should I be talking to?'**

People Who Have Transformed Their Careers

Some of the material which follows originally appeared in *Coaching at Work* magazine (see www.coaching-at-work.com).

The article looks at the way we make career changes and what gets in the way of finding more satisfying work. The case studies set out below are from JLA clients who built their career change around ideas contained in this book.

ADVICE FOR THE RUDDERLESS

Dealing with the major obstacles in career coaching

Career coaching is about helping clients to explore the difference between comforting fantasies and goals. Working fantasies are important – imagining yourself on a desert island may be a healthy antidote to the drudgery of work. However, these are pipe-dreams that we have no intention of acting upon, while goals require activity, first steps.

For me, the heart of career coaching is the question '*how is this decision going to be made?*'. If the question is, as it is for many, '*what do I feel called to do?*', the routine straight-line thinking we do in business life rarely works. Exciting career change involves taking at least one risky step, which is usually asking the question 'what if …?'. That requires divergent, right-brain thinking, and often a dumping of conventional wisdom about what's out there, and what kind of people enjoy exciting careers.

WILL BEALE, HEAD OF PROGRAMME MANAGE-MENT, World Wildlife Fund

Will studied Natural Sciences and Chemical Engineering before joining Unilever. He worked in research, manufacturing and new product development, but after ten years had a strong impulse to find his ideal career path.

Will began feeling apprehensive, but threw himself positively into the process: *'I spent three months undertaking informational interviews with about 40 people in my target fields. I learned a lot but it was also quite a tough time, especially for my family.'*

Will applied for a wide range of jobs – business, NGOs, public sector. His dream was to work for an organization actively contributing to animal protection. When a job at the WWF entered his sights he felt he had found the perfect match: *'It seemed ideal but honestly I did not expect to get it. However, by this time my application, interview and negotiation skills were well practised, and I knew how to sell the positive about myself.'*

At WWF Will has moved from quality management to building excellence in conservation management. Will continues to enjoy his work enormously, and recognizes that the change he has made is part of deeper life choices – *'it's an analytical role but requires a lot of people skills. I have travelled widely (while endeavouring to minimize flights) and have a much broader perspective on the world. Through the whole process of change, my personal faith and my prayer life were very important in sustaining me towards finding my mission in life.'*

CHRIS WEBB, Freelance Graphic Designer about to change direction

Although Chris was studying Classics at university, working on the university newspaper revealed a talent for design, so after graduating he found a job as a graphic designer working for an engineering company. When the recession hit he was made redundant, still in his early 20s. Chris had written off for several advertised positions but was not getting short-listed, so was talking about alternative career paths, even though they were far less interesting to him. Everyone advised Chris that this was a time to get a 'sensible' job, and that there was no point applying for jobs in the graphic design field, which is competitive even in boom times.

He was about to give up on the idea of creative work. Chris writes: 'Using the Skill Cards showed me that I really was drawn to creative work, but also that I had people and analytical skills.' When asked what he would do if all jobs paid the same, it was clear that Chris wanted to at least once in his career try the world of illustration.

The next step was to rethink his job search at a time when the market was laying off graphic designers every day. Chris reveals how, even with little experience, the hidden job market opened up: 'I learned not to look for advertised jobs, but to find people who are doing interesting things and may need help.' By making direct approaches to organizations who were not advertising, and demonstrating both skill and enthusiasm, Chris had two job offers within a fortnight of his change of strategy.

12 months later Chris has had experience of both in-house work and freelance work as an illustrator and cartoonist. What next? 'Possibly not graphic design, but something that draws upon creative, people and business skills – and I've already set up several conversations with people who might be able to make that happen'.

BETH GRANT, Property Manager, West Sussex

When she first came to John Lees Associates, Beth had been unable to work for 3 years following an accident at work resulting in a long-term shoulder problem. Initially she could see very few work options and was worried about the kind of reception she would get from employers as a job seeker with long-term health problems and a long period out of the labour market.

Beth worked with JLA consultant Caroline Humphries. She was encouraged by the fact that the exercises she was offered were tailored to her particular circumstances: 'All of the exercises completed were incredibly thought provoking and were excellent in really helping you to think about what it is you want from a job and from life. Even though some of these were testing, with the amazing support I was fortunate enough to have, the end results far outweigh the difficult soul-searching moments.'

Not only that, the work she did boosted her confidence: 'At all stages we celebrated the progress I had made and it was refreshing to be reminded of how far I had come.' With her consultant's knowledge, advice, encouragement and guidance Beth found herself in a position to start looking at retraining and returning to work with a clearer understanding of her skills and the messages she needs to communicate to employers. She has learned to place the focus on what she can do rather than on her limitations: 'My self-confidence and self-belief has rocketed and using techniques I have learnt through my journey with Caroline I have confidence I will eventually find the right job for me at the right time.'

Beth is now looking at moving into an HR or similar administrative role where she can use her good organizational skills but also tap into her curiosity about people.

> Beth adds: 'When I first met with Caroline I was struggling to even contemplate the thought of returning to some form of work and did not believe it would be possible to change this. I am delighted to say I was proved wrong!'

Decision making is in fact a form of controlled discovery, and that only works where career changers are prepared to step to the edge of their comfort zone, and sometimes beyond. All of the case studies here did exactly that – rejecting initial advice from recruitment consultants about what was the realistic, no-brainer next step, they all pursued active enquiries with actual post-holders, often exploring several fields of work at the same time.

It's all about moving into active mode, taking control. In passive mode many of us can't seem to find the energy to take the obvious first step, even when we have great contacts. Pinning down what gets in the way (fear of rejection, poor self-image, a need for certainty and concrete outcomes) is the job of the creative career coach, who needs to be a mix of magician and touchline encourager. So the real work isn't focused on activity at all, but what prevents it. What gets in the way of that first phone call? Interestingly, the steps to success are often baby steps – very often all that's required is to ask a friend or colleague for one piece of information.

The real art is helping clients to set goals *without getting in the way of them*. We are all gifted at blocking our own best ideas; it's too easy to find an inner negative voice. Change makes us more vulnerable than usual to fear of rejection or ridicule.

SIMON BARBER, CHIEF EXECUTIVE, 5 BOROUGHS PARTNERSHIP NHS TRUST

Chartered Accountant Simon Barber left United Utilities and a long career in the commercial world, after undertaking a senior role in Your Communications.

Simon began with a review of his history: *'I felt that my skills and experience could be useful to the public sector, ideally in the NHS, and that this would be more personally rewarding. I learned to take my time and really use the opportunity to examine where I wanted to go next, to identify what I enjoyed doing and what really drives me. It seemed a tall order to move role and sector.'*

A clear strategy developed: *'I learned the power of developing a network – of simply picking up the phone or sending a short letter to ask how I might help in my target sector. This took me outside my comfort zone – I had been very confident in the internal network of UU but I was very reluctant to approach people I didn't know.'*

Simon learned a great deal from new contacts inside the sector, who pointed to the value of short-term assignments. The turning point came when Simon received a 'no' letter on a permanent job at Christie's Hospital, then turned it into a conversation about the organization's needs and into a breakthrough short-term assignment.

For Simon *'that moved the conversation from the theoretical to the specific'*. Simon focused on the way health authorities were required to make radical changes by the Department of Health, and became appointed as the Turnaround Director for a high profile PCT where he reduced a deficit of £42.6m by just under £14m in 12 months.

Having started with recruiters telling him that a move into the health sector was all uphill, Simon became Chief Executive of 5 Boroughs Partnership Trust (a specialist mental health trust covering Warrington, St Helens, Knowsley, Wigan and Halton), beating 50 other applicants to the job, many of whom had far more health sector experience.

HEATHER GROSSMAN, DIRECTOR OF ASSETS AND RESOURCES FOR STOKE ON TRENT & STAFFS FIRE AND RESCUE SERVICE

Heather had been Finance Director of a £50m turnover public sector organization for 12 years and was *'overdue for a change'*. At her first session Heather displayed a dissatisfaction with the 'same old' choices being offered her by the marketplace.

Heather strongly wanted to make the transition into a broader role: *'I knew I would have difficulty finding the right role because employers like to recruit people who have done the role somewhere else whereas I was looking for something new.'*

'JLA asked me to describe my perfect role, where I would be working, who I would be working with, what I would be doing, and helped me build up a checklist which I could measure opportunities by.'

Heather switched from a policy of unsuccessfully applying for a wide range of roles to targeting specific organizations and asking immediately to what extent the organization would welcome someone from outside the sector.

The Fire Service role was particularly attractive to Heather because her father had been a fire fighter. She was impressed with Staffordshire's record on community safety, performance and cost reduction, and also felt that the planned PFI programme for fire stations matched her experience of property development.

Heather steeled herself for an interview. As a person with no fire service experience she expected to fall at the first hurdle: *'I learned that "being myself" was the most important thing at interview, and that the key to being successful was preparation, and then more preparation. The result? I now have a role which fascinates me every minute of every day, and gives me the opportunity to work with some great people. You can't ask for more than that, can you?'*

I often ask clients to define what would be the best and the worst outcome. The best is usually modest (an enjoyable job that hits most of their career drivers), while the worst can be catastrophic. We give far more energy to the dark picture – the one that will whisper to you at 2 o'clock in the morning 'You'll never get a job ...'. There are external factors (the economy, location, industry decline) and real constraints (age, health, qualifications), but none are as powerful as the individual's mindset.

Clients are most responsive in the opening stages, when they are reflecting on who they are, and self-absorption provides a fascination high. The critical stage is to get clients to begin looking outwards to find out what the world of work has to offer. Career coaching is goal-oriented, and requires clients to manage their own futures. To do this, clients have to turn their attention outwards to real organizations and real jobs – a vital *research* step not to be confused with job search.

Strategies for coaches to help individuals who lack confidence to make an uncomfortable career change:

▌ Flagging the issue up at the beginning of the process: 'By *session 4 you might be saying to me ...'.*

▌ Coaching clients from the outset to plan to deal with rejection. It is, after all, the most common experience of job-seekers since you are likely to be rejected for far more jobs and interviews than accepted.

▮ Encouraging clients to set up a support group – two people who will encourage new ideas, remind you of past successes and encourage increased networking.

▮ Getting the client to come up with a reason to begin informational interviews. Once a client has spotted an area of work that looks interesting, then it's only a matter of time before paper and screen sources of information don't deliver enough. If the client prompts the idea of speaking to real people, it works.

▮ Finding quick wins. If they start with people they know well enough to phone without a moment's hesitation, they can get some positive results. I get clients to commit to contacting three named people they already know and trust.

▮ Probing how a client would undertake this activity if they were doing it for someone else – stepping out of their personal situation prompts a wide range of new ideas.

▮ Forming a strong link between a client's passions and their research. If it's a field of work they really care about, they will find a way of discovering more.

▮ Build on synchronicity – connections and opportunities will sometimes just happen. Encourage your client to push on doors that appear to be opening unassisted ... .

▮ Making connections directly for a client. Setting up meetings with past clients, friendly employers, recruitment consultants ... .

What we love to do, of course, is to turn the world into easy choices. The nation's favourite is to play the real/ideal game: 'Either I have a job I love OR I get a job that will pay the bills.' If you turn the world into black and white, grey becomes inconvenient, but practitioners will tell you that gradual career change is far more common than overnight transformation.

Useful Websites

This Appendix lists a wide selection of interesting and useful websites. You can find additional and updated links at www.johnleescareers.com.

JOB BOARDS

www.noras.co.uk
The National Online Recruitment Survey (NORAS) profiles the major UK job boards, segmenting the data by more than 40 categories including industry sector, location, seniority and experience. The site contains a free online tool which helps you to select job boards.

www.alljobsuk.com
Job board portal listing the major and specialist job board sites and a list of the top UK job boards.

www.indeed.co.uk
An aggregator site that collects jobs from newspapers and other sources including employer job boards.

www.simplyhired.co.uk
Consolidates jobs from the top job boards, content sites, newspapers, organizations and company career sites.

www.whatjobsite.com
A job board directory you can search by job role, industry sector and location.

www.workhound.co.uk
Offers an aggregated vertical search of more than 700,000 UK job listings sourced from job boards, employment services and company job postings.

www.gumtree.com/jobs
A site that offers an alternative local community approach and carries a wide range of job ads.

www.cv-library.co.uk
Covers jobs from 90 industries from a range of recruitment agencies and employers.

CAREERS INFORMATION AND EXPLORATION

The links below give you information to help you explore a wide range of potential careers.

www.careerhorizons.net
Career Horizons contains a wide range of tools for career development – reader discounts available, see page 134.

www.careermotivation.co.uk
Your chance to take the Career Motivation Indicator, a tool which builds on John Lees' Career Hot Buttons – again, reader discounts available, see page 134.

www.w3-therapist.co.uk/ques-intro.php
'What Do You Enjoy?' is a free online profile of what a person enjoys doing, particularly useful during a period of job loss or enforced career transition.

www.prospects.ac.uk
Site aimed at graduates but a useful resource for all job seekers. Allows you to explore types of jobs, how you get into them, typical pay, training and promotion routes.

www.workingforacharity.com
Promotes the voluntary sector as a positive career option for those seeking paid employment in the sector.

4talent.channel4.com/getstarted/kickstart
Information on careers in the media

www.nhscareers.nhs.uk
Information on careers in the NHS

**www.direct.gov.uk/en/Employment/Jobseekers/
JobsAndCareers/DG_4003112**
Links and information on the different types of public
sector careers.

careersadvice.direct.gov.uk
The Directgov website contains a wide variety of careers
information.

www.careersa-z.co.uk
A-Z of careers provided by Learn Direct which lists careers
information.

www.careershifters.org
An exciting site for career changers.

www.cipd.co.uk/subjects/lrnanddev/careermand
The Chartered Institute of Personnel and Development
(CIPD) site on career management which includes best
practice for career and outplacement consultants.

www.myexecutivecareer.com
www.newlifenetwork.co.uk
www.mygraduatecareer.com
Rich sources of advice and resources for redundant
executives, life changers and new graduates.

SOCIAL MEDIA

The explosion of social makes it an interesting space for job
searchers.

www.linkedin.com
LinkedIn is an interconnected network of business
professionals from around the world, representing 150

industries and 200 countries. The LinkedIn help pages
contain useful tips on how to use LinkedIn as a job searcher.

www.facebook.com
A social network of over 400 million users worldwide,
often also used as a business networking tool.

www.twitter.com
A free social networking site that enables its users to send
and read messages. Twitter can be a useful way of
communicating to an audience and building a following.

www.zoominfo.com
Gathers publicly-available business information which is
then compiled into profiles. You can search caches – earlier
versions of the site – which is useful when looking up
people's backgrounds.

www.youtube.com
Contains a wide variety of video clips from organizations,
experts and enthusiasts and a huge range of free material
on interview preparation and using social media.

www.123people.com
A people search tool that extracts from Web images, videos,
email addresses, social networking and Wikipedia profiles.

www.xing.com
A business networking site with over eight million
members from 200 countries. Its job portal boasts 30,000
expert groups and international networking events.

www.naymz.com
A professional networking platform which scores
professionals according to their reputations.

mashable.com/2009/01/05/job-search-secrets
The secrets of using social media to conduct your job
search.

**www.time.com/time/business/article/0,8599,
1903083,00.html**

How to use Twitter and Facebook to find a new position.

**fly4change.wordpress.com/2008/08/10/your-
facebook-professionalism-policy-balancing-your-
relationships-on-and-off-the-clock/**

Useful pointers on how to use Facebook within a work
context.

www.bnet.com/2403-13070_23-219860.html

How to make the most of LinkedIn to build relationships.

www.how-to-really-use-linkedin.com

Allows you to download a free PDF guide on getting the
best out of LinkedIn.

www.twitjobsearch.com

A product from WorkDigital which also runs Workhound.

www.jobsite.co.uk/twitter.html

How to receive personalised job tweets on Twitter.

SELF-EMPLOYMENT

www.johnleescareers.com

Contains a free Self-Employment Inventory.

www.businesslink.gov.uk

Start-up tips and links to further information.

www.springwise.com

A network of 'spotters' that scan the globe for smart new
business ideas, delivering inspiration to entrepreneurial
minds.

www.peopleperhour.com

Helps people with problems or work to be done to connect
with independent freelancers.

www.thebfa.org
British Franchise Association – contains a list of members and a searchable directory for different types of franchising.

www.businessesforsale.com
Businesses for sale in the UK searchable by location and type of business.

www.daltonsbusiness.com/BusinessListings.aspx
The online business website for *Daltons Weekly*.

www.top-consultant.com
Dedicated to consultancy work – contains headlines from the world of consulting, career opportunities, networking events and seminars.

www.interimmanagement.uk.com/pages/home.aspx
Links and information on Interim Management including links to agencies. Also provides a quarterly survey on the interim market.

www.london.edu/facultyandresearch/research/docs/TysonReport.pdf
Report on the recruitment and development of Non-Executive Directors.

TRAINING

www.open.ac.uk
Open University.

www.learndirect.co.uk
Information and advice on courses nationwide.

www.vision2learn.com
e-learning service which offers online courses leading to UK-recognized qualifications, which you can study from home or work.

WORKING PARENTS

www.womenlikeus.org.uk/home.aspx
Women Like Us is an award-winning social enterprise set up to support women with children to find flexible, part-time work.

www.workingmums.co.uk
Dedicated to working mothers with home-based jobs and careers information.

www.mumandworking.co.uk/index.asp
Online job directory of part-time jobs for working parents.

www.jobs4mothers.com
Online jobs board for flexible work.

childcarefinder.direct.gov.uk
Directory of childcare resources containing information on schools and childcare.

www.netmums.com
A unique local network for parents, offering a wealth of information on a wide range of issues on both a national and local level.

OTHER USEFUL WEBSITES

www.moneysavingexpert.com
Dedicated to saving consumers money on products and services which contains one of the UK's largest Web communities.

www.volunteering.org.uk
Contains information on volunteering in different sectors.

graduatetalentpool.direct.gov.uk
Ways of finding an internship for graduates.

www.adviceguide.org.uk
Online help from the Citizens Advice Bureau covering a whole range of topics

www.hays.co.uk/salary-guides.aspx
Salary comparison guide from Hays.

www.rec.uk.com
The Recruitment & Employment Confederation – includes a list of member agencies.

www.mya4e.com/Home.aspx
A4E delivers frontline public services such as Flexible New Deal, Connect to Work and Train to Gain. Their website contains useful information on job seeking and claiming benefits.

Index